"The thing about Dan's cooking is that he somehow manages to extract more flavor out of every ingredient than one would think possible. It's always seemed like magic to me—but in this book he reveals the secrets behind that magic, showing us the techniques he uses, and some of the go-to items in his pantry. This book is a beautiful summary of the many extraordinary things Dan has learned during his lifetime in the kitchen."
—WILL GUIDARA, RESTAURATEUR

"Being fortunate enough to live in Dan Kluger's neighborhood, Loring Place—a legacy of a kitchen in many ways—I am blessed to have a home away from home. Dan's food and this book are filled with beauty, simplicity, big flavor, and color. He is the Wizard of Oz to our family and has been our home away from home for some time now. Bring him into your home with this book."
—RACHAEL RAY, HOST OF *THE RACHAEL RAY SHOW*

"I met Dan in the Union Square Greenmarket years ago when I asked his advice on a new leafy green I had never seen. Over the years, I have personally crowned Dan the 'King of Vegetables,' for the most imaginative and incredibly delicious vegetable dishes . . . so much so, that those are the ones I gravitate toward at Loring Place—not an easy feat for a meat eater!"
—LELA ROSE, FASHION DESIGNER

"Chasing Flavor?? Dan Kluger 'caught' flavor long ago! I've been eating his food in his restaurants for over a decade. Now he's showcasing all of the ways he builds, layers, and creates his tantalizing dishes for all of us to make at home. I'll be firing up his Fried Shrimp with Szechuan Salt and Chile Aioli tonight!"
—BOBBY FLAY, CHEF AND STAR OF FOOD NETWORK'S *BEAT BOBBY FLAY*

"Dan's gift of instinctually knowing how to layer flavor and texture in every single bite is mind-blowing. After years of mastering the science of taste, in this book, he breaks it down so you and I can create the magic in our own kitchens. The art of a good char and the dance of sweet, sour, and spice transforms a good dish into a fabulous dish. You're going to have so much fun in these pages!"
—ELVIS DURAN, HOST OF *ELVIS DURAN AND THE MORNING SHOW*

"This book of Dan Kluger's is everything I hoped it would be, and more. It's informative, utterly gorgeous, and one I will keep out on my kitchen counter for years to come. He's a chef who truly expresses himself through memorable food, and it's why I continue to chase him wherever he goes."
—TIFFANI THIESSEN, AUTHOR OF *PULL UP A CHAIR*

Chasing
Flavor

Chasing Flavor

Techniques

and

Recipes

to

Cook

Fearlessly

DAN KLUGER

AND NICK FAUCHALD

PHOTOGRAPHS BY EVAN SUNG

HOUGHTON MIFFLIN HARCOURT
BOSTON · NEW YORK · 2020

For my parents, who taught me that respect,
courage, and hard work pay off. And to my amazing
wife, Hannah, who taught me to follow my dreams,
and our two wonderful daughters, Ella and Georgia,
who support me every day with their love.

———

For information about permission to reproduce selections
from this book, write to trade.permissions@hmhco.com
or to Permissions, Houghton Mifflin Harcourt Publishing
Company, 3 Park Avenue, 19th Floor, New York, New York
10016.

hmhbooks.com

Library of Congress Cataloging-in-Publication Data
Names: Kluger, Dan, author. | Fauchald, Nick, author.
Title: Chasing flavor : techniques and recipes to cook
    fearlessly / Dan Kluger and Nick Fauchald ; photographs by
    Evan Sung.
Description: Boston : Houghton Mifflin Harcourt, 2020. |
    Includes index. | Summary: "In his debut cookbook, James
    Beard Award-winning chef Dan Kluger shares 190 recipes
    to help home cooks master flavor and technique"—
    Provided by publisher.
Identifiers: LCCN 2020016361 (print) | LCCN 2020016362
    (ebook) | ISBN 9781328546333 (hardback) | ISBN
    9781328546524 (ebook)
Subjects: LCSH: Cooking. | Creative ability in cooking. |
    Cooking—Technique. | LCGFT: Cookbooks.
Classification: LCC TX714 .K5824 2020 (print) | LCC TX714
    (ebook) | DDC 641.5—dc23
LC record available at https://lccn.loc.gov/2020016361
LC ebook record available at https://lccn.loc.gov/2020016362

Food styling by Rebekah Peppler
Prop styling by Maya Rossi
Book design by Allison Chi and Melissa Lotfy

Printed in China

TOP 10 9 8 7 6 5 4 3 2 1

Contents

Acknowledgments

I want to take a moment to thank not only everyone who has helped make this book possible, but also those who helped me build the career that led me to it.

Thank you to Norm Faiola and Peter Ricardo, who sparked my interest in the food business, and to Leon Genet, who introduced me to luminaries such as Danny Meyer, who gave me a shot and made me a believer in taking care of people. Thank you to Paul Bolles-Beaven, Michael Romano, Kenny Callaghan, Elsie Loh, Stephen Sherman, Karen King, Regina Kohler, Scott Frantangelo, and so many more who opened my eyes and heart to the restaurant business. I'm grateful for the friendship and guidance of the late chef Floyd Cardoz. My years at Tabla restaurant and his mentorship made a greater impact on my career than I had ever let him know; I wish I had. His understanding of balance of flavors and textures helped me form my own style of cooking. His lesson of "always cook from the heart" taught me the importance of truly loving what I was cooking and allowing that to shine through to the plate. He will forever be in my ear as I cook. And to those who worked with me at Tabla and challenged me to be a better leader and helped me become a better cook: Terry Coughlin, Ty Kotz, Ben Pollinger, Tracy Wilson, Kevin Richer, Mohan Ismail, Randy Garutti, and many others.

Thank you to Jennie Enterprise, Francesca Giessmann, Daniel Rabia, and the employees and members of the Core Club, who gave me the confidence to be "the chef." To Dan and Linda, Steve and Amy, Jonathan and Stacy Levine, Shawn and Jolyne, Tom Owens, Kathryn St. Andre, and so many more who I met when we opened in 2005, and who still support me today—I have so much love for you all!

To Jean-Georges Vongerichten, Greg Brainin, Danny Del Vecchio, and Phil Suarez for giving me an incredible opportunity at ABC Kitchen and allowing me to make something great of it. Thank you for giving me the knowledge and tutelage in food and business, and being by my side along the way. I am forever grateful for the experience and the friendship.

To some very special friends and wonderful sounding boards: François-Olivier Luiggi, Alison Cayne, Will Manuel, Todd Snyder, Michael Lagnese, Jonathon Cohen, Chris Papanti, and Michael Armilio.

To the many chefs (and non-chefs) who I've admired and looked to for inspiration throughout my career: Alfred Portale, John Adler, Charlie Palmer, Tom Colicchio, Marco Canora, David Chang, Jonathan Benno, Jimmy Lau, Nick Kim, Athena Calderone, Kate Heddings, Michele Ishay-Cohen, Kelly O'Connor, and Lela Rose.

To Noam and Bianca Gottesman, Guy Weltsch, Scott Sublett, Nick Boyle,

Gene and Liz Assaf, Elvis Duran and Alex Carr, Richie Jackson and Jordan Roth, Glenn and Amanda Fuhrman, Danyelle Freeman and Josh Resnick, Dan and Linda Rosensweig, Ed and Wendy Hollander, Pam and Lindsay Drucker Mann, Rich and Peggy Gelfond, Victor Oviedo, Steve and Amy Lipin, Lyor Cohen, James Basille, Alex and Dinorah Zubliagga, Eric Foster, David and Sylvia Hermer, Ted and Betsey Pick, Neil and Elissa Crespi, Constantine and Angela Karides: Thank you for believing in me and for investing in Loring Place.

Thank you to the incredible team of cooks, sous chefs, dining room staff, managers, and office staff that I've been fortunate enough to work with over my career. A huge thanks to the past and present crew at Loring Place: We couldn't have opened the restaurant or grown it to where we are today without Karen Shu (an incredibly important part of LP as well as the inspiration behind some of the recipes in this book), George Kantlis, Natalie Johnson, Diana Valenzuela, Slav Dobrow, Ann Marie Del Bello, Christine Ra, Michaelangelo Calvarido, Jessica Pearlman, Jill Levy, Caitlin Giamario (a pillar of Loring Place), Andrew Espinal, Jay Reusi, Amanda Perkins, Meghan Amato, Nikki Solanick, and the incredible Scott Reinhardt. Last but not least, a very special thanks to my longtime friend and chef Seth Seligman and the amazing Kendra Cusack, who are both my rocks at work and handle everything I throw at them with grace.

A very special thank-you to my agent, David Black, for encouraging me to write a cookbook and connecting me with Rux Martin at Houghton Mifflin Harcourt, who brought me onboard. Thanks to Raquel Pelzel, who started the wheels in motion, and to Nick Fauchald, who turned a bunch of recipes and ideas into a book. His writing and leadership has made this book what it is. Thank you to the entire team at HMH for helping to make an amazing book: Deb Brody, Sarah Kwak, Emma Peters, Allison Chi, Marina Padakis, Melissa Lotfy, Kevin Watt, and our copy editor, Deri Reed. Thank you to Jono Pandolfi for loaning some amazing plates for the book and to Laurel Dragonetti for bailing me out throughout the photo shoots and prepping like a maniac. And I am ever grateful to Evan Sung, one of the most amazing photographers out there, who was able to work magic with prop stylist Maya Rossi and food stylist Rebekah Peppler to create something so beautiful.

Last but not least, I owe a huge thank-you to my family. To my parents for instilling my work ethic and passion for food. To my father, for the countless hours watching cooking shows with me, and to my mother, who taught me how to bake. To my brother, whose love for food has pushed me to know more than him simply for that reason. To my amazing wife, whose love and support has given me the confidence to sustain this career and do what I love doing. And to my wonderful girls, who give me a reason to get up and work hard every day.

Introduction

In 1995, I was a student in Syracuse University's food service program and was asked to show around a special visitor who'd be speaking at my school that day: Danny Meyer.

At the time, the restaurateur had recently opened his second establishment, Gramercy Tavern, and his first, Union Square Cafe, was considered one of New York City's best restaurants.

I took Danny to the Carrier Dome, where they put "Welcome Danny Meyer" in big lights on the scoreboard. Then we ate lunch. At the end, I asked if I could do a summer internship with him, and he connected me with his managing partner at Union Square Cafe, Paul Bolles-Beaven. I didn't know it at the time, but this was my first real step to becoming a chef and, eventually, a restaurateur.

My internship at Union Square Cafe was everything you would expect from one of the country's most influential restaurants. It was informative, challenging, and eye-opening, but most of all it taught me about hospitality. I learned how much time, effort, and training it required to offer guests exceptional service, and I filed these lessons away in case I ever had the opportunity to run my own restaurant.

After I graduated, I returned to Union Square Cafe to work in the front of the house. My duties there ranged from answering phones and hosting to taking wine inventory. Curious about what was happening in the back of the house, I spent my days off in the organized chaos of the restaurant's kitchen. There, sous chefs Kenny Callaghan, Stephen Sherman, and Elise Loh put me to work while opening their hearts and minds to me.

A few months later, I realized that I didn't have the patience to work as a host for a couple of years until a management position opened up. As I started to look around for another job, Michael Romano, the restaurant's executive chef, offered me a position as prep cook. I accepted and spent the next six months peeling potatoes, frying calamari, and cleaning artichokes. I loved the work, and became competent enough to move up through the kitchen ranks over the next couple of years, amassing knowledge about cooking, teamwork, and hustle. Michael had an incredible knowledge of French and Italian cooking, and Elise had an extensive palate for Asian flavors.

While cooking at Union Square Cafe, I also met Floyd Cardoz, who was preparing to open

another Danny Meyer restaurant, Tabla. The food he was developing for Tabla was unlike anything I'd seen or tasted: Rooted in his Indian culture, he executed the elevated French techniques he'd perfected as the chef de cuisine at the esteemed Lespinasse. I liked Floyd's demeanor in the kitchen: He was kind, respectful, and always willing to teach me something new. We hit it off, and he asked me to come work with him. I started at the newly opened Tabla in 1998 as a line cook, and eventually became the restaurant's first chef de cuisine. I learned a lot during the seven years I cooked with Floyd, not only about technique and Indian ingredients, but most importantly about how to balance sweet, sour, spicy, salty, and bitter

flavors, as well as how contrasting temperatures and textures can make a dish so much fun to eat. This experience laid the groundwork for how I cook today.

I eventually ran out of rungs to climb at Tabla, so Floyd connected me with Tom Colicchio, who hired me for a project he was consulting on, a members-only organization in Midtown Manhattan called the Core Club. Leading up to the opening, I honed my skills at Tom's restaurant, Craft, along with Damon Wise, Craft's executive chef. Together, Tom and Damon helped me build the confidence to be the Core Club's executive chef when it opened. I developed breakfast, lunch, and dinner menus that adhered to my approach of using seasonal ingredients, manipulated as little as possible, while balancing the flavors and textures I'd developed at Tabla.

At every one of my restaurant jobs, I spent as much time in the Union Square Greenmarket as possible, not only to source food, but to find inspiration. So it's no surprise that my next job came from a connection there. One day I was at the market, visiting one of my favorite farmers, Franca Tantillo. She turned to me and said, "Hey, Dan, do you know Jean-Georges Vongerichten?" The famous chef was nearby, picking out some cucumbers. She made an introduction, and two days later I was interviewing with him for a job. I accepted a position as the chef of the Mark Hotel, where I was not only fortunate enough to be part of a buzzy hotel opening, but I also became part of Jean-Georges's team of roving chefs who opened restaurants in Arizona, Atlanta, Washington, D.C., and beyond. This team was led by JGV's longtime chef and VP of operations, Danny Del Vecchio. Danny is an incredible person who versed me in Jean-Georges's cuisine, but more importantly taught me a lot about organization. He was a master at building teams and opening restaurants, and I count him as not only a dear friend but a mentor.

Once the Mark Hotel was open for room service, Jean-Georges came to me with the opportunity of a lifetime, ABC Kitchen. His business partner, Phil Suarez, ran two restaurants inside the ABC Carpet & Home building, and I had already spent some time there helping out. (I was also fortunate enough to befriend the restaurants' general manager, George Kantlis, who would help me open Loring Place years later.) Phil and Jean-Georges wanted to revamp the restaurants with something more "farm to table," which was then still a nascent concept in New York. Jean-Georges

knew how influential the Greenmarket was to my cooking, and thought I was a natural fit to be the chef of ABC Kitchen. I couldn't have been more excited.

While we prepared to open ABC Kitchen, I soaked up everything that Jean-Georges shared with me. Our palates were very similar—we both loved the high notes that acidity and spicy ingredients bring to a dish—so I didn't feel like there was a huge learning curve. Greg Brainin, Jean Georges's culinary director, also had an amazing palate, along with a devotion to technique. made an incredible impact on my cooking. We opened ABC Kitchen in 2010, and the accolades and awards soon started pouring in. I had access to amazing local ingredients and the freedom to cook my style of food: sophisticated but approachable and affordable, familiar yet always exciting and boldly flavored. My four-year tenure at ABC was an amazing experience, and I'm forever grateful for the opportunity that Phil, Jean-Georges, Greg, and the ABC Home team gave me. They helped me hone my skills, sharpen my palate, and made me a better leader. But most of all, they inspired me to become an entrepreneur and open my own place.

I found the space for my restaurant, Loring Place, in 2014, but it took another two years to finally open our doors. Like this cookbook, Loring Place is a culmination of my experiences cooking in some of New York's best restaurants over the past twenty years, and an opportunity to spread my wings.

How to Use This Book

Over the years, so many diners and friends have asked me how to re-create at home what I've served them at my restaurant. It's easy for me to put together a dish, but it's very difficult for me to explain the hows and whys of what I've cooked—at least on the spot.

So I dedicated myself to putting it down on paper. My goal, however, isn't to simply give you a collection of recipes to follow to the letter. That is a great place to start, of course, but I want you to get so much more out of this book. I want you to see how I build and balance flavors—specifically acidic, sweet, salty, and spicy ones—to create dishes that are exciting from the first bite through the last. I also want you to come away with an understanding of texture: how a little bit of crunch can make a good dish great, or why I slow-roast a piece of fish instead of searing it in a pan.

Regardless of your competence in the kitchen, this book will teach you some new cooking techniques. You'll learn the importance of using a wire rack when roasting vegetables, how to blend and emulsify sauces and dressings so they're silky smooth, and how to get the most out of a hot grill. Some chefs like to flaunt their technique on the plate. In most cases I like to hide my technique, to make complicated dishes look simple and approachable.

Most of all, I want this cookbook to elevate your appreciation for high-quality ingredients and your dedication for sourcing them. So many of my recipes are inspired by the farmers market and the treasures I discover there. Every restaurant I've worked at during my career has been within a short stroll from the Union Square Greenmarket, and I spend every free moment I can spare there, talking with farmers and tasting everything they'll let me sample. Like many chefs these days, I try to cook with the seasons, letting whatever looks best at the market lead the way. As such, I've ordered the recipes in each chapter according to the time of the year, working from early spring at the beginning of each section through the winter at the end. And while you can cook many of these recipes throughout the year, you'll always get the most flavorful results if you use fresh products at their peak of the season. If you've ever needed a little push to do more shopping at local farmers markets and less shopping at the supermarket, let this cookbook be it. Any time you need some inspiration, visit your farmers market and see what vegetables, fruit, and proteins grab your attention, then come back here to decide what to cook with it.

With all of these goals in mind, I put a lot of thought into how to present the recipes in this cookbook. I believe that every recipe should leave you with something beyond a tasty dish, whether it's a new technique, an underappreciated ingredient, a surprising flavor pairing, or a single element—such as a sauce, dressing, crunchy topping, or pickle—that becomes part of your cooking repertoire. I've tried to make these "takeaways" as obvious as possible by calling them just that: Every recipe in his book calls out a main takeaway, and most will leave you with more than one gift that you can apply to other recipes as well as your own creations.

Most of the recipes in this book are inspired by dishes that I've cooked at my current restaurant, Loring Place, or the restaurants I've worked at in the past, including Union Square Cafe, Tabla, Core Club, and ABC Kitchen. Whenever I create a new dish for a restaurant, I write a recipe intended for the kitchen staff. These recipes assume a lot of culinary—and some institutional—knowledge on their part. If I handed you one of these recipes, you'd probably be lost. So we've adapted the recipes for this cookbook—and for you, the home cook—not only by filling in the gaps with specific instructions on the techniques required to cook them, but we've also taken great pains (and I use the word "pain" intentionally) to simplify the recipes as much as possible while still retaining what makes them excellent.

When you look at most of the recipes in this book, you'll see the various elements of the recipe broken out into separate ingredient lists and instructions, as well as a section for finishing and serving the dish. Although it appears slightly unconventional when compared to most cookbooks, this mimics how most restaurant kitchens work: Various parts of a dish are prepared individually—some hours or even days in advance—then assembled right before serving. Tom Colicchio calls this "component cooking," and I think it's a great method for you to follow at home as well. Many of my recipe components can be made in advance, which not only saves you time and lets you plan ahead, but also helps you identify the components—and the takeaways— that you can use more broadly in your cooking. I hope many of these fundamental sauces, dressings, pickles, crunchy toppings, stocks, and so on become your new pantry staples, and that you discover many new uses for them beyond what I suggest in the book.

Lastly, I know many cooks—myself included— prefer to use recipes as inspiration, rather than following them to the letter. I encourage you to do this with my cookbook. If a recipe calls for sugar snap peas and you want to use green beans instead, go for it. If you can't pickle something in time for dinner, swap in another pickle or other acidic ingredient. Hate halibut? Use cod instead. As long as you're striving for synergy in your cooking—a balance of sweet, sour, spicy, and bitter flavors, as well as contrasting textures—you're going to love the results.

Dan's Pantry Staples

You don't need to copy my pantry exactly to make the recipes in this book, but keeping the following ingredients on hand will set you up for success and save you a few trips to the market.

KOSHER SALT

I prefer kosher salt over fine sea salt, as the coarse grains are easier to grab with your fingers and sprinkle evenly when seasoning food. There are two major brands of kosher salt in America: Morton and Diamond Crystal. Unfortunately for home cooks, there's a huge difference between these two brands. While both are made from sodium chloride, Diamond Crystal salt granules are flakier than the denser Morton salt, which means a teaspoon of Diamond Crystal is less salty than a teaspoon of Morton. We cook with Diamond Crystal at my restaurant, and used it to test the recipes in this cookbook as well. If you're using Morton kosher salt to cook these recipes, start with half as much salt as the recipe calls for, and season to taste from there.

FLAKY SEA SALT

When finishing a dish, I often add a sprinkle of flaky sea salt to add texture and little pops of salinity. I love the light, pyramid-shaped flakes of Maldon sea salt, which is widely available. Oregon-based Jacobsen Salt Co. also makes an excellent flaky salt. When I want a little more crunch from a finishing salt, I'll use Maine Sea Salt Company's salt, which is similar to French fleur de sel.

SPICES

Although you'll spot some outliers in my recipes, you can cook most of this book with a handful of spices: black peppercorns, sweet smoked paprika, fennel seeds, cumin seeds, coriander seeds, and red pepper flakes. For maximum freshness (and minimal waste), I recommend buying your spices in small amounts from a shop that sells them in bulk bins, rather than pulling them from the jarred spice rack at the grocery store, as those spices might have been sitting around for ages. I also buy whole spices whenever possible, and grind them as needed.

OLIVE OIL

For everyday cooking, I use California Olive Ranch's mild, fruity Miller's Blend, which is widely available. I also like the brand's Arbequina extra-virgin olive oil for simple vinaigrettes (where the olive oil is a major player) and for drizzling over finished dishes.

VEGETABLE OIL

I try to use non-GMO ingredients whenever possible, so I avoid soybean-based "vegetable oil" and instead use sunflower oil, which has a neutral flavor and high smoke point, making it a great all-around cooking and frying oil.

VINEGAR

I use a *lot* of vinegar in my cooking, as well as many different styles: red and white wine vinegar, champagne vinegar, balsamic vinegar, sherry vinegar, and unseasoned rice vinegar. Sparrow Lane makes great examples of most of these styles, and I also use Villa Manodori's balsamic vinegars, which offer a great value. I also get asked a lot about the difference between white wine and champagne vinegars: Champagne vinegar is less acidic and slightly sweeter than white wine vinegar, so I usually use it in concert with other acidic ingredients.

TAMARI

Because many of our guests avoid gluten, I use tamari instead of soy sauce, which contains wheat. If that's not a concern at home, you can use soy sauce.

ELDERFLOWER SYRUP

If I have a secret ingredient for salad dressings, it's elderflower syrup, which has a flowery aroma and honey-like flavor. My go-to brand is d'Arbo, and Belvoir Fruit Farms makes a great elderflower cordial as well. You'll find elderflower syrup at many high-end grocery stores, and it's readily available online.

MAPLE SYRUP

I use maple syrup to add sweetness and a deep, caramelized flavor to syrups and sauces. The grading system for maple syrups has recently changed, but I typically use what was previously known as "grade B" syrup, and is now called "grade A, dark color and robust flavor."

HONEY

I buy local honey from the farmers market, and suggest you do the same. For most purposes, I use a lighter, floral honey.

SUGAR

For environmental reasons, I use organic, unbleached sugar whenever possible, but you can use regular granulated white sugar without any noticeable difference in flavor.

FLOUR

At Loring Place, we mill most of our flour in-house. But at home I stock King Arthur or Bob's Red Mill brands. I also love the gluten-free flours made by Cup4Cup, which you can purchase online.

DRIED PASTAS

We make most of our pastas in-house at Loring Place, but for cooking at home, I love Rustichella d'Abruzzo and Sfoglini brands.

CANNED TOMATOES

I mostly use fresh tomatoes in my cooking, but when tomatoes aren't in season, I reach for a can of Muir Glen organic tomatoes or Jersey Fresh crushed tomatoes.

MISO

Miso comes in a few styles and flavor profiles, but I mostly use white miso when I want a more mild flavor in vinaigrettes and dressings, and a more robust yellow miso when I want its flavor to be more pronounced or when pairing it with mushrooms and other umami-heavy ingredients. I also love the Momofuku line of hozon, a fermented bean paste similar to miso but made from chickpeas or sunflower seeds.

KOMBU

We use kombu, a type of dried, edible kelp, to flavor stocks and other cooking liquids, as well as for quick-cured fish. You'll find kombu in the Asian section of most supermarkets.

OLIVES

I use a lot of green olives in my dishes and have two favorite varieties: California-grown Sevillano olives, which have a pronounced olive-y flavor, and Italian Castelvetrano olives, which are softer and more mild.

YOGURT

It's always useful to have some creamy, Greek-style yogurt on hand. If you don't make your own, look for Stonyfield, Fage, or Chobani brands at the store, and use whole-milk yogurt whenever possible.

CHEESES

When a recipe calls for Parmesan cheese, I use an imported Parmigiano-Reggiano. Grana Padano is similar in style and makes a great substitute, as does the domestically made Sartori SarVecchio Parmesan from Wisconsin. I also frequently call for fresh goat's milk cheese (or chèvre), and like those made by Coach Farm and Vermont Creamery.

CHILES

Most of my recipes contain chile peppers in one form or another, and I always have a few varieties on hand. I use red finger chiles as the base for my Fermented Chile Sauce (page 252) and thinly sliced as a finishing chile; if you can't find red finger chiles, you can substitute cayenne chile peppers, which are similar in flavor and heat level. With green chiles, I look to jalapeños when I want to use bigger pieces and add crunch to a dish, and serranos when I want more heat or thin slivers. Thai chiles (aka bird's eye chiles) are small and add a lot of heat. You'll find both green and red versions of these; red Thai chiles have fully ripened and have a more pronounced flavor. Lastly, I love the unique fruity flavor of habaneros, and typically leave out their seeds because they're quite spicy. You can use Habanada chiles in their place, a variety that was created to deliver the flavor of habanero without the heat.

CITRUS

Although citrus, like chiles, are a fresh ingredient, I always keep a stock of limes, lemons, and oranges on hand. There's nothing more transformative than a squeeze of fresh citrus to finish a dish.

Dan's Essential Tools

In addition to a set of high-quality pots and pans, this is the gear I use every day in my kitchen.

HIGH-POWERED BLENDER

You don't need a commercial-strength Vitamix to make silky-smooth purees and creamy dressings, but you need something more powerful than the cheap $20 blender you bought for making margaritas in college. At home, I love Breville's line of blenders.

RIMMED BAKING SHEETS

Commercial-grade baking sheets, aka "sheet pans," are easy to find online and at restaurant supply stores. I suggest stocking a few each of half-sheet (13 by 18 inches) and quarter-sheet (9 by 13 inches) sizes.

WIRE BAKING RACK

I almost always use a baking rack when roasting vegetables. The elevated platform allows for more airflow around the food, which means you can evenly brown the ingredient on all sides without having to constantly flip—this is especially helpful when roasting something that's been coated with spices or cheese. Buy one for every size of rimmed baking sheet that you own, and make sure it has bars in a grid (as opposed to lengthwise rows).

INSTANT-READ THERMOMETER

A good thermometer is essential for cooking meat, and very helpful for deep frying as well. I like OXO's thermocouple thermometer, which measures to the tenth of a degree.

MANDOLINE

I use a lot of thinly shaved fruits and vegetables in my cooking, and a mandoline will not only speed up your prep work, but give you more consistent cuts than you can ever achieve with a knife. Japanese Benriner mandolines are very affordable and up to the task—look for one with a julienne attachment.

FINE-MESH SIEVES

I recommend having two fine-mesh sieves in your kitchen: a small, cone-shaped one for sauces and dressings, and a larger basket-style strainer for purees and everything else.

PEPPER MILL

Invest in a high-quality pepper mill with an adjustable grind setting and you'll never regret the purchase. Mine is made by Peugeot, and I've had it forever.

CHEESE GRATERS AND CITRUS ZESTERS

A fine-tooth Microplane (or similar style) rasp grater will tackle most cheese-grating and citrus-zesting duties, but I also have a ribbon grater for making potato ribbons (see page 146), and a box grater or handheld coarse cheese grater for grating tomatoes and breadcrumbs in addition to cheese.

DIGITAL SCALE

The vast majority of measurements in this cookbook have been converted to volume (i.e., teaspoons, tablespoons, and cups) for your convenience, but it's great to have a digital scale around for weighing out ingredients for doughs and baking recipes. I use OXO's digital scale, which has a handy pull-out display, and a smaller jeweler's scale when measuring small amounts of ingredients.

OVEN THERMOMETER

Most home cooks don't realize how far off their actual oven temperature can be from what the dial reads, especially gas ovens. I highly recommend buying a simple oven thermometer—or a few, and placing them around the oven—to make sure you're cooking at the right temperature.

KNIVES

Knives are the most personal tools a cook owns, so you've probably already found some that work for you (and hopefully you're keeping them sharp). If not, I'd invest in a small, sturdy paring knife for fine cuts, a utility knife (for fine cuts of shallots, garlic, and other small ingredients, as well as for butchering chicken), and a good chef's knife (I use a Masanobu VG-10 Gyuto, as well as other knives from Korin). I also highly recommend an offset serrated knife (Zwilling J.A. Henckels makes a great one) for slicing hard vegetables and bread.

CORN ZIPPER

This gadget (mine is made by Kuhn Rikon) is totally not necessary, but it's cheap and you'll probably fall in love with it. It does a much better job than a knife at separating kernels from a corn cob.

Techniques

ESSENTIAL CUTS

Here is a visual guide to the knife cuts I frequently reference in my recipes.

HERBS

My biggest pet peeve in my kitchen is when one of my cooks hacks up some herbs. If you see a big green stain on your cutting board after you've finished chopping herbs, that means you've committed the same kitchen sin: All of that greenness left behind is flavor. I try to cut herbs as few times as possible to avoid bruising them and speeding up oxidation. Instead of running my knife through a pile of herbs, I'll bunch them up into a tight bundle and slice them once. For finely chopped herbs, I'll run my knife through once, turn the herbs, then cut them one more time.

MINT
PARSLEY

WIDE RIBBONS | THINLY SLICED | ROUGHLY CHOPPED | FINELY CHOPPED

BASIL

THINLY SLICED   WIDE RIBBONS   COARSELY CHOPPED

VEGETABLES

CUCUMBERS

ON THE BIAS   OBLIQUES

ONIONS

THINLY SLICED

DICED

FINELY CHOPPED

FENNEL

WEDGES

MATCHSTICKS

CHILES

FINELY CHOPPED

HALF-MOONS

Greg Brainin taught me this trick for finely diced or chopped jalapeños:
Make long slits down the length of the chile, rolling it as you go and leaving
them attached at the stem end, then cut the strips crosswise.

GINGER

CARROTS

OBLIQUES

CUTTING CITRUS SEGMENTS
AND PEELS

SLICING SASHIMI AND CRUDO

When slicing raw fish, a sharp knife is absolutely essential. After that the task is simple: Cut the fish across the grain, wiping your blade between every cut to avoid sticking. If the fish starts to separate (which is common with tuna), turn the fish over and change the angle of your cut to be at a slight angle against the grain.

CURING FISH IN KOMBU

BLENDING CHEESE INTO DRESSINGS AND VINAIGRETTES

You can make an extra-creamy dressing or vinaigrette (without adding any cream or mayonnaise) by blending cheese into the dressing. With hard cheeses (like Manchego and Parmesan), I first break the cheese up into bite-size pieces—there's no need to grate the cheese first, but you certainly can. Once the cheese has been added, blend until the cheese has completely broken down and emulsified into a very smooth, silky dressing. This will take longer than you think, at least a minute with a high-powered commercial blender, and a minute or two longer with most home blenders. Once the dressing looks smooth, have a taste; if it's still grainy, continue blending until it's perfectly silky.

BLANCHING VEGETABLES

A few things will help you be a better blancher. Use a large amount of water (a large saucepan or stockpot is your best vessel) and salt the water heavily—even more than you would a pot of pasta water (I use 1 to 2 cups of salt per gallon of water). Prepare a very icy water bath and set a strainer or colander inside the ice (to make removing the shocked vegetables easy). Then bring the water to a rolling boil before adding the vegetables. If the water stops boiling for more than a few seconds, cover the pot until it returns to a boil.

MAKING CRISPY SHALLOTS

21

SHAPING PIZZA DOUGH

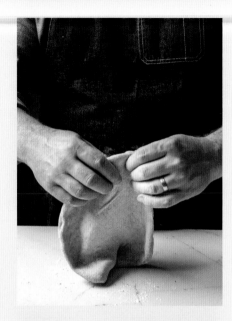

MAKING RICOTTA CAVATELLI

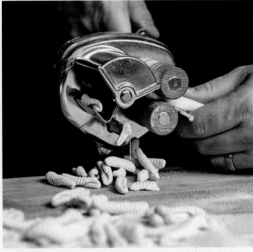

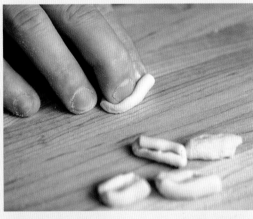

Building Blocks of Flavor

At many restaurants (including mine), we break our dishes down into many mini recipes, or components. This allows us to divide the labor among multiple cooks, makes it easy to prepare some components ahead of time, and gives me building blocks that I can use to develop new dishes. Here, I've organized the components of the recipes in this book to help you do all of these things, but most of all, I want you to use them to inspire your own new kitchen creations.

PICKLES & PRESERVES

Bell Pepper Chutney 223
Caramelized Onions 44
Dried Cherry Tomatoes 43
Garlic Confit 112
Grilled Cucumber
  Pickles 101
Lemon Jam 32
Lavender-Pickled
  Peaches 99
Marinated Kohlrabi 52
Marinated Olives 104
Marinated Peppers 315
Mushroom Jam 238
Orange Marmalade 301
Pickled Carrots 263
Pickled Cherry-Pepper
  Relish 63
Pickled Cauliflower 117
Pickled Fennel 92
Pickled Fresno Chiles 93
Pickled Ginger 115
Pickled Green
  Tomatoes 219
Pickled Jalapeños 227
Pickled Mixed Peppers 318
Pickled Peppers 215
Pickled Ramps 154
Pickled Red Finger
  Chiles 182
Pickled Red Onions 55
Pickled Shallots 308
Pickled Vegetable
  Salad 79
Pickled Watermelon
  Radishes 74
Quick Kohlrabi Kimchi 223
Quick Preserved
  Lemons 249
Roasted Cherry
  Tomatoes 312
Roasted Tomatoes 203
Shallot Confit 250
Soppressata-Tomato
  Jam 216
Sweet-Sour Onions 348

SAUCES

Apple Gastrique 188
Barbecue Sauce 259
Broken Chile Sauce 145
Carrot Barbecue
  Sauce 263
Carrot-Ginger Dip 50
Carrot-Hazelnut
  Romesco 54
Cheese Sauce 208
Chickpea Sauce 321
Chile Sauce 236
Corn Béchamel 214
Corn Sauce 219
Crushed Tomato
  Sauce 211
Fermented Chile
  Sauce 252
Green Hot Sauce 109
Grilled Scallion
  Rémoulade 230
Herbed Goat Cheese 154
Honey-Butter Hot
  Sauce 268
Lime Yogurt 101
Maple-Chile Glaze 72
Maple-Lime Glaze 185
Miso Glaze 327
Miso-Herb Sauce 164
Mushroom Ragu 241
Orange-Ginger Puree 124
Peach-Apricot Puree 176
Peach-Tomato Sauce 309
Pomegranate Glaze 278
Quick Tomato Sauce 201
Red Hot Sauce 130
Red Wine Vinegar
  Glaze 278
Sunchoke Sauce 341
Sweet and Sour Carrot
  Sauce 147
Sweet and Spicy Sauce
  257/305
Tamarind Sauce 327
Yogurt Sauce 325

STOCKS

Corn Stock 48
Chicken Stock 75
Infused Chicken
  Stock 264
Kombu Tea 240
Tomato Water 212

TOPPINGS

Almond-Herb
  Topping 309
Candied Walnuts 160
Caramelized
  Onions 44
Charred Shallots 179
Corn Fritters 56
Crispy Garlic 246
Crispy Goat
  Cheese 123
Crispy Onions 170
Crispy Shallots 88
Fried Capers 325
Fried Chickpeas 31
Fried Pumpkin
  Seeds 167
Ginger-Scallion
  Topping 172
Herbed
  Breadcrumbs 277
Horseradish
  Gremolata 294
Kombu Spray 50
Lime Yogurt 101
Orange-Chile
  Topping 306
Parmesan
  Croutons 110
Potato Ribbons 146
Sesame Clusters 134
Spiced Popcorn 48
Spicy
  Breadcrumbs 224
Spicy Granola 188
Sunchoke Chips 126
Szechuan Salt 34
Winter Spice Mix 192

Starters
&
Soups

———

CONTINUES ➡

Baby Artichokes
WITH WINE GLAZE

MAKES 4 SERVINGS

This rustic one-pot dish can play either as a starter or a side, maybe next to a piece of roasted fish (the wine glaze will serve double duty as a sauce). You can make this with full-grown artichokes, but I much prefer baby artichokes, which are more tender and don't require as much prep work. Which brings us to . . .

THE TAKEAWAY

Cleaning and prepping baby artichokes is easier than for their adult counterparts. You don't have to remove as many leaves, and the furry choke is edible (a little bit of choke from an adult artichoke can taint an entire dish with bitterness). Let color be your guide when prepping baby artichokes: Trim away anything that's dark green, and leave the rest.

---

8 to 10 baby artichokes

¼ cup extra-virgin olive oil

2 large garlic cloves, thinly sliced

2 teaspoons kosher salt

¾ cup white wine

¼ cup Castelvetrano olives, pitted and coarsely chopped

1 teaspoon red pepper flakes

1 cup roughly chopped mint

½ cup roughly chopped basil

Pinch of sugar

2 tablespoons fresh lemon juice

WITH A small, sharp knife, cut off the artichoke stems. Remove the tough exterior leaves. Cut off the top third of the artichokes and trim any tough parts. Quarter the artichokes lengthwise.

IN A large skillet, heat the oil over medium-high heat. Add the artichokes and cook, stirring occasionally, until they're well browned on all sides and just tender when pierced with a knife. Add the garlic and salt and cook, stirring frequently, until golden brown, 2 to 3 minutes. Add ½ cup of the wine, increase the heat to high, and simmer until most of the liquid has evaporated. Add the olives, red pepper flakes, mint, basil, and a pinch of sugar. Add the remaining ¼ cup wine and bring the liquid to a boil, then add the lemon juice and stir well; the liquid should form a glaze that coats the artichokes. Serve.

Hummus

WITH RADISHES AND CRISPY CHICKPEAS

MAKES 8 SERVINGS

I started making hummus back in my Tabla days, and it's since become the go-to snack in my house. My hummus is far from minimalist; I blend in some garlic confit, pickled onions, and a good amount of lemon juice. For added crunch, I set aside some of the cooked chickpeas and fry them right before I'm ready to serve the hummus. The difference between good and great hummus starts at the market: A high-quality tahini will add the fresh, nutty sesame flavor that this recipe needs. I use the Seed + Mill brand, which is made in New York City.

THE TAKEAWAY

In addition to sourcing good tahini, the secret to excellent hummus is to cook the chickpeas past the point where they're tender, but stop before they start to completely fall apart. Then let your food processor or blender do the rest of the work—it's impossible to over-puree the hummus.

1 cup dried chickpeas

½ teaspoon baking soda

Kosher salt

¾ cup Pickled Red Onions (page 55)

½ cup Garlic Confit (page 112)

½ cup tahini, well stirred

¾ cup extra-virgin olive oil

¼ cup fresh lemon juice

Kosher salt

IN A bowl, cover the chickpeas by at least 2 inches of water (they'll soak up more than you'd expect). Add the baking soda and 1 tablespoon salt and stir until dissolved. Let the chickpeas soak at room temperature for at least 8 hours or overnight. Drain and rinse.

PLACE THE soaked chickpeas in a saucepan and cover with 8 cups water. Bring the water to a boil, then reduce the heat and simmer until the chickpeas are very tender and starting to fall apart, 45 to 60 minutes. As they cook, give the chickpeas an occasional stir and skim off any foam or skins that come to the surface.

DRAIN THE chickpeas, reserving the cooking liquid. Set aside 1 cup of the drained chickpeas for frying.

IN A food processor, combine the pickled onions and garlic confit. Puree until finely chopped. Add the drained chickpeas, tahini, olive oil, lemon juice, and 1 tablespoon salt. Puree until very smooth, thinning the hummus out with a bit of cooking liquid if needed (the hummus should be thick enough to support a radish stuck into it). Season to taste with salt. If you want an extra-smooth hummus, pass it through a tamis or fine-mesh strainer, using a rubber spatula to press it through. The hummus is best served right away, but you can cover and refrigerate it for a day or two. Let warm to room temperature before serving.

FRIED CHICKPEAS

MAKES 1 CUP

Vegetable oil, for frying   Kosher salt

1 cup cooked chickpeas
 (from Hummus,
 opposite)

IN A small saucepan, heat 1 inch of oil to 375°F. Dry the chickpeas well with paper towels. Fry the chickpeas, stirring frequently, until they're golden brown, 4 to 5 minutes. Drain on paper towels and season with salt.

FOR SERVING

2 cups Hummus   Fried Chickpeas

1 teaspoon ground   2 cups breakfast
 cumin   radishes, halved
                          lengthwise if large
1 teaspoon sweet
 smoked paprika

SPREAD THE hummus in the base of a platter or large shallow bowl. Sprinkle with the cumin and paprika. Sprinkle the fried chickpeas over the top, then stand the breakfast radishes in the hummus and serve.

Crispy Spiced Cauliflower
WITH LEMON JAM AND CHILES

MAKES 4 SERVINGS

When I worked at Tabla, I fell in love with the combination of cauliflower and Indian spices. Over the years I've run with this idea in both raw (see the Pickled Cauliflower, page 117) and cooked cauliflower. What makes this dish memorable, though, is the texture you achieve when both roasting and frying cauliflower. The roasting stage infuses the vegetable with the intense spice paste, then a quick dip in hot oil crisps it up and turns it into fun finger food. We use this technique for making Butternut Squash Fries (page 57), and it works well with broccoli, sunchokes, and potatoes as well.

THE TAKEAWAY

A small swipe of tart lemon jam will balance out the deeply spiced cauliflower. You'll have some left over, and you'll be glad you do. Think of it as a super-concentrated condiment that adds big flavor in small doses: a few dots next to a piece of fish or roasted vegetables will completely transform the dish. But achieving its smooth, silky texture requires more blending than you'd expect. Keep scraping down the side of the blender carafe, and blend it at full speed for a full 3 or 4 minutes.

---------- SPICE PASTE ----------

1½ teaspoons black peppercorns

1½ teaspoons coriander seeds

1½ teaspoons fennel seeds

½ teaspoon cumin seeds

1½ teaspoons yellow mustard seeds

2 large garlic cloves, smashed

One 1½-inch piece ginger, peeled and chopped

¼ teaspoon sweet smoked paprika

½ teaspoon red pepper flakes

½ teaspoon turmeric

3 long strips lemon zest (no pith)

1½ teaspoons kosher salt

IN A small skillet, toast the peppercorns, coriander, fennel, cumin, and mustard seeds over medium heat until fragrant, 2 to 3 minutes. Grind the seeds and add to a blender or mini food processor. Add the remaining ingredients and blend until smooth.

---------- LEMON JAM ----------

MAKES 1 CUP

5 medium lemons

½ cup fresh lemon juice, strained

1 tablespoon plus ½ teaspoon water

⅓ cup sugar

1 teaspoon kosher salt

Pinch of turmeric

USING A vegetable peeler or sharp knife, peel the lemons, trying to get some of the white pith as well (this will add body to the jam). Roughly chop the lemon peels, then add to a small saucepan. Cover with cold water, bring to a boil, then strain. Blanch the lemon peel two more times; this will make the jam less bitter. Return the blanched lemon peel to the saucepan and add the remaining ingredients. Bring to a simmer and cook until the liquid has reduced to a syrupy texture, about 10 minutes. Transfer to a blender or mini food processer and blend until very smooth, frequently scraping down the bowl. If the puree is too thick to blend, add a splash of water to loosen it up. Scrape the

32

jam into a container and cover with plastic wrap pressed onto the surface. Let cool, then refrigerate until ready to use. The lemon jam can be refrigerated for several days.

─────── CRISPY CAULIFLOWER ───────

1 head cauliflower, cut into bite-size florets

¼ cup water

⅓ cup plus 5 tablespoons all-purpose flour

Spice Paste

Vegetable or canola oil, for frying

⅓ cup cornstarch

⅛ teaspoon baking powder

3 tablespoons vodka

3 tablespoons cold seltzer water

Kosher salt

PREHEAT THE oven to 450°F. Line a large rimmed baking sheet with parchment paper and place a wire rack on top. In a large bowl, toss the cauliflower with the water until evenly coated. Add the 5 tablespoons flour and toss well to coat. Add the spice paste and toss again, until the cauliflower is evenly coated. Arrange the cauliflower on the prepared rack and roast for 10 minutes, or until the cauliflower is crisp-tender and starting to brown. Let cool on the rack for a few minutes while preparing the batter.

IN A medium saucepan, heat 2 inches of oil to 375°F. In a bowl, whisk together the remaining ⅓ cup flour, the cornstarch, and baking powder. Whisk in the vodka and seltzer until smooth. Working in batches, dip the cauliflower into the batter, letting the excess drip off. Fry the cauliflower until crispy and golden brown, about 2 minutes. Transfer to paper towels and sprinkle with salt. Repeat with the remaining cauliflower.

─────── FOR SERVING ───────

Lemon Jam

Crispy Cauliflower

¼ cup Pickled Red Finger Chiles (page 182)

¼ cup roughly chopped cilantro

SPREAD A wide smear of the lemon jam around one side of a shallow serving bowl or platter. Top with the fried cauliflower. Sprinkle the pickled chiles and cilantro over the top and serve.

Fried Shrimp
WITH SZECHUAN SALT AND CHILE AIOLI

MAKES 4 SERVINGS

I love a good spicy mayonnaise and will use it anywhere you'd find regular mayo. I always have some around for tacos, soft-shell crabs, sandwiches (especially banh mi), and anything fried. The two keys to my version are the addition of yellow miso, which adds a layer of umami, and the fermented chile sauce, a kitchen staple that I use frequently. If you don't want to go through the trouble of making your own (though it's really not much trouble at all), substitute some sriracha instead.

THE TAKEAWAY
A sprinkle of Szechuan salt adds the pungent peppercorn's unique, lemony aroma to the crispy fried shrimp, something regular salt and pepper won't do. Keep some of this seasoning on hand whenever you want to add an extra kick to anything that needs S&P (which is basically everything).

CHILE AIOLI

MAKES ABOUT 2 CUPS

¼ to ½ cup Fermented Chile Sauce (page 252)

¼ cup white wine vinegar

3 tablespoons yellow miso

1 tablespoon Tabasco hot sauce (or Red Hot Sauce, page 130)

1½ tablespoons Dijon mustard

2 teaspoons Colman's mustard powder

1 teaspoon kosher salt

2 large egg yolks

1¼ cups sunflower oil

IN A blender or mini food processor, combine the chile sauce, vinegar, miso, Tabasco, Dijon mustard, mustard powder, and salt. Process until smooth. Add the egg yolks and process until mixed. With the machine running, slowly drizzle in the oil until emulsified. Refrigerate until ready to use.

SZECHUAN SALT

MAKES ABOUT 1 TABLESPOON

1 tablespoon Szechuan peppercorns

½ teaspoon black peppercorns

2 teaspoons kosher salt

USING A spice grinder or mortar and pestle, grind the Szechuan and black peppercorns into a fine powder. Transfer to a small container and add the kosher salt. Cover and shake until combined. The Szechuan salt will stay fresh for a couple of weeks.

FOR SERVING

1 tablespoon kosher salt

1 quart water

1 pound shrimp (16–20 per pound size), shells removed (tails intact)

Vegetable oil, for frying

½ cup cornmeal

Szechuan Salt

Lime wedges

Chile Aioli

IN A bowl, whisk the salt into the water until dissolved. Add the shrimp and brine for 15 minutes.

HEAT 1 inch of vegetable oil in a medium saucepan to 375°F. Place the cornmeal in a shallow bowl. Remove the shrimp from the brine and toss in the cornmeal until evenly coated. Working in batches, fry the shrimp until golden brown and cooked through, about 90 seconds. Transfer to a serving bowl and sprinkle with the Szechuan salt. Garnish the bowl with lime wedges and serve with a small bowl of chile aioli.

Spring Pea Soup

MAKES 4 TO 6 SERVINGS

English peas are one of those ingredients that are fantastic when they're super fresh, but quickly lose their flavor the longer they're off the vine. Because this soup is all about showcasing the pea's bright, sweet flavor, I would only use just-picked peas from the farmers market or a CSA (community-supported agriculture), or substitute frozen peas, which have locked in that flavor at its peak. If you see fresh peas at the grocery store, it's guaranteed they'll be disappointing. This is a great soup to serve in smaller portions as a starter to a decadent meal.

- 1 pound English peas, either very fresh or frozen
- 1 cup loosely packed tarragon leaves
- 2 cups loosely packed parsley
- 1½ cups loosely packed mint leaves
- 1 bunch scallions, thinly sliced (about 1½ cups)
- 1 tablespoon chopped jalapeño chile (seeds removed)
- Kosher salt and freshly ground black pepper
- 1 lemon, for zesting
- ¼ cup plain yogurt
- 4 radishes, cut into matchsticks
- 12 chive blossoms or 2 tablespoons chopped fresh chives

BRING A large saucepan full of heavily salted water to a boil and prepare an ice bath. Blanch the peas until tender, 60 to 90 seconds. Transfer to the ice bath to cool, then transfer to a blender.

WORKING WITH one herb at a time, blanch the tarragon, parsley and mint for 8 to 10 seconds per batch and transfer to the ice bath. Then blanch the scallions for 15 seconds and transfer to the ice bath. When cool, transfer the herbs and scallions to the blender.

ADD THE jalapeño to the blender along with 2 cups water. Blend the soup until very smooth (this will take longer than you think), thinning it out with a little more water if needed. Pass the soup through a fine-mesh sieve into a bowl, pressing on the solids to extract as much liquid as possible. Season the soup with salt and pepper to taste and refrigerate until cold.

LADLE THE soup into chilled bowls. Drizzle some yogurt over each bowl and grate some lemon zest on top. Garnish with a sprinkle of radishes and chive blossoms (or chopped chives). Serve.

THE TAKEAWAY

This soup calls for a whopping 6 cups of fresh herbs, which means keeping their vibrant green color intact requires some work. Blanching the herbs will lock in their color and ever so slightly mellow their flavor, which will let them support—rather than dominate—the peas.

When you're making this soup, it's also a great time to blanch some extra herbs and freeze them for long-term storage. After they've been blanched and cooled, squeeze out as much water as possible, roughly chop them, then place them in small freezer bags, pushing the herbs to make a thin, even layer. When you want to use them (in a soup, stew, or sauce), simply break or snip off a piece.

Chicken Liver Mousse

MAKES 4 TO 6 SERVINGS

I was never a fan of chicken liver until I was a young cook at Union Square Cafe, when chef Michael Romano made an Italianized version of the classic French dish by adding pancetta to his recipe. It was an eye-opening experience, and I've loved chicken liver mousse ever since. This is my homage to that dish, made lighter and smoother by adding a lot of butter and a healthy dose of Cognac.

─────── CHICKEN LIVER MOUSSE ───────

1 pound chicken livers, cleaned

Kosher salt and freshly ground black pepper

¾ cup diced pancetta

¾ cup diced onion

⅔ cup Cognac

4 teaspoons extra-virgin olive oil

10 sage leaves

½ cup (1 stick) unsalted butter, at room temperature

1 teaspoon sugar

SPREAD THE livers out on paper towels and season generously with salt.

IN A large skillet, cook the pancetta over medium heat until some of the fat has rendered, about 5 minutes. Add the onion and cook, stirring, until caramelized, 10 to 15 minutes. Turn off the heat and add about a quarter of the Cognac, stirring it into the onion mixture and scraping up any browned bits in the pan. Scrape the contents of the pan into a bowl and wipe the skillet clean.

IN THE same skillet, heat the olive oil over high heat until almost smoking. Add the chicken livers and brown on all sides, 3 to 4 minutes. Pour off any fat in the pan and add the onion mixture. Add the remaining Cognac and carefully flambé (if the Cognac doesn't light immediately, tilt the pan toward the flame or use a long lighter or match if cooking on an electric stovetop). Shake the pan until the flames subside and cook until almost all of the liquid has evaporated and the livers have reached an internal temperature of 165°F. Turn off the heat and stir in the sage.

TRANSFER THE contents of the skillet to a food processor and add the butter, 1 tablespoon salt, and the sugar. Pulse until almost smooth but still slightly chunky. Season to taste with salt and pepper. Transfer the mousse to a serving container (you can put it all in a small casserole dish, or divide it between smaller jars or ramekins). Cover with plastic wrap, lightly pressing the wrap to the surface of the mousse so that it doesn't oxidize. Refrigerate until set, roughly 4 to 6 hours. The mousse can be made a day or two in advance.

─────── FRIED SAGE LEAVES ───────

Vegetable oil

12 sage leaves

Kosher salt

IN A medium saucepan, bring 1 inch of oil to 365°F. Working in batches, add the sage leaves and briefly fry until crisp, a few seconds per batch. Transfer to paper towels and season with salt.

─────── FOR SERVING ───────

1 tablespoon champagne vinegar

1 tablespoon extra-virgin olive oil

Salt and freshly ground black pepper

Chicken Liver Mousse

Fried Sage Leaves

Crostini or grilled bread

IN A small bowl, whisk the vinegar and oil together until emulsified. Season to taste with salt and pepper.

USING THE back of a spoon, make a few shallow dimples in the chicken mousse. Drizzle the vinaigrette into the holes. Garnish the mousse with the fried sage leaves and serve with crostini.

THE TAKEAWAY

Chicken liver mousse is rich, rich, rich, so it needs something to lighten it up. Add a vibrant acidity by making little divots in the top of the mouse, then filling them with a simple vinaigrette. Take this idea and run with it using different vinaigrettes and condiments, especially the Honey-Mustard Vinaigrette from the Roasted Brussels Sprouts on page 175.

Heirloom Tomato Toasts

MAKES 4 SERVINGS

At Union Square Cafe, we made a traditional tomato bruschetta that has inspired many tomato-and-bread dishes since. This dish is so much more than tomatoes on bread, however. It starts with selecting the best tomatoes. At the farmers market, I look for ones that are firm but fully ripe, which I can tell from looking at the color around the stem: It should match the rest of the tomato. A lot of recipes will have you salt tomatoes ahead of time to release some of the juices, but here I season the tomatoes right before layering them on the toast; any liquid they release gets soaked up by the cheese and bread, making every bite that much more interesting.

——— THE TAKEAWAY ———

There's a surprising amount of finesse needed to toast the bread just right. Think of it like a steak: You want to create a crispy crust on the outside without overcooking the middle. Then hit the toasted bread with some Parmesan and give it a quick broil, which will result in the best cheesy bread you've ever had.

Four ½- to ¾-inch-thick slices rustic Italian bread (sourdough bread also works)

Extra-virgin olive oil

1 cup finely grated Parmesan cheese

1 pound multicolored heirloom tomatoes, cut crosswise in ¼-inch slices, slices halved if large

Kosher salt and freshly ground black pepper

Flaky sea salt

PREHEAT THE broiler and place a wire rack inside a rimmed baking sheet. Arrange the bread in a single layer on the rack and drizzle both sides with olive oil. Broil the bread, flipping halfway through, until light golden brown, about 2 minutes per side. Remove from the oven and immediately sprinkle one side of each piece generously with Parmesan cheese, pressing gently with your fingers to help it adhere. Return to the oven and broil just until the cheese begins to melt, 30 to 60 seconds. Transfer the bread to a serving platter.

ARRANGE THE tomato slices on a plate or platter and season with kosher salt and pepper. Shingle the tomatoes, seasoned side down, on top of each slice of bread. Sprinkle the flaky salt over the top, along with some more pepper. Drizzle with olive oil and serve.

39

Fluke Sashimi
WITH DRIED TOMATOES, STRAWBERRIES, AND OLIVES

MAKES 4 SERVINGS

Tomatoes and strawberries are such good partners that you can often apply the same cooking technique to both. In this case, I take a cue from a fresh tomato sauce and grate strawberries to make the base of a dramatic, red-hued dressing. I also love the intense flavor and texture of semi-dried cherry tomatoes (you'll also find them in the Baked Ricotta recipe on page 43), so I apply the same oven-drying technique to both tomatoes and strawberries (as well as olives). The strawberry-olive dressing could work with any raw-fish preparation, and would also work as a chunky dressing for delicate greens, such as baby butterhead or young chicories.

——— QUICK-CURED FLUKE ———

10 ounces skinless very fresh fluke

2 sheets of kombu

PLACE THE fluke between the sheets of kombu, then wrap in plastic and refrigerate for 2 to 4 hours (the kombu will soften as the fish cures). Discard the kombu and thinly slice the fish across the grain.

——— STRAWBERRY-OLIVE DRESSING ———

MAKES 1 CUP

2 cups whole strawberries (preferably smaller ones)

¼ cup chopped Sevillano or Castelvetrano olives

¼ cup chopped kalamata olives

½ cup halved cherry tomatoes

¼ cup plus 1 tablespoon oil from Marinated Olives (page 104) or extra-virgin olive oil

¼ cup fresh lime juice

1 tablespoon elderflower syrup or 1½ teaspoons honey

2½ teaspoons kosher salt

PREHEAT THE oven to 200°F and line a rimmed baking sheet with parchment paper. Measure 1½ cups of strawberries and cut them in half. Arrange the halved strawberries in a single layer on one-third of the baking sheet. Arrange all the chopped olives in a single layer on one-third of the baking sheet, and the tomatoes on the remaining section. Bake until the ingredients are shriveled and mostly dried (but still have some chew), 1 to 2 hours. Set the dehydrated strawberries aside for garnishing the dish. Place the dehydrated olives and tomatoes in a bowl.

USING THE large holes of a box grater, grate the remaining ½ cup strawberries (you should have ¼ cup). Add to the dehydrated olives and tomatoes along with the oil, lime juice, elderflower syrup, and kosher salt and stir well. The dressing can be made a few hours ahead of time, but is best used the same day.

——— FOR SERVING ———

Quick-Cured Fluke

Kosher salt

Strawberry-Olive Dressing

Flaky sea salt

Dehydrated strawberries (from dressing, above)

2 tablespoons chopped fennel fronds

2 tablespoons chopped tarragon

SEASON ONE side of the fluke with kosher salt. Arrange the fish, seasoned side down, on a serving plate. Spoon the dressing over the fish and sprinkle with flaky salt. Sprinkle the dehydrated strawberries, fennel, and tarragon over and serve.

THE TAKEAWAY

This recipe contains three different semi-dehydrated ingredients: strawberries, olives, and cherry tomatoes. I love the way this technique concentrates the flavors of each ingredient without completely drying them out. They become slightly chewy, but don't taste at all cooked. This is a great way to add big flavor to a dressing or garnish without adding too much moisture to the dish.

THE TAKEAWAY

Finishing a cheesy dip with a quick pass under the broiler adds a lot to the dish. It caramelizes the cheese on top, creating a nice textural contrast to the creamy molten cheese below. It also lightly chars and intensifies the flavors of the cherry tomatoes. Keep this trick in mind anytime you're baking something cheesy.

Baked Ricotta
WITH DRIED CHERRY TOMATOES

MAKES 8 SERVINGS

When I was developing the menu for Loring Place, everyone wanted us to serve seasonal toasts like the ones I'd become known for at ABC Kitchen. But I felt like our food culture had already hit "peak toast," so I came up with seasonal variations of this baked ricotta. The simple, creamy ricotta base—I add some mozzarella to give it a slightly stringy cheese pull—is a great platform for all kinds of toppings, including kabocha squash, fava beans, mushrooms, or anything else that can stand up to the heat. You can also keep this super simple and just finish the broiled cheese with chopped herbs and a drizzle of olive oil.

—— RICOTTA MIXTURE ——

16 ounces whole-milk ricotta

8 ounces fresh mozzarella cheese, grated

⅓ cup grated Parmesan cheese

1 tablespoon chopped oregano

1 teaspoon garlic oil from Garlic Confit (page 112) or extra-virgin olive oil

2 teaspoons kosher salt

1 large egg plus 1 egg yolk

COMBINE ALL ingredients in a large bowl and stir until well combined.

—— SPICY VINAIGRETTE ——

MAKES ABOUT ⅓ CUP

2 tablespoons extra-virgin olive oil

3 tablespoons white wine vinegar

One ½-inch piece red finger chile

½ teaspoon Aleppo pepper flakes

½ teaspoon kosher salt

½ teaspoon sugar

⅛ teaspoon sweet smoked paprika

COMBINE ALL ingredients in a blender or mini food processor and blend until emulsified.

—— DRIED CHERRY TOMATOES ——

1 cup cherry tomatoes, halved through the equator (not the stem end)

2 tablespoons extra-virgin olive oil

Kosher salt

PREHEAT THE oven to 300°F and line a rimmed baking sheet with parchment paper. In a bowl, toss the tomatoes with the olive oil. Arrange the tomatoes, cut side up, on the baking sheet and season with salt. Bake until the tomatoes are slightly shriveled but still juicy inside, 35 to 45 minutes. Transfer to a bowl and set aside.

—— FOR SERVING ——

Ricotta Mixture

Dried Cherry Tomatoes

3 tablespoons finely grated Parmesan cheese

3 tablespoons Spicy Vinaigrette

1 tablespoon Crispy Garlic (page 246)

Flaky sea salt

2 tablespoons finely shredded basil

1 tablespoon finely shredded mint

Pinch of ground cinnamon

Grilled bread or crostini

INCREASE THE oven to 500°F. Spoon a ½-inch layer of ricotta mixture into an 8-inch cast-iron skillet or similarly sized shallow baking dish. Dot the top of the ricotta with the tomatoes, cut side up, and sprinkle evenly with the Parmesan. Bake until the ricotta mixture starts to bubble, 5 to 8 minutes. Remove the dish from the oven and turn on the broiler. Broil the ricotta until lightly browned on top, 2 to 3 minutes. Drizzle with the vinaigrette and sprinkle the crispy garlic, flaky salt, basil, mint, and cinnamon over the top. Serve with grilled bread or crostini for dipping.

Baked Ricotta

WITH KABOCHA SQUASH, CARAMELIZED ONIONS, AND MINT

MAKES 8 SERVINGS

Here's another version of my baked ricotta, using the same cheesy base, but this time topping it with kabocha squash, a sweet variety from Japan. I first roast cubes of squash until they're soft and fluffy, then toss them with sweet-and-sour caramelized onions to make another gooey starter that's perfect for kicking off a fall or winter dinner—or pair it with a salad for lunch!

THE TAKEAWAY

I create extra layers of flavor in caramelized onions by adding apple cider vinegar and maple syrup after cooking the onions until they're well browned, then boiling the liquid until it's thickened. These sweet-sour onions are great with all kinds of grilled meats, and make a fantastic addition to a grilled cheese sandwich.

—— CARAMELIZED ONIONS ——

2 tablespoons extra-virgin olive oil

1 large Spanish onion, halved and thinly sliced

½ teaspoon kosher salt

½ cup apple cider vinegar

¼ cup maple syrup

IN A medium skillet, heat the olive oil over medium heat. Add the onions and salt and cook, stirring frequently, until golden brown, about 20 minutes. Add the vinegar and maple syrup, increase the heat to medium-high, and bring to a boil. Reduce until the liquid is syrupy, 3 to 5 minutes. Remove from the heat.

—— ROASTED SQUASH ——

½ small kabocha squash, peeled, seeded, and cut into 1-inch pieces (about 2 cups)

1 tablespoon extra-virgin olive oil

¼ teaspoon kosher salt

Red pepper flakes

MEANWHILE, PREHEAT the oven to 500°F and line a rimmed baking sheet with parchment paper. In a bowl, toss the squash with the olive oil, salt, and a large pinch of red pepper flakes. Spread the squash in an even layer on the prepared baking sheet and roast, tossing halfway through, until the squash is tender and golden, about 13 minutes.

—— RICOTTA MIXTURE ——

16 ounces whole-milk ricotta

8 ounces fresh mozzarella cheese, grated

⅓ cup grated Parmesan cheese

1 tablespoon chopped oregano

1 teaspoon oil from Garlic Confit (page 112) or extra-virgin olive oil

2 teaspoons kosher salt

1 large egg plus 1 egg yolk

COMBINE ALL ingredients in a large bowl and stir until well combined.

Caramelized Onions

Roasted Squash

Ricotta Mixture

**1 tablespoon thinly
sliced mint**

Flaky sea salt

**Grilled bread or
crostini**

IN A bowl, combine the caramelized onions and roasted squash and gently stir. Spoon a ½-inch layer of ricotta mixture into an 8-inch cast-iron skillet or similarly sized shallow baking dish. Top with the squash mixture. Bake until the ricotta mixture starts to bubble, 5 to 8 minutes. Remove the dish from the oven and turn on the broiler. Broil the ricotta until lightly browned on top, 2 to 3 minutes. Sprinkle with the mint and flaky salt. Serve with grilled bread or crostini for dipping.

Tomato-Raspberry Gazpacho

MAKES 4 SERVINGS

I love pairing summer fruits with tomato: Strawberries, peaches, watermelon—all are perfect. But raspberries in particular have a big, distinguishable punch that can stand up to lots of savory flavors. Here, I combine them with tomatoes to make a deeply flavored soup that can be quickly thrown together for a starter, light dinner, or lunch. Just leave enough time to thoroughly chill the soup before serving, and keep it cold by refrigerating your soup bowls as well. While some gazpachos are chunky, this one is meant to be silky smooth.

THE TAKEAWAY

When seasoning soups, you'll often find that they taste blander as they cool down. Keep this in mind when making a cold soup like gazpacho, and taste it after it's fully chilled. You'll likely need to add more salt and acid, but it's safer to season right before serving rather than overcompensate when the soup is warmer.

GAZPACHO BASE

3 cups raspberries

2 Persian cucumbers or ½ English cucumber, peeled and roughly chopped

3 large beefsteak tomatoes, roughly chopped

1 teaspoon chopped red finger chile

¾ cup diced bread

¼ cup extra-virgin olive oil

½ medium shallot, peeled

1½ teaspoons fresh lime juice

1 tablespoon sherry vinegar

1 tablespoon kosher salt

1 teaspoon sugar

COMBINE ALL ingredients in a blender or food processor and puree until smooth. Pass through a fine-mesh strainer into a bowl, pressing on the solids to extract all of the liquid. Refrigerate until cold, then taste and adjust seasoning as needed with more salt, sugar, lime juice, or vinegar.

FOR SERVING

1 lime

Gazpacho Base

½ cup raspberries

1 Persian cucumber or ¼ English cucumber, peeled and diced

1 cup cherry tomatoes, halved

Extra-virgin olive oil

1 tablespoon thinly sliced mint

1 tablespoon chopped tarragon

Flaky sea salt

USING A sharp knife, cut the peel and pith off the lime. Working over a bowl, cut the lime between the membranes to release the segments. Dice the segments into small pieces.

DIVIDE THE gazpacho among four chilled bowls. Top with the lime, raspberries, cucumber, and tomatoes. Drizzle the soups with olive oil, sprinkle with the herbs and flaky salt, and serve.

Vegetable Crudités
WITH CARROT-GINGER DIP

MAKES 8 SERVINGS

If you've eaten in a Japanese restaurant, you're probably familiar with the carrot-ginger dressing that usually comes on a salad towards the beginning of the meal. I fell in love with this flavor combination at sushi restaurants during college, and have been playing with it ever since. This iteration was inspired by a party we threw at home, when I was staring down a platter of crudités and trying to come up with a dip that was vegetable based. Texture is key to making this bright dip memorable: Keep pureeing it until it's the texture of a smooth chocolate mousse. When selecting vegetables for your crudités, try to get a good mix of colorful vegetables, and remember to cut them into one- or two-bite pieces. No double dipping!

─────── CARROT-GINGER DIP ───────

MAKES 2 CUPS

6 medium carrots, peeled and cut into ¼-inch-thick slices (about 2 cups)

1 tablespoon rice vinegar

3 tablespoons white miso

One 1-inch piece ginger, peeled and roughly chopped

1½ tablespoons sriracha (store-bought or homemade, page 68)

4 teaspoons tamari or soy sauce

1 teaspoon kosher salt

¼ cup sunflower or vegetable oil

3 tablespoons fresh lime juice

PREHEAT THE oven to 325°F. Place the carrots and a splash of water in a shallow baking dish. Cover with foil and bake until tender, about 30 minutes. Transfer to a blender and add the vinegar, miso, ginger, sriracha, tamari, and salt. Blend until very smooth; the ideal texture is mousse-like and should take several minutes of blending to achieve. With the blender running, slowly stream in the sunflower oil until emulsified. Transfer to a container and let cool for a few minutes, then stir in the lime juice. The dip can be made a day or two ahead of time and refrigerated until ready to use.

─────── KOMBU SPRAY ───────

MAKES ⅔ CUP

Two 6-by-6-inch pieces kombu

⅔ cup water

One 3-inch strip orange zest

IN A saucepan, combine the kombu, water, and zest. Bring to a boil, remove from the heat, cover, and let sit for 10 minutes. Strain and transfer to a spray bottle. The kombu spray can be refrigerated for a couple of days.

─────── FOR SERVING ───────

Carrot-Ginger Dip

4 cups mixed vegetables cut into bite-size pieces, such as:

  Fennel wedges

  Halved radishes (with greens attached, if possible)

  Baby carrots (with greens attached, if possible)

Kohlrabi spears

Broccoli florets

Persimmon wedges

Cauliflower florets

Blanched asparagus

Blanched sugar snap peas

Blanched green beans

Kombu Spray

SPREAD SOME carrot-ginger dip in the bottom of a shallow serving bowl. Insert the vegetables lengthwise into the dip so they form a colorful bouquet that hides most of the dip below. Spritz the vegetables with the kombu spray and serve.

50

Crudité platters are usually a visual representation of unfulfilled potential: a few piles of raw vegetables, usually dried out from sitting around too long, next to a bowl of some white-colored dip. You can save yourself (and your guests) from crudité boredom with just a few spritzes of a flavorful spray. I infuse water with kombu and orange to create a seasoning spray that adds a subtle—but impactful—umami flavor to raw vegetables. Take this idea and run with it: You can make sprays with all sorts of ingredients and bases (try adding some vinegar or citrus juice to the water). Spritz some over your next crudité platter and watch it disappear. Use any leftover spray on your next salad.

Arctic Char Sashimi
WITH SESAME-CHILE CONDIMENT

MAKES 4 SERVINGS

This raw fish starter works with all sorts of seafood, thanks to the chunky condiment that accompanies it. I was inspired to make it after having a piece of raw salmon at my local sushi joint, which was drizzled with a sesame-chile oil. I layer on more textures and flavors: pungent ginger, crunchy fried garlic, smoky-fruity gochugaru flakes, and funky miso paste. It's similar in texture to the Broken Chile Sauce I spoon over grilled asparagus (page 145), giving you little chunks of intense flavor swimming in a slightly smoky infused oil. I always keep some of this condiment in the fridge because it tastes great with any fish preparation, on top of rice bowls, spooned over broccoli, green beans, and much, much more.

——— THE TAKEAWAY ———

In addition to the sesame-chile condiment, this recipe contains a bonus takeaway: marinated kohlrabi. Sometimes you want a crunchy vegetable garnish that isn't as punchy as a pickle, but is still packed with flavor. In times like this, I'll make a simple infusion—here, mint leaves steeped in lemon juice. It only takes an hour or two for the kohlrabi to soak up the marinade's bright flavor, but it becomes something way more interesting than the raw vegetable. Try this technique with other crunchy vegetables like fennel, jicama, or cucumbers, or on fruits like apples, pears, or watermelon.

——— MARINATED KOHLRABI ———

1 cup mint leaves

⅔ cup fresh lemon juice

1 small kohlrabi, peeled and cut into ¼-by-1½-inch batons (about 1 cup)

IN A small saucepan, combine the mint and lemon juice. Heat over low heat until just before the liquid begins to simmer, then turn off the heat. Using a wooden spoon, gently muddle the mint. Let steep for 30 minutes, then strain into a bowl. Add the kohlrabi to the liquid, cover, and refrigerate for at least 1 hour, or up to 24 hours.

——— SESAME-CHILE CONDIMENT ———

MAKES ABOUT 1 CUP

⅔ cup Paprika Oil (page 186)

4 teaspoons finely chopped ginger

1½ teaspoons kosher salt

3 tablespoons sesame seeds

¼ teaspoon red pepper flakes

1 tablespoon Crispy Garlic (page 246)

3 tablespoons sesame oil

2 tablespoons maple syrup

2 teaspoons gochugaru (Korean chile flakes)

1 tablespoon yellow miso

IN A small saucepan, heat the paprika oil over medium-low heat. Add the ginger and salt and cook until the ginger starts to brown, about 2 minutes. Add the sesame seeds and cook until they start to brown, about 2 minutes. Add the red pepper flakes and cook for 1 minute, then add the crispy garlic and turn off the heat. Stir in the sesame oil, maple syrup, gochugaru, and miso until well combined. The condiment can be made ahead and refrigerated for up to 2 weeks.

Marinated Kohlrabi

4 teaspoons thinly sliced mint

10 ounces skinless super-fresh arctic char, thinly sliced across the grain

Kosher salt

Flaky sea salt

½ cup Sesame-Chile Condiment

2 lemon wedges

COVER THE bottom of a serving plate with a single layer of kohlrabi, including a little bit of the mint-infused marinade. Sprinkle the mint over. Season one side of the char with the kosher and flaky salt, then arrange the fish, seasoned side down, over the kohlrabi. Season the top of the fish with both salts, then spoon the sesame-chile condiment over the fish, making sure to distribute some of the chunky parts over each piece. Squeeze the lemon wedges over and serve.

Smoky Japanese Eggplant
WITH CARROT-HAZELNUT ROMESCO

MAKES 4 SERVINGS

I first made carrot romesco for the WastED dinner series at Manhattan's Blue Hill restaurant, where chefs were enlisted to create elevated dishes from everyday kitchen scraps. For my turn in the series, we were given a mess of extra carrots and a pig's head. We made head cheese from the pork, then turned the carrots into a smoky, nutty sauce based on the Spanish staple, which is traditionally made with roasted tomatoes and pine nuts. I've been using my carrot romesco in various dishes ever since. It goes especially well with fish (the classic pairing for romesco), chicken, and green vegetables, and you'll also find it in this book as an accompaniment for Crispy Potatoes and Sunchokes on page 168. Here, it's paired with Japanese eggplant, which picks up a smoky flavor from the broiler. But if you have a charcoal grill, do what we do at my restaurant and cook the eggplant in smoldering embers to get an extra-smoky flavor.

THE TAKEAWAY

Cooking carrots in their own juice might seem like overkill, but it really intensifies their flavor. This technique was popularized in the nouvelle cuisine era in France and by Charlie Trotter and Jean-Georges Vongerichten here in America. I apply it to all kinds of vegetables, including beets, parsnips, and fennel, and you can try it with poached fruit as well.

——— CARROT-HAZELNUT ROMESCO ———

MAKES ABOUT 3 CUPS

4 medium carrots, cut into ¼-inch slices

1 cup carrot juice

½ cup fresh orange juice

2 tablespoons fresh lemon juice

1 tablespoon plus ¾ teaspoon sugar

¼ cup toasted hazelnuts, skins removed

¼ cup toasted almonds

1 garlic clove, mashed into a paste

1½ teaspoons chipotle powder

1 teaspoon hot smoked paprika

2 teaspoons kosher salt

4 teaspoons white wine vinegar

¼ cup plus 2 tablespoons extra-virgin olive oil

3 tablespoons almond oil (if you can't find almond oil, use hazelnut oil)

IN A small saucepan, combine the carrots, carrot juice, orange juice, lemon juice, and 1 tablespoon sugar. Bring to a boil, then lower the heat and simmer, covered, until the carrots are tender, 8 to 10 minutes. Transfer the carrots to a bowl and continue simmering the liquid until it's thick enough to coat the back of a spoon. Turn off the heat and return the carrots to the pan.

PLACE THE hazelnuts and almonds in a food processor and pulse until finely chopped. Transfer to a medium bowl. To the food processor, add the carrots and their reduced liquid, the garlic, chipotle powder, paprika, salt, vinegar, and the remaining ¾ teaspoon sugar. Turn the machine on and slowly stream in the ¼ cup olive oil and the almond oil; the mixture should form a chunky puree. Scrape into the bowl with the nuts and stir in the remaining 2 tablespoons olive oil. The romesco can be made ahead and refrigerated for up to 1 week.

PICKLED RED ONIONS

MAKES ABOUT 2 CUPS

1 large red onion, halved and thinly sliced

1 tablespoon cumin seeds

1 tablespoon coriander seeds

2 teaspoons fennel seeds

1½ teaspoons yellow mustard seeds

1 dried red chile

1 dried bay leaf

1¾ cups apple cider vinegar

2 tablespoons sugar

PLACE THE onion in a sterilized pint-size jar.

IN A small skillet, toast the cumin, coriander, fennel, and mustard seeds over low heat until fragrant, about 30 seconds. Let cool. Add to the jar along with the chile and bay leaf.

IN A small saucepan, combine the vinegar and sugar. Bring to a boil, stirring until the sugar dissolves. Pour over the red onions and let cool to room temperature. Let sit for at least 1 hour before using, or seal the jar and refrigerate for up to 2 weeks.

SMOKY JAPANESE EGGPLANT

4 Japanese eggplants

PREHEAT THE broiler (use the high setting if you have the option). Place the eggplants on a baking sheet and broil, turning once or twice, until charred all over and just tender when pierced with a knife, but holding their shape, 4 to 5 minutes. Transfer the eggplants to a cutting board. When cool enough to handle, peel them with a paring knife. Cut the eggplants crosswise into 1-inch pieces.

FOR SERVING

½ cup Carrot-Hazelnut Romesco

Smoky Japanese Eggplant

¼ cup diced Pickled Red Onions

Extra-virgin olive oil

Lemon wedge

Flaky sea salt

1 tablespoon chopped parsley

1 tablespoon chopped mint

1 tablespoon thinly sliced scallion greens

Warm mini pitas or quartered pitas

SPREAD THE romesco in the bottom of a serving plate. Top with the eggplant pieces, cut-side down. Sprinkle with the pickled onions. Drizzle with olive oil and a squeeze of lemon. Sprinkle the salt and herbs over the top. Serve with pitas.

Beet Green and Chickpea Soup
WITH CORN FRITTERS

MAKES 4 TO 6 SERVINGS

Most cooks throw away beet greens without giving them a second look. But they're delicious, packed with nutrients, and both the stems and greens can be used much like Swiss chard.

THE TAKEAWAY

I wanted to give this soup a crunchy garnish, like a crouton, but more elevated. The cheesy cornmeal fritters do the trick, and they're easy enough to throw together. Keep these fritters in mind anytime you want an unexpected accompaniment to soups, stews, or chili, or serve them as a snack.

CHICKPEA SOUP

3 tablespoons extra-virgin olive oil

1 large white onion, quartered and thinly sliced

2 garlic cloves, thinly sliced

Kosher salt and freshly ground black pepper

1 tablespoon tomato paste

1 pound beet greens (from 2 bunches), well washed, leaves roughly chopped, and stems cut into 1- to 2-inch pieces

7 cups water

One 15-ounce can chickpeas, rinsed and drained

IN A medium saucepan, heat the oil over medium heat. Add the onion, garlic, and 1 tablespoon salt. Cook, stirring occasionally, until softened, about 5 minutes. Add the tomato paste and cook, stirring, for 1 minute. Add the beet stems and cook, stirring occasionally, until they just begin to soften, about 4 minutes. Add the beet leaves and cook until wilted, about 3 minutes. Add the water and bring to a boil. Reduce the heat to medium-low and simmer for 20 minutes. Add the chickpeas and simmer for 15 minutes. Season the soup with salt and pepper.

CORN FRITTERS

¾ cup water

1 tablespoon unsalted butter

¼ cup fine ground yellow cornmeal

½ teaspoon kosher salt, plus more for seasoning the fritters

½ teaspoon finely ground black pepper

½ cup finely grated Parmesan cheese

1 large egg

1 tablespoon Aleppo pepper or 1½ teaspoons crushed red pepper flakes

Vegetable oil, for frying

WHILE THE soup is cooking, combine the water and butter in a small saucepan. Bring to a simmer over medium-high heat, then whisk in the cornmeal. Reduce the heat to low and cook, stirring occasionally, until the cornmeal reaches the texture of a soft polenta, about 15 minutes. Stir in the salt, black pepper, and cheese. Cook, stirring, for 1 minute longer. Add the egg and Aleppo and whisk constantly to make sure the egg is distributed evenly. Remove from the heat and let cool slightly.

ADD 1 inch of vegetable oil to a medium saucepan and heat to 350°F. Working in batches, drop the cornmeal batter into the hot oil, a rounded tablespoon at a time, and fry, turning a few times, until golden all over, 3 to 4 minutes. Transfer to a paper towel–lined plate and sprinkle with salt.

FOR SERVING

Chickpea Soup

Corn Fritters

DIVIDE THE soup among bowls and top each with a couple of fritters. Serve.

56

Butternut Squash Fries
WITH LEMON-PARMESAN AIOLI

MAKES 6 TO 8 SERVINGS

When I serve guests this appetizer, they always ask "What's in the aioli?" When I list the ingredients, they can't believe how simple it is. The secret is the miso: Not only does it add richness (and eliminate the need for eggs or mayonnaise), it adds a depth of flavor you can't quite place. A ton of grated Parmesan also helps.

The creamy aioli actually started as a dressing for potato salad, then became a dip as I added more and more miso. It also makes a great spread for sandwiches. Here, it's the perfect accompaniment for crispy fried squash, or any other vegetable you want to swap in—I'd start with asparagus, zucchini, or green beans.

THE TAKEAWAY

Whenever I make a tempura-like batter for fried vegetables, I add a good amount of vodka to the mixture, which yields a much crispier coating. This is because vodka evaporates more quickly than the water in the batter, which dries out the batter more quickly and creates large bubbles that result in an airy and incredibly crispy crust.

ROASTED BUTTERNUT SQUASH

1 medium butternut squash (about 2 pounds)	3 tablespoons chopped sage
⅓ cup extra-virgin olive oil	1½ teaspoons red pepper flakes
Finely grated zest of 1 medium lemon	1 teaspoon kosher salt
	1 teaspoon freshly ground black pepper

PREHEAT THE oven to 375°F and place a wire rack in a rimmed baking sheet. Peel the squash and cut it in half crosswise between the neck and the bulb. Cut the bulb in half, scoop out the seeds, and cut the flesh into ½-inch wedges. Cut the neck into fries about 3 inches long and ½ inch thick.

IN A mixing bowl, combine the oil, lemon zest, sage, red pepper flakes, salt, and black pepper and stir to combine. Add the squash and toss well to coat (you want the spices to stick to the squash).

ARRANGE THE squash on the prepared baking sheet and roast until just tender when pierced with a paring knife, 20 to 25 minutes. Set aside and let cool to room temperature. (The roasted squash can be made ahead and refrigerated for a few hours.)

LEMON-PARMESAN AIOLI

MAKES 2 CUPS

Finely grated zest of 4 lemons	4 teaspoons chopped rosemary
½ cup fresh lemon juice	1½ teaspoons kosher salt
2 tablespoons champagne or white wine vinegar	1 teaspoon freshly ground black pepper
¼ cup plus 2 teaspoons yellow miso paste	½ cup extra-virgin olive oil
3 cups finely grated Parmesan cheese	

CONTINUES ➡

57

IN A blender, combine the lemon zest and juice, vinegar, miso, Parmesan, rosemary, salt, and black pepper. Blend until very smooth. With the blender running, slowly add the olive oil. Refrigerate until ready to use; the aioli can be made up to 2 days ahead.

BUTTERNUT SQUASH FRIES

Canola or peanut oil, for frying

¾ cup all-purpose flour, plus 1 cup for dredging

¾ cup cornstarch

½ cup vodka

½ cup seltzer water

Roasted Butternut Squash

Kosher salt

¼ cup finely chopped parsley

HEAT 2 inches of oil in a medium saucepan until it reaches 375°F on a deep-fry thermometer.

IN A medium bowl, whisk together the ¾ cup flour and the cornstarch. Combine the vodka and seltzer in a mixing cup and whisk the liquid into the dry ingredients until smooth.

PLACE THE remaining flour in a shallow bowl. Working in batches, dredge the roasted squash in the flour, then dip them in the batter, letting the excess drip off. Fry the squash in batches, stirring frequently, for 1½ to 2 minutes, until crisp (the batter will not brown very much). Transfer the fried squash to paper towels and sprinkle with salt and chopped parsley. Let the oil return to 375°F between batches.

TO SERVE, transfer the squash to a platter and serve with the Lemon-Parmesan Aioli on the side.

Creamy Tomato and Cauliflower Soup

MAKES 4 SERVINGS

Cauliflower and tomato were a common pairing in the Indian-style food I cooked at Tabla, but this recipe was born out of a desire to merge two of my favorite American soups: cream of cauliflower and cream of tomato. This is an easy one-pot meal that you can serve with Parmesan croutons (which you'll find in the Heirloom Tomato Panzanella on page 109), but I also love it with a grilled cheese sandwich. It freezes well, too, so make a double batch and save some for a cold winter day.

── THE TAKEAWAY ──

By adding cauliflower and pureeing the heck out of it, you can make cream of tomato soup with very little dairy. (I add a little crème fraîche for extra richness, but you can turn this into a vegan-friendly soup by skipping the dairy altogether.) Cauliflower won't overpower most vegetable-based soups, so keep this trick in mind anytime you're making a pureed soup.

One 14½-ounce can whole peeled tomatoes

3 tablespoons extra-virgin olive oil

1 medium Spanish onion, thinly sliced

Kosher salt

2 large garlic cloves, thinly sliced

1 head cauliflower, cored and cut into 1-inch pieces

3 cups water

½ cup crème fraîche

1 tablespoon plus 2 teaspoons sherry vinegar, plus more for seasoning

── FOR SERVING ──

Chopped chives

Freshly cracked black pepper

Extra-virgin olive oil

2 cups Parmesan Croutons (page 110)

CRUSH THE tomatoes in a bowl with your hands.

IN A large saucepan, heat the olive oil over medium-low heat. Add the onions and a big pinch of salt and cook, stirring frequently, until the onions are very soft, 5 to 7 minutes. (The onions shouldn't take on any color; lower the heat if they begin to brown.) Add the garlic and cook until soft, about 2 minutes. Add the tomatoes, cauliflower, and water. Bring to a simmer, cover, and cook over low heat until the cauliflower is very tender, 10 to 15 minutes. Turn off the heat and stir in the crème fraîche.

BLEND THE soup until smooth, either with an immersion blender or by transferring to a standing blender. Wipe out the saucepan and pass the soup through a fine-mesh strainer back into the pan, pressing on the solids. Stir in the vinegar and season the soup to taste with salt and more vinegar, if needed. Divide among bowls and garnish each with chives, black pepper, a drizzle of olive oil, and Parmesan croutons. Serve.

Salmon Tartare
WITH PICKLED CHERRY-PEPPER RELISH, CRUNCHY VEGETABLES, AND GARLIC TOASTS

MAKES 4 SERVINGS

Here's a super-flavorful (and color-saturated) starter you can assemble while the rest of your dinner is in the oven. It's relatively easy to find super-fresh salmon worthy of tartare and other raw preparations (once again, ask your fishmonger which of their salmon is freshest). But if you can't find any, this dish can also be made with cold-smoked salmon—at Loring Place, we give our salmon a quick sauna in the cold smoker to add another layer of flavor.

You can surely skip the garlic toasts and serve it with crackers or crostini, but you'll be missing out on a cool technique for making intensely garlicky bread. Mashing garlic confit and butter together helps infuse the entire slice of toast with flavor, and once you make garlic bread this way, you'll never go back.

THE TAKEAWAY

The pickled cherry-pepper relish that becomes the dressing for the cubed salmon has potential beyond this dish. Make a double batch and use the leftovers as a sandwich spread, or serve alongside other fish or chicken dishes. You can also mix it with mayonnaise to make a creamier condiment. We use homemade whole-grain mustard in our relish. Try making mustard yourself, then compare it to the store-bought stuff to see why we go through the extra effort.

WHOLE-GRAIN MUSTARD

MAKES ABOUT 2 CUPS

1 cup apple cider vinegar

⅔ cup filtered water

2 tablespoons elderflower syrup

⅓ cup yellow mustard seeds

⅓ cup brown mustard seeds

1 tablespoon kosher salt

COMBINE ALL ingredients in a bowl and stir well. Cover the bowl and let sit at room temperature for 8 hours. Transfer half of the mustard to a blender or food processor and blend until smooth. Add the remaining half and pulse the machine a few times to break up the seeds, leaving the mustard coarse. Transfer to a container, cover, and let sit at room temperature for 2 days before using. The mustard can be refrigerated for up to 6 months.

PICKLED CHERRY-PEPPER RELISH

MAKES ABOUT ⅔ CUP

4 pickled cherry
peppers, drained,
seeds removed
(if any), and finely
chopped (about
¼ cup)

¼ cup finely chopped
Pickled Red Onions
(page 55)

¼ cup whole-grain
mustard, store-
bought or homemade
(page 62)

⅓ cup champagne
vinegar

4 teaspoons kosher salt

COMBINE ALL of the ingredients in a small bowl
or storage container and refrigerate until ready
to use, up to 1 week.

GARLIC TOASTS

4 cloves Garlic Confit
(page 112)

4 tablespoons unsalted
butter, softened

6 slices pullman or pain
de mie bread, crusts
removed

PREHEAT THE oven to 425°F and place a wire
rack in a rimmed baking sheet. In a small bowl,
mash the garlic confit into a paste. Add the butter and mash until combined. Spread the garlic
butter on both sides of the bread. Place on the
rack in the pan and bake until golden brown,
8 to 10 minutes. Cut the bread diagonally into
triangles.

FOR SERVING

6 ounces fresh salmon,
cut into ¼-inch dice

1 tablespoon extra-
virgin olive oil, plus
more for drizzling

⅓ cup Pickled
Cherry-Pepper Relish

2 tablespoons diced
cucumber

¼ cup diced celery

1 tablespoon chopped
parsley

1 tablespoon chopped
fennel fronds

1 tablespoon thinly
sliced scallion greens

Flaky sea salt and
freshly ground black
pepper

Garlic Toasts

IN A small bowl, mix the salmon with the olive oil
and cherry-pepper relish. Arrange the salmon
mixture in the middle of a serving plate. Top with
the vegetables and herbs. Drizzle with some more
olive oil, sprinkle with flaky salt and pepper, and
serve with the garlic toasts.

Farro and White Bean Soup
WITH HERB OIL

MAKES 8 TO 10 SERVINGS

Now here's a soup I would consider a full meal. I created it for Food & Wine *magazine, loading it up with beans, farro, tomatoes, and Swiss chard and topping it with a fragrant herb oil. It's a soup you can probably make any night of the week without having to run to the store (just be sure to plan ahead so you can soak the beans overnight). This recipe will also leave you with some leftover Swiss chard stems, which you can use to make the Grilled Chard Stems on page 169.*

——— FARRO AND WHITE BEAN SOUP ———

Kosher salt

1 cup dried Great Northern beans

¾ cup farro

¼ cup extra-virgin olive oil

1 small Spanish onion, thinly sliced

½ cup diced carrots

½ cup diced celery root

4 large garlic cloves, thinly sliced (3 tablespoons)

One 28-ounce can diced tomatoes

1 bunch Swiss chard, leaves coarsely chopped, stems reserved for another use

Freshly ground black pepper

IN A bowl, whisk 6 tablespoons salt into 4 cups water until dissolved. Add the beans and soak for at least 8 hours, or overnight.

DRAIN THE beans and place in a medium saucepan. Cover the beans with at least 4 inches of water and bring to a boil. Lower the heat and simmer the beans until tender, about 1 hour and 15 minutes. Drain, reserving 3 cups of the cooking liquid.

MEANWHILE, PLACE the farro in a small saucepan and cover with 2 inches of water. Add 1 table-spoon salt and bring to a boil. Cook the farro until al dente, about 20 minutes. Drain.

IN A medium saucepan, heat the olive oil over medium heat. Add the onion and a pinch of salt and cook, stirring occasionally, until softened but not browned, about 7 minutes. Add the carrots, celery root, and garlic and cook, stirring occasionally, until the vegetables begin to soften, about 5 minutes. Add the tomatoes with their juices and cook over medium-high heat, stirring occasionally, until the juices have reduced by half, 8 to 10 minutes. Add the reserved cooking liquid from the beans and 7 cups water and bring to a simmer. Stir in the beans, farro, and Swiss chard and simmer over medium heat until the chard is wilted, about 5 minutes. Season to taste with salt and pepper.

——— HERB OIL ———

MAKES ABOUT 1 CUP

2 tablespoons finely chopped parsley

1 tablespoon finely chopped rosemary

1 tablespoon finely chopped thyme

1 tablespoon finely chopped oregano

½ jalapeño chile, seeded and finely chopped

1½ teaspoons finely grated lemon zest

1 cup extra-virgin olive oil

Kosher salt

IN A medium bowl, whisk the herbs with the jalapeño, lemon zest, and olive oil. Season to taste with salt. The herb oil can be made 1 day ahead and refrigerated until ready to use.

——— FOR SERVING ———

Farro and White Bean Soup

Herb Oil

1 cup freshly grated Parmesan cheese

LADLE THE soup into bowls and top each with some of the herb oil. Sprinkle with the Parmesan and serve.

THE TAKEAWAY

In my restaurant, we often make an herb oil that involves blanching herbs, blending them with oil, and straining the liquid. While not difficult, this process takes time, and I don't like spending a lot of time on soup. This simplified herb oil is made by chopping a bunch of herbs (you can speed things up by chopping them all together at the same time), then letting them briefly infuse the oil. A drizzle of this fragrant oil can be used to finish other soups, as well as pizza and roast chicken. If you make it a few hours or a day ahead, it'll get even more flavorful.

Arctic Char Crudo
WITH GRILLED POMELO AND BLOOD ORANGE DRESSING

MAKES 4 SERVINGS

I always have at least one crudo dish on the menu at Loring Place, but the fish we use will vary depending on whatever super-fresh seafood my purveyor can get at the time. You should take the same approach at home. Shop at a market you trust (preferably a seafood-focused spot, as they'll put a premium on freshness), tell the fishmonger your crudo intentions, and ask him or her what's up to the task. You don't need to ask for "sushi grade" fish, as that term is unregulated and doesn't really mean anything. Another great place to find crudo-worthy fish is at a Japanese or Korean market: They often have a wide selection of fish that's been sourced specifically for raw preparations.

Classic Italian-style crudo is usually simply dressed with olive oil, salt, and citrus. My crudos are hardly classic, but I like to take those same elements and amplify them, as well as adding texture. Here, I add texture both with raw vegetables in the dressing—much like shallots add crunch to a mignonette—as well as a juicy pop of grilled citrus. Leftover dressing will be great with any kind of cooked fish or grilled chicken.

——— BLOOD ORANGE DRESSING ———

MAKES 1½ CUPS

1 medium blood orange	1 tablespoon maple syrup
2 tablespoons fresh lemon juice	½ teaspoon finely grated ginger
2 tablespoons red wine vinegar	2 teaspoons kosher salt
2 tablespoons extra-virgin olive oil	¼ teaspoon freshly ground black pepper

1 scallion, white part only, thinly sliced	¼ cup diced carrots (⅛-inch dice)
½ red finger chile, finely chopped (with seeds)	¼ cup diced parsnips (⅛-inch dice)

USING A sharp knife, cut the peel and pith off the blood orange. Working over a bowl, cut half of the orange between the membranes to release the segments. Dice the segments, then return them to the bowl. Squeeze the remaining orange into the bowl; you should have about 1 tablespoon juice. Add the remaining ingredients and gently stir to combine. Let sit for at least 1 hour before serving to allow the flavors to marry.

——————— FOR SERVING ———————

1 pomelo or grapefruit	½ cup Blood Orange Dressing
Sugar	
One 10-ounce fillet of very fresh arctic char or salmon	Flaky salt
	Extra-virgin olive oil
	2 tablespoons thinly sliced mint

PREPARE A hot grill or preheat a grill pan over high heat. Using a sharp knife, cut the peel and pith off the pomelo. Working over a bowl, cut the pomelo between the membranes to release the segments. Pat the pomelo segments dry, then dust with sugar. Grill the pomelo segments, turning once with a spatula, until charred, about 30 seconds per side (if the segments don't easily release from the grill when nudged with the spatula, wait a few seconds and try again). Break or cut each segment into three pieces and arrange on a large plate.

USING A super-sharp knife, slice the char into ⅛-inch-thick slices, rinsing your knife under cold water between slices to prevent sticking. Arrange the char slices over the grilled pomelo. Spoon the blood orange dressing over the fish. Finish with the flaky salt, a drizzle of olive oil, and the mint. Serve.

66

——— THE TAKEAWAY ———

Grilling citrus to the point where it's deeply
charred turns something that's sweet,
sour, and bitter into something incredibly
savory. It'll add an unexpected depth
to any dish you pair it with, from salads
and composed vegetable dishes to raw
and cooked seafood. I like to dust citrus
segments with sugar before grilling them,
which helps speed up caramelization—
otherwise, it might take too long to get a
good sear before the citrus begins to cook.
This is a great cheat for other ingredients
as well: I will unabashedly sprinkle a bit
of sugar on vegetables, pork, steak—
even burgers!—before throwing them on
the grill. Give it a try and you'll see some
astonishing results.

Bay Scallop Crudo
WITH HOUSE SRIRACHA

MAKES 4 SERVINGS

This elegant starter comes together in a snap, once you finish making your own sriracha (more on that in the takeaway). I love the natural sweetness of bay scallops and how it pairs with the spicy, slightly acidic hot sauce, but if you can't find bay scallops, you can thinly slice larger scallops—just make sure they're very fresh.

—— THE TAKEAWAY ——

Why make your own sriracha? I like the bottled stuff as much as anyone else, but once I perfected the recipe for our house-made sriracha, it's hard to go back. Charring the chiles and garlic gives this version a much deeper flavor, and habaneros lend their distinctive citrusy, floral flavor. Taste it alongside the bottled stuff and see for yourself.

—————— HOUSE SRIRACHA ——————

MAKES ABOUT 1⅓ CUPS

8 ounces red cayenne chiles, stems and seeds removed

4 ounces red habanero chiles, stems and seeds removed

6 garlic cloves, cut into ¼-inch slices

2 tablespoons plus 2 teaspoons kosher salt

1 tablespoon sugar

2 teaspoons filtered water

⅓ cup white wine vinegar

HEAT A nonstick or cast-iron skillet over medium-high heat. Add the chiles and garlic and cook, stirring a few times, until slightly charred and toasted, 5 to 7 minutes. Transfer to a blender or food processor and add the salt, sugar, and water. Pulse until finely chopped, then transfer to a very clean container and cover with cheesecloth. Let ferment at room temperature for 3 days. Transfer to a blender and add the vinegar. Puree until very smooth. Transfer to a sterilized jar or storage container and refrigerate for up to 1 month.

——————— FOR SERVING ———————

10 ounces bay scallops or thinly sliced dry-packed diver scallops

Extra-virgin olive oil

Kosher salt

Flaky sea salt

¼ cup House Sriracha

2 lemon wedges

Fresh horseradish, for grating

1 lemon, for zesting

1 tablespoon finely chopped tarragon

4 teaspoons Crispy Garlic (page 246)

IN A bowl, drizzle the scallops with olive oil and toss well. Season with a pinch each of kosher and flaky salt and toss again. Arrange the scallops on a serving platter and spoon small dots (or use a squeeze bottle) of sriracha on and around the scallops. Drizzle the scallops with more olive oil and squeeze the lemon wedges over. Finely grate some horseradish and lemon zest over the dish. Season with more flaky salt and sprinkle the tarragon and crispy garlic over. Serve.

Parsnip Soup
WITH SAUTÉED MUSHROOMS

MAKES 4 TO 6 SERVINGS

Confession: I'm not that big on soup. I don't consider it a complete meal by itself, so when I do make soup, it's usually eaten alongside a sandwich or salad. But when I'm short on time and need to throw something together, soup is a good option. For this reason, I try to minimize the amount of knife work required and either make a chunky soup (like the Beet Green and Chickpea Soup on page 56) or a pureed soup like this one. If you have guests with dietary restrictions, keep this recipe in your back pocket—it's vegan and gluten-free.

THE TAKEAWAY

As with the beet green soup, I like pairing simple, rustic soups with more dramatic garnishes. Instead of bread and cheese here, I reach for a mixture of mushrooms, which I sauté until they're both crispy and chewy, adding lots of texture and savory flavors to an otherwise simple soup.

PARSNIP SOUP

3 tablespoons extra-virgin olive oil

1 large white onion, diced

4 large garlic cloves, thinly sliced

1 tablespoon kosher salt

2 pounds parsnips, trimmed, peeled, and cut into ½-inch pieces

7 cups water

IN A medium saucepan, heat the oil over medium heat. Add the onion, garlic, and 1 tablespoon salt and cook, stirring, until softened, about 5 minutes. Add the parsnips and cook, stirring occasionally, until the outsides of the parsnips are slightly softened, about 10 minutes. Add the water and bring to a boil. Reduce the heat to medium and simmer until the parsnips are very tender, about 30 minutes. Let cool slightly, then transfer the soup to a blender (or use an immersion blender) and puree until smooth, working in batches if necessary. Keep warm.

SAUTÉED MUSHROOMS

2 tablespoons extra-virgin olive oil

12 ounces mushrooms (I like trumpet and cremini, but use whatever you can find)

Kosher salt and freshly ground black pepper

1 teaspoon finely grated lemon zest

2 tablespoons fresh lemon juice

1 tablespoon thinly sliced red finger chile

1 tablespoon chopped parsley

1 scallion, thinly sliced

WHILE THE soup is cooking, heat the olive oil in a medium skillet over high heat. Add the mushrooms and ½ teaspoon salt. Cook the mushrooms, stirring occasionally, until deeply caramelized, about 5 minutes. Scrape the mushrooms into a bowl and add the lemon zest and juice, the chile, parsley, and scallion. Toss to combine. Season to taste with salt and pepper.

FOR SERVING

Parsnip Soup

Sautéed Mushrooms

Extra-virgin olive oil

Flaky sea salt and freshly ground black pepper

LADLE THE soup into bowls and top with the mushrooms. Drizzle with olive oil, sprinkle with flaky salt and a few grinds of pepper, and serve.

69

Quick-Cured Salmon
WITH FENNEL AND CITRUS VINAIGRETTE

MAKES 4 TO 6 SERVINGS

There's a huge difference in texture and flavor between raw salmon and gravlax or other styles of cured salmon. This quick cure falls somewhere between the two, closer to the raw side of the spectrum. Coating the fish in seasoning and wrapping it in kombu for a few hours will draw out some of the fish's moisture and infuse it with plenty of flavor, without making it something that begs for a bagel. The quick-cure method works on all kinds of fish as well, and you have plenty of room to play around with different spices and seasonings. At my restaurant, we use fatty salmon bellies for this dish—if you can find some, use them.

—— THE TAKEAWAY ——

In addition to the quick-cure technique, this recipe is hiding a small, but very useful, lesson. Tossing finely diced onion into a hot skillet will give you that great caramelized onion flavor, but retain most of the crunch of raw onions. Use this trick whenever you want a similar effect, whether it's in a dressing, sauce, or vinaigrette.

—— QUICK-CURED SALMON ——

1 tablespoon fennel seeds

1 tablespoon coriander seeds

¼ cup sugar

¼ cup flaky sea salt

½ cup packed chopped fennel fronds

Finely grated zest of 1 lemon

Finely grated zest of 1 small orange

1 Thai chile pepper, thinly sliced

2 large sheets of kombu (large enough to cover the salmon)

1 pound center-cut skinless Atlantic salmon

IN A small skillet, toast the fennel and coriander seeds over medium heat until fragrant, 2 to 3 minutes. Grind the seeds and add to a bowl. Add the sugar, salt, fennel, citrus zest, and chile pepper and mix well. Spread half the curing mix in a thin layer on one sheet of the kombu. Place the salmon on top. Spread the remaining mix on top of the salmon, then place the other sheet of kombu on top. Wrap the kombu in a clean kitchen towel (or several layers of paper towels), then wrap everything tightly in plastic wrap (the kombu will soften as it cures). Refrigerate for 4 to 6 hours (4 hours for thinner fillets, 6 hours for thicker ones).

—— FENNEL AND CITRUS VINAIGRETTE ——

1 lemon

1 medium orange

½ cup finely diced red onion

¼ cup plus 2 tablespoons extra-virgin olive oil

2 tablespoons chile powder

¼ cup finely diced fennel

1 teaspoon elderflower syrup or ½ teaspoon honey

½ teaspoon kosher salt

USING A sharp knife, cut the peel and pith off the lemon and orange. Working over a bowl, cut between the membranes of the lemon to release three segments. Cut each segment into a few pieces and place in a mixing bowl. Repeat with the orange. Squeeze the remaining lemon to measure out 2 tablespoons of the juice and add to the mixing bowl. Repeat with the orange.

HEAT A skillet over high heat. In a small bowl, toss the onions with the 2 tablespoons olive oil. When the skillet is very hot, add the onions and cook, stirring, until they're lightly charred but still crunchy, about 1 minute. Remove from the heat and stir in the chile powder. Let cool for a few minutes, then scrape into the bowl with the citrus segments. Add the remaining ¼ cup olive oil, the fennel, elderflower syrup, and salt.

FOR SERVING

Quick-Cured Salmon

Fennel and Citrus
  Vinaigrette

Extra-virgin olive oil

Flaky sea salt

2 tablespoons thinly
  sliced mint

2 tablespoons chopped
  cilantro

UNWRAP THE salmon, then rinse away the cure and pat dry. Using your longest, sharpest knife at a sharp angle, cut the salmon on the diagonal into thin slices (about ⅛ inch thick), rinsing and wiping the blade between slices to prevent sticking.

ARRANGE THE salmon slices in a circle on a serving plate. Scatter the vinaigrette over the top. Drizzle with olive oil and sprinkle with the salt and herbs. Serve.

Chicken Nuggets
WITH MAPLE-CHILE GLAZE AND CELERY ROOT

MAKES 4 TO 6 SERVINGS

General Tso's chicken is one of the most famous Chinese-American dishes. It's one of my favorites, and a loose inspiration for this dish. The glaze that coats the crispy little bites of fried chicken has gone through many iterations, but I landed on a spicier, Latin-flavored version. While you could serve these sweet-spicy nuggets with rice and call it homemade takeout, I like making the protein a secondary player to vegetables. Here, the big-flavored chicken is balanced by a creamy celery root puree and some crunchy pickled watermelon radishes or carrots (though pretty much any pickled vegetable can be swapped in).

THE TAKEAWAY

The spicy and sweet maple-chile glaze that coats the fried chicken here is surprisingly versatile. Use it as a sauce for roast chicken, grilled pork chops, or a steak, or as a glaze on fattier cuts of fish (e.g., salmon, tuna, or arctic char). It's great on broccoli and Brussels sprouts, too.

MAPLE-CHILE GLAZE

1 dried ancho chile
1 dried pasilla chile
½ cup maple syrup
½ cup fresh lime juice
1 teaspoon kosher salt

1 red finger chile, seeded and finely chopped (about 2 tablespoons)
2 teaspoons red pepper flakes

IN A skillet, warm the ancho and pasilla chiles over medium-high heat until toasted, about 5 minutes. Let cool slightly, then remove the stems. Finely grind the chiles in a spice grinder. Measure out 1 tablespoon of the chile powder, saving the rest for another use.

IN A small saucepan, combine the 1 tablespoon of chile powder, the maple syrup, lime juice, and salt. Bring to a boil and reduce by half. Add the finger chile and red pepper flakes and let cool completely. The glaze can be made ahead and refrigerated for up to 1 week.

CELERY ROOT PUREE

¼ cup extra-virgin olive oil
4 garlic cloves, thinly sliced
1 medium shallot, thinly sliced

1 medium celery root, peeled and coarsely chopped
2 cups water
2 teaspoons kosher salt

IN A small saucepan, combine the olive oil and garlic. Sweat over medium-low heat until softened, about 3 minutes. Add the shallots and cook until soft, about 4 minutes. Add the celery root, water, and salt. Bring to a simmer, cover, and cook over medium-low heat until the celery root is very tender, 15 to 20 minutes. Strain, reserving the cooking liquid. Blend the celery root mixture until completely smooth, adding a bit of cooking liquid if necessary. Return to the saucepan and keep warm until ready to use.

CONTINUES ➡

72

GLAZED CHICKEN NUGGETS

Vegetable or canola oil, for frying

1 pound boneless, skin-on chicken thighs (about 6 thighs)

½ cup cornstarch

¼ teaspoon baking powder

1 teaspoon kosher salt

Maple-Chile Glaze

IN A medium saucepan, heat 2 inches of oil to 360°F. Meanwhile, cut the chicken thighs into 2-inch pieces. In a shallow bowl, whisk together the cornstarch, baking powder, and salt. Toss the chicken pieces in the cornstarch mixture, shaking off any excess. Working in batches, fry the chicken until well browned and cooked through, 2 to 3 minutes. Transfer the chicken to a bowl and immediately toss with the maple-chile glaze until well coated.

PICKLED WATERMELON RADISHES

MAKES ABOUT 2 CUPS

8 medium watermelon radishes, diced or thinly sliced (about 2 cups)

2 cups red wine vinegar

¼ cup sugar

1½ teaspoons kosher salt

PLACE THE radishes in a sterilized pint-size jar. In a small saucepan, combine the vinegar, sugar, and salt. Bring to a boil, stirring until the sugar and salt dissolve. Pour over the radishes and let cool to room temperature. Use immediately or seal the jar and refrigerate for up to 2 weeks.

FOR SERVING

1 cup Celery Root Puree

Glazed Chicken Nuggets

½ cup diced Pickled Watermelon Radishes and/or Pickled Carrots (page 263)

4 teaspoons Crispy Garlic (page 246)

1 tablespoon roughly chopped cilantro

1 tablespoon thinly sliced mint

SPREAD THE celery root puree on a platter or in a large, shallow bowl. Top with the chicken and drizzle some of the leftover glaze from the bowl around the dish. Sprinkle the pickles, crispy garlic, and herbs over the top and serve.

Matzo Ball Soup

MAKES 8 TO 10 SERVINGS

My family used to make matzo ball soup for Passover, and we had an ongoing (and mostly unspoken) contest for who can make the most flavorful soup with the lightest matzo balls. In my version, I break with convention and fold beaten egg whites into the matzo ball mixture to make them extra-fluffy. I also add an herb-packed soffritto to the matzo mix, a nod to the matzo ball soup we served at Tabla's unleavened bread bar during the Passover holiday.

THE TAKEAWAY

Any great chicken soup starts with good homemade chicken stock. But when making the matzo soup, I amplify the chicken flavor by using the stock to poach a whole chicken. But instead of simmering the chicken in stock, I like to bring the stock to a boil, then turn off the heat, cover the pot, and wait 30 minutes—which is exactly enough time to cook the chicken through. (If you're using an especially large chicken, add a few extra minutes of poaching time.) You can use this trick anytime you want a perfectly poached chicken—and an extra-flavorful stock.

CHICKEN STOCK

MAKES ABOUT 1 GALLON

4 pounds chicken wings	2 garlic cloves, smashed
6 quarts water	4 parsley sprigs
1 large onion, diced	1 rosemary sprig
2 celery stalks, chopped	2 thyme sprigs
2 medium carrots, chopped	1 bay leaf
	1 tablespoon black peppercorns

PLACE THE chicken wings in a stockpot and cover with the water. Bring to a gentle simmer over medium heat, skimming any foam from the surface as needed. When the liquid begins to simmer, add the remaining ingredients. Return to a gentle simmer and cook for 4 to 6 hours. Strain the stock through a fine-mesh sieve, discarding the solids. The chicken stock can be refrigerated in an airtight container for up to 4 days, or frozen for up to 3 months.

CHICKEN SOUP

One 3- to 4-pound whole chicken	2 celery stalks, chopped
Kosher salt	1 leek, white and light green parts only, halved and thinly sliced
2 tablespoons extra-virgin olive oil	1 teaspoon black peppercorns
2 garlic cloves, thinly sliced	2 bay leaves
One 1-inch piece ginger, peeled and thinly sliced	2 basil sprigs
2 medium carrots, chopped	5 parsley sprigs
1 large onion, chopped	1 rosemary sprig
	1 gallon Chicken Stock

A DAY before making the soup, rinse the chicken and pat dry. Using 1 teaspoon salt per pound, season the chicken all over. Set a wire rack inside a rimmed baking sheet and place the chicken on top. Refrigerate for at least 6 hours, or up to 24 hours.

CONTINUES ➡

IN A stockpot, heat the olive oil over medium-low heat. Add the garlic and ginger and cook, stirring, for 3 minutes. Add the carrots, onion, celery, leek, peppercorns, and 1 tablespoon salt and cook, stirring, until the vegetables are softened, 5 to 7 minutes. Add the chicken, bay leaves, basil, parsley, and rosemary. Add the stock and bring to a boil over high heat. Cover the pot, turn off the heat, and wait 30 minutes.

AFTER 30 minutes, the chicken should be cooked through (an instant-read thermometer inserted into the thickest part of a leg should register 165°F). If the chicken isn't done after 30 minutes, bring the liquid to a simmer and cook until it's finished.

REMOVE THE chicken from the pot and discard the skin. Shred the meat and set aside. Strain the soup through a fine-mesh sieve, discarding the solids. Return the soup to the pot and season to taste with salt.

MATZO BALLS

1 tablespoon extra-virgin olive oil	One 4.5-ounce box matzo meal
2 garlic cloves, minced	1 tablespoon chicken or duck fat
1 teaspoon finely chopped fresh ginger	3 large egg yolks
Kosher salt	1 tablespoon chopped chives
2 tablespoons minced onion	1 tablespoon chopped dill
½ jalapeño chile, minced (with seeds)	1 tablespoon chopped parsley
1 teaspoon finely chopped parsley	⅓ cup plus 2 tablespoons seltzer water
1 teaspoon finely chopped oregano	4 large egg whites

IN A small skillet or saucepan, heat the olive oil over medium-low heat. Add the garlic, ginger, and ½ teaspoon salt and cook, stirring, for 2 minutes. Add the onion and jalapeño and cook, stirring, until the onion is translucent, about 4 minutes. Remove from the heat and stir in the finely chopped parsley and oregano. Let the soffritto cool, then transfer to a large bowl. Add the matzo meal, chicken fat, egg yolks, chives, dill, chopped parsley, and 1 teaspoon salt. Add the seltzer and stir to combine.

USING A stand mixer fitted with the whisk attachment (or a handheld electric mixer), beat the egg whites until they hold stiff peaks. Fold the egg whites into the matzo mixture until combined. Using oiled hands, shape the matzo mixture into Ping-Pong–size balls (you should have enough to make about 10 balls).

FOR SERVING

Chicken Soup	Shredded chicken (from the chicken soup, above)
Matzo Balls	
4 medium carrots, thinly sliced (about 1 cup)	½ cup chopped dill
	¼ cup chopped chives
1 turnip, cut into small dice	

BRING THE soup to a simmer. Add the matzo balls to the soup, cover the pot, and gently simmer until cooked through, 20 to 25 minutes. Using a slotted spoon, transfer the matzo balls to serving bowls (1 matzo ball per bowl). Add the carrots, turnip, and shredded chicken to the soup and simmer until the chicken is warmed through and the vegetables are slightly softened, about 5 minutes. Divide the soup among the bowls, garnish with the dill and chives, and serve.

Crispy Pork Belly Confit

WITH CITRUS GLAZE AND PICKLED VEGETABLES

MAKES 6 TO 8 SERVINGS

Pork belly has become a hallmark entrée of many restaurants, but I prefer to eat this fatty cut in smaller doses, rather than a large, sticky hunk as a main course. Because the belly is so rich—especially after slow cooking in duck fat—it needs a lift. In this dish, that lift comes from a bright citrus glaze that coats the seared belly (make sure you toss them together as soon as the pork comes out of the pan, so the glaze will adhere). A scattering of pickled vegetables finishes the job, adding a complementary crunch to the soft, pillow-y pork.

——— THE TAKEAWAY ———

You really can't mess up confit belly pork, and the confit process yields my ideal pork belly texture: meat that's tender but not mush, with plenty of fat intact—like a great piece of thick bacon. I treat our pork belly confit like unsmoked bacon, cutting it up into lardons for salads, or crisping thin slices to use in a killer BLT. I intentionally have you make double the amount of confit than you need for the recipe, so you have some left over to play with.

——— PORK BELLY CONFIT ———

3 pounds boneless, skinless pork belly

2 cups rendered duck fat

PREHEAT THE oven to 225°F. Place the pork belly, fatty side up, in a baking dish (use one just large enough to fit it) and pour the fat over the top, enough to submerge the pork. Cover the dish with foil and bake until the pork is very tender, about 4 hours. Let cool to room temperature, then strain the fat (reserve for another use). Wrap the pork belly in plastic wrap and refrigerate overnight.

——— CITRUS GLAZE ———

¼ cup sugar

1 tablespoon water

1 tablespoon finely chopped ginger

1½ teaspoons kosher salt

1 tablespoon finely grated orange zest and ¼ cup strained fresh orange juice (from 1 to 2 oranges)

2 tablespoons finely grated Meyer lemon zest and ½ cup strained fresh Meyer lemon juice (from 2 Meyer lemons*)

½ teaspoon finely ground black pepper

IN A small saucepan, combine the sugar and water. Melt the sugar over medium heat, without stirring, until it turns a light amber color. Add the ginger and salt, turn off the heat, and add the orange and lemon zest and the pepper. Wait a couple of minutes (this allows the citrus zest to "bloom"), then add the orange and lemon juices. Bring the mixture to a boil and reduce until syrupy. Turn off the heat and let cool.

*If you can't find Meyer lemons, use ½ cup orange juice and ¼ cup regular lemon juice (instead of the ¼ cup orange juice and ½ cup lemon juice), and substitute regular lemon zest for the Meyer lemon zest.

CONTINUES ➡

77

────── PICKLED VEGETABLE SALAD ──────

1 red finger chile,
thinly sliced

½ medium fennel bulb,
thinly sliced

2 medium radishes,
thinly sliced
(preferably on a
mandoline)

2 cipollini onions or
¼ medium red onion,
thinly sliced

1 small turnip, thinly
sliced (preferably on
a mandoline)

1 teaspoon fresh
rosemary needles

1 teaspoon coriander
seeds

½ cup white wine
vinegar

¼ cup sugar

PLACE THE chile and all of the vegetables in a heatproof bowl. Combine the rosemary and coriander in a cheesecloth bundle and add to the vegetables. In a small saucepan, combine the vinegar and sugar and bring to a boil, stirring until the sugar is dissolved. Pour over the vegetables and let cool to room temperature. Discard the cheesecloth bundle. Cover and refrigerate until ready to use (the pickles can be made a day or two in advance).

────── FOR SERVING ──────

1 pound Pork Belly
Confit, cut into
1-inch cubes (save the
rest of the confit for
another use)

Citrus Glaze

Pickled Vegetable
Salad

3 tablespoons fines
herbes (equal parts
finely chopped
chervil, chives,
parsley, and tarragon)

Flaky sea salt

HEAT A large skillet over medium-high heat. Working in batches, add the pork and brown on all sides. Add some of the glaze and toss until the pork is well coated, then transfer to a bowl. Repeat with the remaining pork and glaze.

ARRANGE THE pork in a shallow serving bowl. Scatter the pickled vegetables over the top and sprinkle with the fines herbes and salt. Serve.

Salads

———

85   Charred Sugar Snap Pea Salad with Manchego Vinaigrette

Manchego Vinaigrette

86   Butterhead Lettuce with Cashew Vinaigrette

Cashew Vinaigrette

87   Roasted Summer Bean Salad with Toasted Hazelnuts and Sungold Tomatoes

Hazelnut Vinaigrette

88   Little Gem Salad with Sesame-Soy Dressing and Crispy Shallots

Crispy Shallots | Sesame-Soy Dressing

91   Asparagus and Puntarelle Salad with Seared Poached Eggs

Lemon Vinaigrette | Pickled Fennel

Charred Sugar Snap Pea Salad
WITH MANCHEGO VINAIGRETTE

MAKES 4 SERVINGS

When I worked for Jean-Georges at ABC Kitchen, he encouraged us to combine raw and cooked versions of the same ingredient in a dish, which results in contrasting textures and flavors. Here, I apply this idea to snap peas—quickly blanching half and charring the rest in a skillet—and toss them with a cheesy vinaigrette that reminds me (in a good way) of the peppery bottled salad dressings I loved growing up. My dressing is made creamy by pureeing Manchego cheese in a blender until it completely breaks down and emulsifies. This will take longer than you think, so keep blending until the dressing is completely smooth.

———— MANCHEGO VINAIGRETTE ————

MAKES ABOUT 1 CUP

3 tablespoons buttermilk, well shaken

¼ cup plus 1½ teaspoons champagne vinegar

1½ tablespoons fresh lemon juice

¼ cup plus 1½ teaspoons extra-virgin olive oil

3 ounces Manchego cheese, coarsely grated (about ¾ cup)

1½ teaspoons kosher salt

¾ teaspoon freshly ground black pepper

IN A blender, combine all ingredients and blend until very smooth, scraping the side of the carafe as needed. The dressing can be made up to 1 day ahead and refrigerated until ready to use.

— BLANCHED AND CHARRED SNAP PEAS —

4 cups sugar snap peas (about 1 pound), strings removed

1 tablespoon extra-virgin olive oil

1 teaspoon kosher salt

BRING A medium saucepan of salted water to a boil and prepare an ice bath. Blanch 2 cups of the snap peas until bright green and crisp-tender, 30 to 45 seconds, then transfer to the ice bath. When cool, transfer the peas to paper towels to drain.

HEAT A skillet (preferably cast-iron) over high heat. In a mixing bowl, toss the remaining 2 cups snap peas with the oil and salt. When the skillet is very hot, working in batches to not crowd the pan, add the peas and let them char on one side without moving them around, 30 to 45 seconds. Turn the peas over and char the other side, then transfer to a plate and let cool to room temperature before assembling the salad.

———————— FOR SERVING ————————

Blanched and Charred Snap Peas

4 globe radishes, cut into small wedges

¼ cup finely chopped mixed herbs (such as parsley, tarragon, and chives)

Flaky sea salt

2 cups baby lettuce (such as arugula or romaine)

Manchego Vinaigrette

½ cup coarsely grated Manchego cheese

½ red finger chile, thinly sliced

Freshly ground black pepper

IN A mixing bowl, combine the blanched snap peas and charred snap peas with the radishes, half of the herbs, and a big pinch of flaky salt; toss to combine. Divide the lettuce among four plates and top with the snap pea mixture. Drizzle with the dressing (about 2 tablespoons per plate) and garnish with the cheese, sliced chile, and remaining herbs. Grind some pepper over each salad and serve.

Butterhead Lettuce
WITH CASHEW VINAIGRETTE

MAKES 4 SERVINGS

This seemingly simple fork-and-knife salad is surprisingly filling and offers lots of big flavors, thanks to the chunky cashew vinaigrette and a generous shower of herbs. You can find butterhead lettuce at the supermarket year-round, but don't hesitate to make this salad with other farmers market finds.

THE TAKEAWAY

Butterhead lettuce is mild, so it can take on a flavorful dressing. The cashew vinaigrette is an example of a dressing that begins with infusing olive oil with the flavor of toasted nuts, then gets cooled down with more olive oil and additional flavorful ingredients. This technique can work with all kinds of nuts; I do something similar with the Pistachio Vinaigrette on page 158.

CASHEW VINAIGRETTE

MAKES ABOUT 1 CUP

¾ cup extra-virgin olive oil

½ cup chopped raw cashews

1 Thai chile, thinly sliced (with seeds)

¼ cup champagne vinegar

1 tablespoon fresh lemon juice

1 teaspoon kosher salt

¼ teaspoon freshly ground black pepper

IN A medium skillet, heat ¼ cup of the olive oil over medium heat. Add the cashews and cook, stirring, until golden brown, 5 to 7 minutes. Stir in the remaining ½ cup olive oil and the chile and stir to combine. Scrape the contents of the skillet into a small bowl and stir in the vinegar, lemon juice, salt, and pepper.

FOR SERVING

2 tablespoons chopped oregano

2 tablespoons chopped chives

2 tablespoons thinly sliced mint

Cashew Vinaigrette

2 heads butterhead lettuce, halved

2 radishes, thinly sliced (use a mandoline if you have one)

½ cup chopped green olives

Freshly cracked black pepper

COMBINE ALL the herbs in a small bowl. Add about half of the herbs to the vinaigrette. Place the lettuce halves, cut side up, on four serving plates. Spoon some of the vinaigrette over each lettuce half. Top each salad with some of the radishes and olives, sprinkle with the remaining herbs, and finish each salad with some freshly cracked black pepper. Serve.

Roasted Summer Bean Salad

WITH TOASTED HAZELNUTS AND SUNGOLD TOMATOES

MAKES 4 TO 6 SERVINGS

Today I'm known as a vegetable fanatic, but I grew up almost exclusively on boiled vegetables and didn't think much of them until I learned the transformative power of caramelization. Once I started roasting, grilling, and sautéing vegetables, it completely changed the way I approach fresh produce. I didn't start roasting summer beans until recently, but it quickly became one of my favorite ways to prepare them—dry heat unlocks lots of flavor you can't get by boiling or steaming.

THE TAKEAWAY

One thing you give up when roasting beans (and other similar vegetables) is their crunchy texture. Here, I reintroduce crunch to the dish with the vinaigrette, using toasted hazelnuts (and their oil) to enhance the otherwise straightforward dressing.

HAZELNUT VINAIGRETTE

MAKES ABOUT 1 CUP

1 medium shallot, finely chopped

¼ cup toasted and coarsely chopped hazelnuts

¼ cup champagne vinegar

2 tablespoons fresh lemon juice

1½ teaspoons kosher salt

¼ teaspoon freshly ground black pepper

¼ cup extra-virgin olive oil

2 tablespoons hazelnut oil

IN A bowl, whisk together the shallot, hazelnuts, vinegar, lemon juice, salt, and pepper with a fork until combined. Slowly whisk in the oils until emulsified. The vinaigrette can be made up to 1 day ahead; refrigerate until ready to use.

ROASTED SUMMER BEANS

1 pound mixed summer beans (such as Romano beans, wax beans, or green beans), cut into 2- to 3-inch pieces

¼ cup extra-virgin olive oil

1 teaspoon kosher salt

¼ teaspoon freshly ground black pepper

PREHEAT THE oven to 425°F. Bring a large saucepan of salted water to a boil and prepare an ice bath. Working in batches, blanch the beans for 1 minute, then transfer to the ice bath to cool. Drain the beans and pat dry with paper towels.

ON A baking sheet, toss the beans with the olive oil and season with salt and pepper. Roast until the beans are just tender and lightly browned in spots, 8 to 10 minutes.

FOR SERVING

Roasted Summer Beans

Hazelnut Vinaigrette

¼ cup fines herbes (equal parts finely chopped chervil, chives, parsley, and tarragon)

1 serrano chile, halved lengthwise and thinly sliced crosswise

1 cup Sungold (or other small) tomatoes, halved

Extra-virgin olive oil

Flaky sea salt

IN A large bowl, toss the beans with the vinaigrette, fines herbes, and chile. Let sit for a few minutes to allow the beans to soak up the dressing. Spread the mixture on a serving plate or in a shallow bowl. Top with the tomatoes, drizzle with olive oil, sprinkle with flaky salt, and serve.

Little Gem Salad
WITH SESAME-SOY DRESSING AND CRISPY SHALLOTS

MAKES 4 SERVINGS

The dramatic presentation of this salad—each head of Little Gem lettuce is opened like a flower blossom—makes it an eye-catching dish to serve at the start of a dinner party. You can also combine several heads of lettuce in a large bowl to make an edible centerpiece for the table. Little Gems come in two colors, green and ruby red, so use a mix of both if you can find them at the farmers market. The dressing is based on that classic Japanese combination of soy sauce, rice vinegar, and sesame oil, which is aggressive enough to stand up to the Little Gems and other heartier greens.

CRISPY SHALLOTS

MAKES ABOUT 1 CUP

2 large shallots, peeled and thinly sliced into rings (use a mandoline if you have one), about ½ cup

2 cups vegetable or canola oil

PLACE THE shallots in a medium saucepan and cover with the oil. Place over medium heat and cook, stirring constantly, until the shallots are until light golden brown. Pour the shallots and oil through a fine-mesh strainer and gently press with a spoon or ladle to squeeze out all of the oil. The shallots will continue to cook, so work quickly. Spread the shallots out on paper towels (they will crisp up as they cool). The shallots can be made up to 1 week ahead; store in an airtight container.

SESAME-SOY DRESSING

MAKES ABOUT 1 CUP

¼ cup fresh lemon juice

4 teaspoons tamari or soy sauce

4 teaspoons rice vinegar

1 teaspoon sesame oil

1 teaspoon kosher salt

1 teaspoon honey

½ cup extra-virgin olive oil

COMBINE ALL ingredients in a blender and blend until smooth.

FOR SERVING

4 heads Little Gem lettuce, rinsed and shaken dry

½ cup Sesame-Soy Dressing

¼ cup finely chopped mint

¼ cup finely chopped basil

½ cup Crispy Shallots

1 red finger chile, thinly sliced

Coarsely ground black pepper

TRIM ABOUT ¼ inch from the root ends of the lettuce heads, leaving the head intact. Place one head of lettuce, root side down, in a small serving bowl and spread the leaves apart to open the lettuce like a blossom. Repeat with the remaining lettuce. Drizzle about 2 tablespoons dressing over each head of lettuce. Sprinkle one-quarter of the herbs, shallots, and chile over each head of lettuce, and finish each with a couple grinds of black pepper. Serve.

THE TAKEAWAY

Crispy shallots are a popular topping in Vietnamese and Thai cuisines, and they're a staple in my kitchen as well. I use them anytime I want to add some crunch and a toasty flavor to a dish. Make a big batch (they'll last for several days, maybe weeks, at room temperature) and you'll find yourself throwing them on top of salads, pastas, soups, and more. Starting the shallots in cold oil helps cook out all of their moisture, which yields a crispier product. Make sure you constantly stir the shallots as they cook, and strain them when they're a shade lighter in color than how you want them to end up; they'll continue cooking after you take them out of the pot, and it's better to err on the side of undercooked shallots than to burn them.

Asparagus and Puntarelle Salad
WITH SEARED POACHED EGGS

MAKES 4 SERVINGS

Puntarelle isn't easy to find, but if you spot a head of this long-stemmed chicory (whose proper name is Catalonian chicory) at the farmers market, grab it! The outer leaves are too bitter to use in this salad, so strip them away to find the celery-like stalks at the core. If you can't find puntarelle, you can substitute Belgian endive or a mix of endive and dandelion greens.

This knife-and-fork salad is a study in contrasting textures. A nest of crunchy asparagus, puntarelle, and pickled fennel hides a secret below: a poached egg that's been seared in a skillet to caramelize the white parts and warm up the runny yolk. When you break into it, the yolk mixes with the lemon vinaigrette, creating a Caesar-like dressing. This is definitely a cheffy technique (especially if you follow the sous-vide poaching directions in the Takeaway, right), but it's an impressive feat of dinner table magic. If you don't want to go through the trouble, substitute fried eggs—just make sure the yolks are runny.

THE TAKEAWAY

We don't do a lot of sous vide cooking at my restaurant, but we do use our immersion circulators for making perfectly poached eggs. Not only does it make poaching eggs a painless task, it allows us to poach a big batch in their shells, then refrigerate them until they're needed. Some folks reheat sous vide–poached eggs in hot water or even in the oven, but we like to sear them briefly in a hot skillet, which not only rewarms the yolks, but also browns the whites to add another layer of flavor. If you have an immersion circulator at home, heat the water to 147°F, add your eggs, and cook them for 1 hour, then chill the eggs until you're ready to crack and sear.

LEMON VINAIGRETTE

MAKES ABOUT ¾ CUP

- 2 teaspoons finely grated lemon zest plus 2 tablespoons juice
- ¼ cup champagne vinegar
- 1 tablespoon Dijon mustard
- 2 teaspoons kosher salt
- ½ teaspoon freshly ground black pepper
- ¼ cup sunflower oil
- 3 tablespoons extra-virgin olive oil

COMBINE THE lemon zest and juice, vinegar, mustard, salt, and pepper in a blender and blend until smooth. With the machine running, slowly drizzle in the oils until emulsified.

CONTINUES ➡

PICKLED FENNEL

MAKES ABOUT 2 CUPS

1 fennel bulb, cored and thinly sliced

2 cups white wine vinegar

2 tablespoons sugar

1½ teaspoons kosher salt

PLACE THE fennel in a sterilized pint-size jar. In a small saucepan, combine the vinegar, sugar, and salt. Bring to a boil, stirring until the sugar and salt dissolve. Pour over the fennel and let cool to room temperature. Let sit for at least 1 hour before using, or seal the jar and refrigerate for up to 2 weeks.

FOR SERVING

4 poached eggs

½ cup Lemon Vinaigrette

2 bunches asparagus, woody parts trimmed, thinly sliced on the bias (about 4 cups)

1 head puntarelle (inner core and a few outer leaves) or 2 Belgian endives, thinly sliced on a sharp bias

1 cup julienned Pickled Fennel

¼ cup chopped Sevillano or other green olives

1 serrano chile, halved lengthwise and thinly sliced crosswise

¼ cup fines herbes (equal parts finely chopped chervil, chives, parsley, and tarragon)

Extra-virgin olive oil

Flaky sea salt

Freshly ground black pepper

HEAT A nonstick skillet over medium-high heat. Add the poached eggs and cook until lightly browned on two sides, about 30 seconds per side. Divide the eggs among four shallow serving bowls and spoon about 1 tablespoon dressing over each.

IN A mixing bowl, combine the asparagus, puntarelle, pickled fennel, olives, chile, and herbs. Add the remaining ¼ cup dressing and toss to coat. Divide the salad among the bowls, mounding it over the eggs so they're hidden. Drizzle the salads with olive oil, season with flaky salt and pepper, and serve.

Corn and Herb Salad
WITH LIME VINAIGRETTE

MAKES 4 TO 6 SERVINGS

Here's another salad where mild-flavored butter-head lettuce is reinforced with a mess of leafy herbs. It's the kind of dish you can prepare inside, then finish next to the grill as soon as the corn comes off. Lime and corn are old flavor buddies, but so are lime and tomatoes, so keep this lime vinaigrette in mind next time you have a surplus of tomatoes.

THE TAKEAWAY

I cook corn a few different ways, depending on the flavor I want from it. But charring corn directly on a hot grill is one of the best ways to add smoky flavors to a salad. It caramelizes easily and really absorbs the flavor of the grill. As always, you'll have the best result if you cook over charcoal or wood, and get that grill very hot.

LIME VINAIGRETTE

Finely grated zest of 1 lime

¼ cup fresh lime juice

¼ cup plus 1 tablespoon extra-virgin olive oil

1 tablespoon liquid from the Pickled Fresno Chiles, or champagne vinegar

1 teaspoon kosher salt

½ teaspoon freshly ground black pepper

½ teaspoon honey

COMBINE ALL the ingredients in a small bowl and whisk until blended. The vinaigrette can be made up to 1 day ahead and refrigerated.

PICKLED FRESNO CHILES

MAKES ABOUT 1 CUP

½ cup champagne vinegar

1 teaspoon kosher salt

4 Fresno chiles, thinly sliced (with seeds)

IN A small bowl, whisk the vinegar and salt until the salt is dissolved. Place the chiles in a sterilized jar or storage container and cover with the vinegar. Let rest at least 15 minutes before using, or seal and refrigerate for up to 2 weeks.

CROUTONS

Six ¼-inch-thick slices crustless sourdough bread

3 tablespoons extra-virgin olive oil

PREHEAT THE oven to 375°F. Arrange the bread on a rimmed baking sheet and brush all over with the oil. Toast until golden brown and crunchy, about 10 minutes. Let cool slightly, then break or chop the bread into small croutons.

FOR SERVING

6 ears corn, shucked

½ cup parsley leaves

½ cup cilantro leaves

½ cup chopped basil

2 tablespoons chopped tarragon

½ cup Pickled Fresno Chiles

6 small radishes, thinly sliced (about ½ cup)

1 pint Sungold (or other small) tomatoes, halved

Lime Vinaigrette, to taste

1 head butterhead lettuce, leaves separated

Croutons

Freshly ground black pepper

PREPARE A hot grill. Grill the corn, turning frequently, until charred all over, about 10 minutes. Let cool, then cut off the kernels into a large bowl. Add the herbs, chiles, radishes, tomatoes, and vinaigrette and toss well. Arrange the lettuce leaves in a large salad bowl and top with the corn salad. Sprinkle with croutons and pepper and serve.

Strawberry, Cucumber, and Tomato Salad

MAKES 4 TO 6 SERVINGS

In many of my salads, I pack as much flavor and texture as possible into the dressing, using it to bridge other ingredients or add layers of complexity to the dish. Not so with this salad! Here, I only need the simplest of vinaigrettes—vinegar, oil, and salt—to tie everything together. Why? Because I'm using two ingredients that are loaded with flavor: super-sweet, apricot-colored Sungold tomatoes and strawberries, which become even more intense with a turn on the grill. As with any strawberry-based dish, try to skip the supermarket and seek out locally grown strawberries in the late spring and early summer. There are hundreds of varieties grown in the U.S.; Tristar and Earliglow are two of my favorites, but I generally buy the smallest berries on offer, which will have the most intense flavor.

THE TAKEAWAY

Strawberries can really take the heat of a grill, but it's vital to season them right before you throw them on, or they'll become too wet to get a good sear. It can be tricky to grill smaller strawberries, so use a wire grill basket, which also prevents you from having to move the strawberries around with tongs, which can easily damage them.

RED WINE VINAIGRETTE

¼ cup red wine vinegar

2 tablespoons extra-virgin olive oil

½ teaspoon kosher salt

WHISK ALL the ingredients in a small bowl until the oil is emulsified.

FOR SERVING

4 cups strawberries, hulled and halved (large berries quartered)

2 tablespoons extra-virgin olive oil, plus more to taste

Kosher salt

Sugar

1 medium English or 4 Persian cucumbers, cut into ½-inch obliques (about 2 cups)

1 pint Sungold tomatoes, halved

2 teaspoons finely chopped jalapeño chile (with seeds)

¼ cup basil ribbons (¼-inch ribbons)

¼ cup mint ribbons (¼-inch ribbons)

Red Wine Vinaigrette

Flaky sea salt

PREPARE A hot grill or preheat a grill pan over high heat. In a medium bowl, toss 1½ cups of the strawberries with the oil and season with kosher salt and sugar. Grill the cut side of the strawberries until charred, about 1 minute (be careful not to overcook the strawberries; you want them to keep their structure). Transfer to a large bowl and add the raw strawberries, cucumbers, tomatoes, jalapeño, and herbs. Add the vinaigrette and toss well. Transfer to a serving bowl, drizzle with olive oil, season with flaky salt, and serve.

Summer Beans

WITH LAVENDER-PICKLED PEACHES AND GOAT CHEESE

MAKES 4 SERVINGS

This dish is proof that what grows together, goes together. In this case, three summertime ingredients—peaches, beans, and lavender—are united in a crunchy salad that's sturdy enough to bring to a backyard barbecue. Selecting the right peaches is the most important step in this recipe: Look for ones that are just ripe, but still firm enough to hold their shape and have a little bit of bite. The best place on the peach to test for ripeness is where the stem attaches to the fruit: It should give a little when you gently press it. Although this is a quick pickle, where hot brine is poured over the peaches, you want to cool the pickles down as quickly as possible after you combine everything; otherwise, the peaches can get too soft.

THE TAKEAWAY

The zippy vinaigrette is another reminder that pickling liquid is a bonus gift we receive from making pickles, and it can replace or supplement other acidic ingredients in dressings, brines, and more.

LAVENDER-PICKLED PEACHES

MAKES ABOUT 4 CUPS

4 medium peaches (they should be slightly underripe, but not hard)	1½ cups white wine vinegar
1 Thai chile, split lengthwise	1½ cups water
2 tablespoons lavender leaves (from 2 sprigs)	⅓ cup sugar
	2½ teaspoons kosher salt

BRING A medium saucepan of water to a boil and prepare an ice bath. Add the peaches and blanch until the skins begin to loosen, about 30 seconds. Transfer to the ice bath to cool. Peel, pit, and cut the peaches into 1-inch wedges. Place in a sterilized quart-size jar.

COMBINE THE chile and lavender in a cheesecloth sachet, tie with string, and add to the peaches. In a small saucepan, bring the vinegar, water, sugar, and salt to a boil. Pour over the peaches and transfer the jar to the ice bath to cool quickly. When cool, remove the sachet, seal the jar, and refrigerate until ready to use. The peaches will keep for a couple of weeks.

PICKLED PEACH VINAIGRETTE

MAKES ABOUT ½ CUP

4 teaspoons finely chopped shallots	1½ teaspoons kosher salt
⅓ cup pickling liquid from the Lavender-Pickled Peaches	½ teaspoon sugar
	¼ cup extra-virgin olive oil
2 tablespoons fresh lime juice	

COMBINE THE shallots and pickling liquid and let sit for 2 hours. Strain the liquid and discard the shallots. Transfer the liquid to a small saucepan, bring to a simmer, and reduce by half. Let cool.

CONTINUES ➡

COMBINE THE reduced pickling liquid, lime juice, salt, and sugar in a bowl and whisk to combine. Slowly whisk in the olive oil until emulsified.

BRING A pot of salted water to a boil and prepare an ice bath. Blanch the beans until crisp-tender, about 2 minutes. Transfer to the ice bath to cool, then drain and cut into 2- to 3-inch pieces on the bias.

IN A mixing bowl, toss the beans with the vinaigrette, jalapeño, and half the herbs. Transfer to a shallow serving bowl and scatter the peaches, goat cheese, and remaining herbs on top. Sprinkle with the lavender and flaky salt and serve.

FOR SERVING
---

1 pound mixed summer beans (such as Romano beans, wax beans, or green beans)

⅓ cup Pickled Peach Vinaigrette

2 teaspoons finely chopped jalapeño chile

¼ cup fines herbes (equal parts finely chopped chervil, chives, parsley, and tarragon)

1 cup Lavender-Pickled Peaches

¼ cup crumbled goat cheese

½ teaspoon finely chopped lavender

Flaky sea salt

Crushed Cucumbers
WITH YOGURT AND CHILES

MAKES 4 SERVINGS

Every year I cook at an event in Las Vegas with one of my cooks, and our first meal there is always at Noodles, a pan-Asian restaurant in the Bellagio Hotel. We order pork buns, dumplings, and two orders of their crushed cucumber salad, which is the inspiration for this dish. I wanted this salad to show-case the various ways you can prepare a cucumber, as well as the many varieties of cukes we find at the farmers market. Gently crushing cucumbers allows them to soak up the marinade, while grilling thin strips of cucumber before immersing them in brine adds a new dimension of flavor to cucumber pickles. Although this salad has lots of Asian flavors and is an amazing accompaniment for noodles, it also goes great with grilled fish and chicken.

——— THE TAKEAWAY ———

Grilling vegetables before pickling them is an easy way to elevate your pickle game. You can do this with cucumbers, of course, but also fennel, leeks, radishes, carrots, and other thinly sliced vegetables, as well as many kinds of fruits (see the Strawberry, Cucumber, and Tomato Salad on page 94). You need a very hot grill or grill pan to get a quick sear before the vegetable starts to cook. At the same time, I'll often grill a slice of onion until it's deeply charred, which boosts the brine's smoky flavor.

——— GRILLED CUCUMBER PICKLES ———

Vegetable oil

One ¼-inch slice yellow onion (from the widest part of the onion)

4 Persian cucumbers, sliced crosswise into ⅛-inch strips (use a mandoline if you have one)

1 cup white wine vinegar

1½ cups water

½ cup sugar

1 tablespoon kosher salt

½ cup chopped dill fronds

1 teaspoon red pepper flakes

2 garlic cloves, smashed

PREPARE A hot grill or preheat a grill pan over high heat. Wipe the grill a few times with vegetable oil to prevent sticking. Grill the onion slice, flipping a couple of times, until very charred, 2 to 3 minutes per side. Pat the cucumber slices dry and grill, flipping once, until charred in spots but still crunchy, about 1 minute per side. Set the onion and cucumbers aside to cool, then transfer to a clean pint-size jar (you may need to cut the onion slice in half to fit).

IN A small saucepan, combine the vinegar, water, sugar, and salt. Warm over medium-low heat, stir-ring, just until the salt and sugar have dissolved. Stir in the dill, red pepper flakes, and garlic. Let the pickling liquid cool to room temperature, then pour over the cucumbers and onion. Seal the jar and refrigerate for at least 8 hours until using, or up to 1 week.

——— LIME YOGURT ———

½ cup Greek yogurt

1 tablespoon extra-virgin olive oil

1 garlic clove, finely grated on a Microplane

1 teaspoon finely grated lime zest

1 teaspoon fresh lime juice

½ teaspoon kosher salt

CONTINUES ➡

101

COMBINE ALL ingredients in a bowl and blend with a fork until well mixed. Refrigerate until ready to use. The yogurt can be made up to 1 day ahead.

—— MARINATED CRUSHED CUCUMBERS ——

2 English cucumbers, peeled, halved lengthwise, and cut crosswise into 4-inch pieces

Kosher salt

Sugar

3 tablespoons rice vinegar

1 tablespoon soy sauce

1 tablespoon sesame oil

2 large garlic cloves, finely grated on a Microplane

½ teaspoon red pepper flakes

PLACE THE cucumber pieces on a cutting board and lightly smash them with the flat side of a chef's knife or a saucepan. They should split slightly, and the seeds will loosen. Wipe away any loose seeds and cut the cucumbers on the bias into 1-inch pieces. Transfer to a colander, add a large pinch each of salt and sugar, and toss. Fill a bowl with ice and place it on top of the cucumbers to help them drain. Drain for 30 minutes, then shake off any excess liquid.

IN A medium bowl, whisk the rice vinegar with the soy sauce, sesame oil, garlic, red pepper flakes, 2 teaspoons salt, and 1 tablespoon sugar until the salt and sugar have dissolved. Add the cucumbers, toss gently, and let sit for at least 2 hours before using, or up to overnight.

—— FOR SERVING ——

Lime Yogurt

1 cup roughly diced cucumbers (I like a mix of lemon, Persian, and Japanese)

Marinated Crushed Cucumbers

1 cup Grilled Cucumber Pickles, plus some of their liquid

¼ cup dill fronds

¼ cup roughly chopped mint

Extra-virgin olive oil

½ Fresno chile, thinly sliced

Flaky salt

SPREAD SOME of the yogurt on the bottom of a serving platter. In a bowl, toss the raw cucumbers with the marinated cucumbers, pickles, dill, and mint. Add a splash each of olive oil and the liquid from the pickled grilled cucumbers. Spoon the cucumber mixture over the yogurt, sprinkle with the chile and flaky salt, and serve.

Tomato and Cucumber Salad
WITH CHICORY, FETA, AND RED WINE VINAIGRETTE

MAKES 4 SERVINGS

This looks like a straightforward summer salad— tomatoes, cucumbers, lettuce—but thanks to a deeply flavored vinaigrette, it tastes like so much more. I add a good bit of elderflower syrup to the dressing to give it a big aroma and honeyed sweetness. Raw garlic and my stomach don't get along, so I will usually blanch garlic if it's destined for a vinaigrette or other raw preparation. It also mellows the garlic's flavor, which helps let the other ingredients shine through in a complex vinaigrette like this one. It might seem like a fussy step, but if you don't love the big flavor of raw garlic, simply cover the garlic with water, bring it to a boil, and drain. Repeat once or twice more with fresh water.

——— THE TAKEAWAY ———

The secret weapon here is the leftover olive oil from our house-marinated olives. We get just as much use, if not more, from the infused oil—which is flavored with olives, chiles, orange zest, and spices— than the olives themselves. We whisk it into vinaigrettes, of course, but also use it as a marinade for fish and as a finishing oil for pizza and vegetable dishes.

——— MARINATED OLIVES ———

MAKES 2 CUPS

2 cups mixed olives (I use Sevillano, Castelvetrano, and kalamata)

2 teaspoons fennel seeds

½ teaspoon red pepper flakes

4 strips orange zest (no pith)

Extra-virgin olive oil

LINE A rimmed baking sheet with a clean towel. Drain and rinse the olives, then spread on the baking sheet to dry for an hour or two.

IN A small skillet, toast the fennel seeds over medium heat until fragrant, about 2 minutes. Add the red pepper flakes and toast until warmed through, about 30 seconds. Place the olives in a pint-size jar or other container and add the toasted spices and orange zest. Add enough olive oil to cover the olives completely and cover. Refrigerate for 1 week before using.

— RED WINE AND OREGANO VINAIGRETTE —

MAKES 1½ CUPS

¼ cup red wine vinegar

¼ cup fresh lemon juice

2 tablespoons elderflower syrup or 1 tablespoon light honey

2 teaspoons finely grated orange zest (from 1 medium orange)

1 medium garlic clove, blanched twice and finely grated on a Microplane (about ½ teaspoon)

½ red finger chile, finely chopped with seeds (about 4 teaspoons)

1 teaspoon kosher salt

½ cup oil from Marinated Olives or extra-virgin olive oil

¼ cup chopped oregano

IN A bowl, combine the vinegar, lemon juice, elderflower syrup, orange zest, garlic, chile, and salt. Slowly whisk in the oil until emulsified, then stir in the oregano. The vinaigrette can be made a day or two ahead of time and refrigerated until ready to use.

─────────── FOR SERVING ───────────

2 cups halved small heirloom or cherry tomatoes

3 Persian cucumbers, half cut into obliques, half cut into ½-inch dice

Kosher salt

1 serrano chile, seeded and finely chopped

⅓ cup thinly sliced basil

½ cup Red Wine and Oregano Vinaigrette

1 head speckled romaine, radicchio, or other chicory, cut into ½-inch ribbons (about 4 cups)

1 spring onion (or 2 scallions), bulb halved and thinly sliced, greens thinly sliced on the bias

2 ounces goat's milk feta, crumbled (about ½ cup)

1 orange, for zesting

Extra-virgin olive oil

Flaky sea salt

Freshly ground black pepper

PLACE THE tomatoes and cucumbers in a bowl and season with kosher salt. Add the chile, basil, and ¼ cup of the vinaigrette and gently toss with your hands.

PLACE THE salad greens in a serving bowl and top with the tomato mixture. Drizzle with the remaining ¼ cup vinaigrette. Scatter the spring onion and feta over the top. Grate some orange zest over the salad, drizzle with olive oil, season with flaky salt and pepper, and serve.

Corn and Shishito Salad

WITH ROASTED RED PEPPER VINAIGRETTE

MAKES 4 SERVINGS

Corn and peppers are a classic pairing, but it usually involves a lot of corn and not much pepper. This dish flips the script, putting the sweet (and slightly smoky) shishito front and center. I try to use the smallest shishitos I can find—their flavor is more pronounced—or you can substitute Padrón peppers if you can't find shishitos. You can cook corn any way you like for this salad, but I prefer to roast un-shucked cobs over a hot grill until the husks are blackened all over, which allows the kernels inside to both steam and lightly char.

RED PEPPER VINAIGRETTE

2 large red bell peppers

¼ cup extra-virgin olive oil

2 tablespoons sherry vinegar

2 tablespoons fresh lime juice

¼ teaspoon smoked paprika

¼ teaspoon ground cumin

Kosher salt and freshly ground black pepper

CHAR THE peppers over the flame of a gas burner (or under a broiler), turning with tongs until blackened and blistered all over, about 10 minutes. Transfer the peppers to a bowl, cover with a plate, and let stand for 15 minutes. Scrape off the skins with a paring knife and wipe the flesh clean with a paper towel. Discard the stem and seeds. Finely dice ¼ cup of the roasted pepper and set aside. Roughly chop the remaining roasted pepper (about ¾ cup) and place in a blender. Add the olive oil, vinegar, lime juice, paprika, and cumin and blend until smooth. Scrape the vinaigrette into a bowl and stir in the finely diced peppers. Season with ¾ teaspoon salt and pepper to taste. The vinaigrette can be made a day or two ahead and refrigerated until ready to use.

FOR SERVING

5 ounces small shishito chiles, stemmed and cut crosswise into 1-inch pieces (about 2 cups)

2 tablespoons extra-virgin olive oil, plus more for drizzling

3 cups cooked corn kernels (grilled, roasted, or sautéed)

Kosher salt and freshly ground black pepper

3 tablespoons fresh lime juice, plus finely grated lime zest for serving

¼ cup mint leaves

¼ cup basil leaves

¼ cup thinly sliced scallion greens

6 ounces baby arugula (about 6 cups)

1 cup Red Pepper Vinaigrette

Flaky sea salt

HEAT A large skillet (preferably cast-iron) over high heat. Add the shishito chiles and cook until blistered, about 2 minutes. Add the olive oil and corn and cook, stirring, until the corn is warmed through, about 1 minute. Remove from the heat and season with kosher salt and pepper. Let cool slightly, then stir in the lime juice, mint, basil, and scallions.

ARRANGE THE arugula in four shallow bowls. Drizzle the vinaigrette on the arugula and top with the corn mixture. Drizzle with olive oil and grate some lime zest over. Season with flaky salt and pepper and serve.

Heirloom Tomato Panzanella

WITH PARMESAN CROUTONS

MAKES 4 SERVINGS

Traditional Italian panzanellas are good, but I've never been a fan of how soggy the croutons get as they soak up the juices from the tomatoes and dressing. This version is my improved panzanella, and it started with perfecting cheese-encased croutons that can soak up some of the salad's other flavors without becoming soggy. Unlike the Heirloom Tomato Toasts on page 39, I season the tomatoes for this salad a few minutes ahead of time to coax out more of their juices, which will mellow out the spicy dressing when you toss everything together. If you don't want to make your own Green Hot Sauce (which I recommend you do!), you can also use green Tabasco sauce.

THE TAKEAWAY

If you make the Parmesan-crusted croutons right, they're amazing. The key is to crisp the bread in the oven first, then coat it twice with Parmesan as it bakes, which helps you build up a shell instead of a single coating of cheese that melts into the bread. These croutons will work on all kinds of salads (and with various kinds of hard cheeses), and they make a great soup garnish as well.

GREEN HOT SAUCE

MAKES ABOUT 2 CUPS

- ½ stalk lemongrass, roughly chopped
- 1 Thai green chile, stemmed
- 1 serrano chile, stemmed
- 2 jalapeño chiles, stemmed
- 1 small Granny Smith apple, cored and roughly chopped
- 4 scallion bottoms (white and light green parts)
- One 2-inch piece of ginger, peeled and roughly chopped
- Finely grated zest of 12 limes
- 2 tablespoons plus 2 teaspoons kosher salt
- 1 tablespoon sugar
- ½ cup plus 2 tablespoons white wine vinegar

COMBINE ALL ingredients except the vinegar in a food processor and process until finely chopped. Transfer to a very clean container and cover with cheesecloth. Let ferment at room temperature for 3 days. Transfer to a blender and add the vinegar. Blend until smooth, then transfer to a sterilized bottle or jar, seal, and refrigerate for up to 1 month.

SPICY GREEN CHILE VINAIGRETTE

MAKES ABOUT 1 CUP

- ¼ cup fresh lemon juice
- 1 tablespoon Green Hot Sauce or green Tabasco sauce
- 1 teaspoon finely chopped serrano chile
- 2 teaspoons kosher salt
- ⅔ cup extra-virgin olive oil

IN A small bowl, whisk together the lemon juice, hot sauce, chile, and salt. Slowly whisk in the olive oil until emulsified.

CONTINUES ➡

PARMESAN CROUTONS

MAKES ABOUT 4 CUPS

One 1-pound loaf of sourdough or country bread, crusts discarded, bread cut into ¾-inch dice

½ cup extra-virgin olive oil

2 teaspoons kosher salt

1 cup grated Parmesan cheese

PREHEAT THE oven to 350°F. In a bowl, toss the bread with the olive oil and salt. Spread the bread on a rimmed baking sheet and bake until it begins to brown and crisp up, 10 to 15 minutes. Sprinkle half of the cheese over the bread and toss well. Bake for 10 minutes, stirring once or twice. Add the remaining cheese, toss well, and bake until the croutons are golden brown and crisp on the outside but still soft enough to chew, about 10 minutes longer.

FOR SERVING

4 medium heirloom tomatoes, cut into 1-inch pieces (about 4 cups)

Kosher salt

¼ cup chopped mixed olives

1 medium red onion, halved and thinly sliced

½ cup roughly chopped parsley

½ cup roughly chopped basil

Spicy Green Chile Vinaigrette, to taste

Flaky sea salt

ARRANGE THE tomatoes on a plate and sprinkle with kosher salt. Let sit for at least 5 minutes. In a serving bowl, toss the olives, onion, parsley, and basil with the vinaigrette to taste. Add the tomatoes (and any accumulated juices) and toss gently. Taste and add more vinaigrette if needed. Sprinkle with flaky salt and serve.

Cobb Salad
WITH YOGURT-BLUE CHEESE DRESSING

MAKES 4 SERVINGS

This is my take on a classic Cobb salad, which I developed for lunching executives when I was the chef at the Core Club (a members-only club in Midtown Manhattan). I wanted to feature a lettuce that was crisp like iceberg, but with more flavor. So I asked Rick Bishop from Mountain Sweet Berry Farm if he could grow me a hearty chicory that had the crunch, but wasn't too bitter. He did exactly that, and continues to grow something called "Dan's Chicory," which we feature in our salad at Loring Place. Where a traditional Cobb is more like a plate full of isolated ingredients, mine is a composed salad with a lighter, tangier dressing. Add a piece of grilled or roasted chicken, and you've got yourself a power lunch.

--- **THE TAKEAWAY** ---

I find most blue cheese dressings to be too heavy, so I lighten mine up with yogurt and more lemon juice, and use a sweet, crumbly blue cheese that won't overpower the rest of the salad. A good blue cheese dressing is both creamy and chunky, so I whisk half of the cheese into the dressing, then fold in the rest for texture.

--- YOGURT-BLUE CHEESE DRESSING ---

MAKES ABOUT 1½ CUPS

½ cup crumbled blue cheese (I like a sweet, crumbly blue like Point Reyes)

½ cup sour cream

½ cup Greek yogurt

2 tablespoons fresh lemon juice

2 tablespoons extra-virgin olive oil

2 tablespoons finely chopped rosemary

½ teaspoon sugar

Kosher salt and freshly ground black pepper

IN A mixing bowl, combine half of the cheese and the remaining ingredients. Whisk until combined, then gently fold in the remaining cheese. The dressing can be made up to 1 day ahead and refrigerated until ready to use.

--- FOR SERVING ---

8 strips thick-cut bacon, cut crosswise into ¼-inch pieces

8 cups mixed chopped lettuce (I like romaine, iceberg, and radicchio)

Blue Cheese Dressing, to taste

1 cup halved cherry tomatoes

1 ripe avocado, diced

PLACE THE bacon in a skillet over medium heat and cook until crisp and browned, 5 to 7 minutes. Using a slotted spoon, transfer the bacon to paper towels; reserve the fat for another use.

IN A salad bowl, toss the lettuce with enough dressing to coat. Scatter the bacon, tomatoes, and avocado over the top and serve.

Field Greens
WITH CRISPY PROSCIUTTO AND SPICY BREADCRUMBS

MAKES 4 TO 6 SERVINGS

Sometimes when I eat raw kale or Swiss chard, I feel like a farm animal. That's why I often give these and other darker greens a quick sauté, which both brings out their natural sweetness and tames some of their bitterness. You want to retain the greens' fresh flavor and crisp texture, so you only need to cook them for about 30 seconds, or until they just begin to soften. Make sure to keep tossing the greens with tongs as they cook, or some will be overcooked while the rest are raw.

If you did a double take when you saw curly parsley listed in the ingredients, hear me out: Curly parsley has had a bad rap for much too long. It has a great bitter-sweet flavor and springy texture, and if you think of it as micro kale, you'll come up with all sorts of uses for it.

You can make this warm salad (which is also a great side for all kinds of meat dishes, pastas, and pizza) anytime from early summer, when the first crops of local kale and Swiss chard hit the market, through early winter after the season's final regrowth has been harvested.

THE TAKEAWAY

If there's one pantry staple from this cookbook that you should always have in your refrigerator, it's my garlic confit. You'll use both the soft, creamy cloves and their garlic-infused olive oil in so many of my recipes. Here, I blend the cloves into a sweet-sour vinaigrette, which gives the dressing enough body to stand up to the hearty greens. An easy way to keep yourself stocked with garlic confit is to buy a few extra heads of garlic whenever you're at the market, then make a batch while you're cooking dinner.

GARLIC CONFIT

MAKES 1½ CUPS

3 heads garlic, cloves peeled

1½ cups extra-virgin olive oil

IN A small saucepan, combine the garlic and oil. Cook over very low heat (it shouldn't bubble) until the garlic is golden brown and very soft, 45 minutes to 1 hour. Let cool to room temperature, then transfer to a storage container and refrigerate for up to 1 month.

——— CREAMY GARLIC VINAIGRETTE ———

MAKES ABOUT ⅔ CUP

4 cloves Garlic Confit

2 tablespoons extra-virgin olive oil

3 tablespoons fresh lemon juice

2 tablespoons sherry vinegar

1 tablespoon honey

1 tablespoon Dijon mustard

¾ teaspoon kosher salt

¼ teaspoon freshly ground black pepper

IN A skillet, warm the garlic confit in the olive oil over low heat until warmed through, about 2 minutes. Transfer the garlic and oil to a blender and add the remaining ingredients. Blend until smooth and creamy.

——— FOR SERVING ———

Extra-virgin olive oil

4 slices prosciutto, chopped

1 bunch dandelion greens, roughly chopped

1 bunch curly parsley, roughly chopped

1 bunch kale, stems discarded, leaves roughly chopped

1 bunch Swiss chard, leaves coarsely chopped, stems reserved for another use (such as the Grilled Chard Stems on page 169)

Creamy Garlic Vinaigrette, to taste

½ cup Spicy Breadcrumbs (page 224)

½ cup coarsely grated Gruyère cheese

Flaky sea salt

Freshly ground black pepper

1 tablespoon chopped chives

IN A large skillet, heat 1 tablespoon olive oil over medium heat. Add the prosciutto and cook, stirring occasionally, until crisp, about 2 minutes. Transfer the prosciutto to paper towels, leaving the oil behind. Add the dandelion greens to the skillet and cook, tossing with tongs, until barely wilted, 30 to 60 seconds. Transfer the greens to a large mixing bowl. Repeat, cooking the parsley, kale, and Swiss chard in separate batches, adding a bit of oil to the skillet between batches if needed. Dress the greens to taste with the vinaigrette, then add the prosciutto and toss. Transfer the greens to a serving bowl and sprinkle with the breadcrumbs and Gruyère. Season with flaky salt and pepper, sprinkle with chives, and serve.

Grilled Cantaloupe, Watermelon, and Kale
WITH YOGURT-POPPY SEED DRESSING

MAKES 4 SERVINGS

This is the dish that made this cookbook possible. Our acquiring editor, Rux Martin, came by Loring Place one day to cook with me. I'd just returned from the farmers market with some cantaloupe, and as we chatted I created this salad, which I'd never made before. I love the combination of yogurt and cantaloupe, so a yogurt dressing seemed right. I borrowed a technique I used a lot at Tabla, where we bloom spices in oil to bring out their flavor, then add them to a dressing or sauce. Yogurt and poppy seeds have an affinity, so they became the base of the salad dressing. I then grilled the cantaloupe to intensify its sweetness and add a slightly smoky note to the salad. A salad needs some green component, so I reached for kale, which can stand up to the rich dressing. I added watermelon for little bursts of juice, some sliced chiles for a bit of heat, and finished the salad with some chopped dill, which helps bind the tart yogurt dressing with the rest of the ingredients. Rux was impressed enough to offer me a book deal, so here we are!

THE TAKEAWAY

Grilled fruit can completely change a dish. A quick sear over a hot grill will caramelize the fruit's flesh, turning sweet into savory, with some added smoky and bitter flavors as well. With larger fruits like cantaloupe and watermelon, I'll first slice the fruit into large planks that are easy to move around the grill, then cut the grilled fruit into smaller pieces when assembling a dish. With smaller fruits, like strawberries, I'll grill them whole. Whenever you're grilling fruit, it's vital that you use a hot fire to ensure you're getting some serious char before the fruit starts to cook through. A hot grill pan or gas grill can do this, but you'll also pick up some smoky flavor if you grill over charcoal or wood.

PICKLED GINGER

MAKES 1 CUP

4 ounces ginger, peeled and very thinly sliced (use a mandoline if you have one), about 1 cup	¾ teaspoon kosher salt
	1 tablespoon sugar
	¼ cup water
	¼ cup unseasoned rice wine vinegar

IN A small bowl, toss the ginger and salt and let sit for at least 30 minutes. In a small saucepan, combine the sugar, water, and vinegar and bring to a simmer. Pour over the ginger and let cool to room temperature. Transfer to a sterilized jar, seal, and refrigerate for at least 4 hours (ideally 24 hours) before using. The pickled ginger can be refrigerated for up to 1 month.

CONTINUES ➡

115

YOGURT–POPPY SEED DRESSING

MAKES ¾ CUP

2 tablespoons extra-virgin olive oil

2 teaspoons poppy seeds

½ cup Greek yogurt

1 tablespoon fresh lime juice

1 tablespoon maple syrup

Kosher salt

IN A skillet, heat the olive oil over medium heat. Add the poppy seeds and turn off the heat. Scrape the contents of the skillet into a bowl and let cool to room temperature. Add the yogurt, lime juice, and maple syrup and whisk to combine. Season to taste with salt.

FOR SERVING

½ cantaloupe (with skin), cut into ½- to ¾-inch planks

Extra-virgin olive oil

Kosher salt and freshly ground black pepper

1 bunch kale, stems discarded and leaved thinly sliced crosswise

Yogurt–Poppy Seed Dressing, to taste

2 cups diced watermelon (½- to ¾-inch dice)

1 serrano chile, halved lengthwise and thinly sliced into half moons

2 tablespoons julienned Pickled Ginger

¼ cup coarsely chopped dill

PREPARE A hot grill or preheat a grill pan over high heat. Brush the cantaloupe slices with olive oil and season with salt and pepper. Grill until nicely charred, 20 to 30 seconds per side. Transfer to a cutting board and let cool, then remove the skin and cut the flesh into ½- to ¾-inch cubes.

IN A salad bowl, toss the kale with some of the dressing until well coated (this will help soften the kale as well). Add the cantaloupe and watermelon and a little more dressing, and toss again. Garnish with the chile, pickled ginger, and dill and serve.

Chopped Salad
WITH PICKLED CAULIFLOWER, GOAT FETA, AND OREGANO VINAIGRETTE

MAKES 4 TO 6 SERVINGS

This is my take on a Greek chopped salad. The dressing reminds me of my mother, who would always have a simple vinaigrette made from oil, vinegar, garlic, and dried oregano on hand. I add a touch of elderflower syrup to my dressing, which is also a nod to my mom and the trips we took to visit her family in England. I discovered elderflower syrup there and fell in love with its floral aroma and honeyed flavor. As a kid I loved mixing it with soda, but once I started cooking with it as a chef, I found that it has a beguiling flavor that bridges other ingredients, especially in salad dressings. Elderflower syrup loves ginger, as well as garlic, soy sauce, and orange. You can probably find the syrup at your local gourmet store (my favorite brand is d'Arbo), or you can order it online.

THE TAKEAWAY ---

I don't like the funky flavor of raw cauliflower, but it makes an amazing pickle. I reached into the Indian spice cabinet to flavor my pickled cauliflower, which adds little pops of big flavor—not only to this salad, but in tacos, in slaws, or as the shining yellow star of a pickle plate.

--- PICKLED CAULIFLOWER ---

MAKES ABOUT 2 CUPS

2 cups small cauliflower florets	¾ teaspoon turmeric
1¼ cups white wine vinegar	¾ teaspoon cumin seeds
1½ teaspoons coriander seeds	½ teaspoon brown mustard seeds
1½ teaspoons red pepper flakes	1 bay leaf
	1 tablespoon sugar
	2 teaspoons kosher salt

PLACE THE cauliflower in a sterilized pint-size jar. In a saucepan, combine the remaining ingredients and bring to a boil. Pour the boiling mixture over the cauliflower, seal the jar, and let sit for at least 30 minutes before using. The pickles can be refrigerated for up to 2 weeks.

--- OREGANO VINAIGRETTE ---

MAKES 1 CUP

¼ cup red wine vinegar	1 tablespoon finely grated orange zest
¼ cup fresh lemon juice	1 teaspoon honey
3 tablespoons elderflower syrup or 1 tablespoon plus 1½ teaspoons honey	2 teaspoons kosher salt
	½ cup extra-virgin olive oil
2 tablespoons finely chopped red finger chile (with seeds)	2 tablespoons finely chopped oregano leaves
3 garlic cloves, finely grated on a Microplane	

IN A bowl, whisk together the vinegar, lemon juice, elderflower syrup, chile, garlic, orange zest, honey, and salt. Slowly whisk in the olive oil until emulsified. Stir in the oregano.

CONTINUES ➡

FOR SERVING

1 head radicchio

1 head Bibb, Boston, or Little Gem lettuce

1 medium carrot, peeled and cut into matchsticks (about 1 cup)

1 medium turnip, peeled and cut into matchsticks (about 1 cup)

8 medium red globe radishes, thinly sliced (about ½ cup)

1 small kohlrabi, peeled, quartered, and thinly sliced (about 1 cup)

Oregano Vinaigrette

4 ounces goat's milk feta, crumbled (about 1 cup)

3 tablespoons chopped parsley

1 cup Pickled Cauliflower

Flaky sea salt and freshly ground black pepper

CUT THE radicchio into four wedges, then chop each wedge into 2-inch pieces, discarding the core. Do the same with the lettuce. Wash the greens and spin dry.

IN A large mixing bowl, toss the lettuce mixture with the carrot, turnip, radishes, and kohlrabi. Pour about ½ cup vinaigrette down the side of the bowl and gently toss the salad with your hands until it's lightly coated. Taste and add more vinaigrette if desired, and toss again.

TRANSFER THE salad to a large serving bowl or individual salad bowls and top with the crumbled feta, parsley, and pickled cauliflower. Sprinkle with flaky salt, grind some black pepper over the top, and serve.

Shaved Brussels Sprout Salad
WITH APPLE DRESSING

MAKES 4 TO 6 SERVINGS

I created this slaw-like salad for a dinner honoring my friend Athena Calderone, the entertaining guru, and her excellent cookbook, Cook Beautiful. *Wherever you encounter Brussels sprouts, you'll often find apples in tow. This recipe is my attempt to pair these flavor bedfellows in a new way. It also happens to be a super-easy dish to throw together for lunch, or as a side dish for dinner or a Thanksgiving feast. Because the dressing is all about fresh flavors, I recommend making it right before you're ready to serve the salad.*

THE TAKEAWAY

Keep this salad dressing in mind for the next time you're stuck in vinaigrette boredom. Juicing fresh fruits and vegetables—and pretty much anything that can be juiced will work—will give you an entirely new palette of flavors to work with. If you have a fancy juicer at home, use it; otherwise, follow my method for pureeing everything together, then straining the liquid. Depending on what ingredients you choose, you may need to add more or less acid or sugar to the dressing to balance out the flavors.

APPLE DRESSING

MAKES 1 CUP

- ½ medium fennel bulb, cored and roughly chopped
- 1 medium Granny Smith apple, peeled, cored, and roughly chopped
- 1 jalapeño chile, seeded and roughly chopped
- 1 tablespoon plus 2 teaspoons fresh lemon juice
- 1½ teaspoons champagne vinegar
- 1½ teaspoons sugar
- 1½ teaspoons kosher salt
- ¼ cup extra-virgin olive oil

IN A blender, combine the fennel, apple, jalapeño, lemon juice, vinegar, sugar, and salt. Blend until smooth, then strain into a small mixing bowl, pressing on the solids to extract as much liquid as possible. Slowly whisk the olive oil into the liquid until emulsified.

FOR SERVING

- 1 pound Brussels sprouts, thinly shaved (use a mandoline if you have one)
- ¼ cup toasted and chopped almonds
- ¼ cup chopped Castelvetrano and/or Sevillano olives
- ¼ cup fines herbes (equal parts finely chopped chervil, chives, parsley, and tarragon)
- Flaky sea salt
- ¾ cup Apple Dressing
- 2 ounces Manchego cheese, thinly shaved with a vegetable peeler
- Extra-virgin olive oil
- Freshly ground black pepper

IN A large mixing bowl, combine the Brussels sprouts with the almonds, olives, and half the herbs. Season with flaky salt and toss well. Transfer to a serving bowl and drizzle with the dressing. Top with the shaved Manchego and remaining herbs. Drizzle with olive oil and grind some pepper over the top. Serve.

Crunchy Fall Vegetable Salad
WITH LEMON-CHILE VINAIGRETTE

MAKES 4 SERVINGS

This healthy slaw-like salad has loads of texture, and can be made with all sorts of crisp fall fruits and vegetables: Parsnips, radishes, jicama, beets, and pears all work well. It's a great side dish for roast pork, or you can add some cooked farro to turn it into a full meal. While arugula is often the main ingredient in salads, I often use it like an herb in salads and pasta dishes, adding its peppery bite to another leafy herb.

——— THE TAKEAWAY ———

There's a reason why you find dried fruit in so many salad bowls, but I especially love pairing them with the earthy flavors of root vegetables and sour vinaigrettes. I'm using standard dried currants and cranberries in this salad, but feel free to play around with more unexpected dried fruits—persimmons, apricots, pluots, figs, and cherries are all excellent—in this salad and beyond.

——— LEMON-CHILE VINAIGRETTE ———

MAKES 1½ CUPS

- ½ cup fresh lemon juice
- 1 tablespoon sugar
- 1 tablespoon finely chopped jalapeño or Fresno chile
- 1 teaspoon Dijon mustard
- 2 teaspoons kosher salt
- ¾ cup extra-virgin olive oil

IN MIXING bowl, whisk together the lemon juice, sugar, chile, mustard, and salt. Slowly whisk in the olive oil until emulsified. The dressing can be made a day or two ahead of time and refrigerated until ready to use.

——— FOR SERVING ———

- ½ medium kohlrabi, peeled and cut into ¼-inch matchsticks (about ¾ cup)
- 1 medium Granny Smith apple, peeled, cored, and cut into ¼-inch matchsticks (about 1 cup)
- 1 medium carrot, peeled and cut into ¼-inch matchsticks (about ¾ cup)
- ½ medium bulb celery root, peeled and cut into ¼-inch matchsticks (about ¾ cup)
- ¼ cup dried cranberries
- ¼ cup dried currants
- ½ cup toasted and roughly chopped almonds
- Lemon-Chile Vinaigrette
- ½ cup roughly chopped mint leaves
- ½ cup roughly chopped basil leaves
- ½ cup chopped dill fronds
- 1 cup baby arugula
- Finely grated lemon zest
- Freshly ground black pepper

IN A large mixing bowl, combine the kohlrabi, apple, carrot, and celery root. Add the cranberries, currants, and almonds (reserving about 1 tablespoon of each for garnish). Add about ⅓ cup vinaigrette and toss well.

IN A separate bowl, combine all of the herbs. Set aside about one-fourth of the mixture for garnish. Add the remaining herbs to the vegetables and toss.

COVER THE bottom of a serving bowl or platter with the arugula and spoon the dressed salad on top. Sprinkle the reserved herbs, cranberries, currants, and almonds on top. Finish with lemon zest and black pepper and serve.

121

Blood Orange and Pomegranate Salad
WITH CRISPY GOAT CHEESE

MAKES 4 SERVINGS

This falls in between a citrus salad and a green salad, but then it throws in a ringer: crispy disks of fried goat cheese. I added this to turn the salad into a meal, but you can skip the fried cheese and sprinkle some crumbled goat cheese over the salad.

THE TAKEAWAY

To get an extra-crispy coating on the fried goat cheese, I double-batter the cheese—flour, egg, flour, egg—before it gets coated in breadcrumbs. Keep this technique in mind for any time you're frying cheese or other high-moisture ingredients.

SHALLOT VINAIGRETTE

MAKES ½ CUP

¼ cup finely chopped shallot

3 tablespoons champagne vinegar

2 tablespoons plus 1 teaspoon fresh lemon juice

1 tablespoon chopped oregano

1½ teaspoons kosher salt

Pinch of freshly ground black pepper

¼ cup extra-virgin olive oil

IN A bowl, combine the shallot and vinegar. Let stand for 1 hour. Drain and reserve 2 tablespoons of the vinegar. Add the shallot and vinegar to a mixing bowl along with the lemon juice, oregano, salt, and pepper. Whisk until combined, then slowly whisk in the olive oil until emulsified.

CRISPY GOAT CHEESE

One 4-ounce log goat cheese

Vegetable oil, for frying

½ cup flour

2 large eggs, beaten

1 cup dry fine breadcrumbs

Kosher salt and freshly ground black pepper

LINE A small baking sheet or plate with parchment paper. Cut the goat cheese into 8 disks and arrange on the parchment. Freeze for 30 minutes to firm up the cheese.

RIGHT BEFORE you're ready to serve the salad, heat 1 inch of vegetable oil in a medium saucepan to 360°F. Place the flour, eggs, and breadcrumbs in separate bowls. Dredge one cheese disk in the flour, then dip in the egg, letting the excess run off. Dredge again in the flour, then the egg, then coat with breadcrumbs. Repeat with the remaining cheese.

WORKING IN batches, fry the cheese until golden brown, about 1 minute. Transfer to paper towels and season with salt and pepper.

FOR SERVING

4 blood oranges

4 cups mesclun mix

Shallot Vinaigrette

½ cup pomegranate seeds

1 tablespoon roughly chopped mint

Crispy Goat Cheese

Flaky sea salt and freshly ground black pepper

USING A sharp knife, cut the peel and pith off the oranges. Working over a bowl, cut the oranges between the membranes to release the segments.

DIVIDE THE greens among four shallow serving bowls. Drizzle each salad with 2 tablespoons of the vinaigrette. Scatter the pomegranate seeds, mint, and blood orange segments over the greens and top each salad with two fried cheese disks. Season with flaky salt and pepper and serve.

Roasted Beets
WITH CRISPY SUNCHOKES AND ORANGE-GINGER PUREE

MAKES 4 SERVINGS

This dish is an exercise in contrasting textures and flavors. Roasted beets are not that interesting to eat by themselves, so I put them atop a bed of citrusy pickled ginger puree, which is pungent, acidic, and sweet. The combination of beets and ginger gives you a great spectrum of flavors, but there's not much texture to be had, so I top them with toasted cashews and a mess of crispy sunchoke chips—a crunchy topping you can also use to add an earthy crunch to a salad, soup, pasta, or vegetable dish. Lastly, some chopped orange segments sprinkled over the dish add little explosions of sweet acidity.

— THE TAKEAWAY —

Light, crispy sunchoke chips are a great crunchy topping for using on salads, as they are here, or as a garnish for braised greens, soups, or chili. Like Crispy Garlic (page 246) and Crispy Shallots (page 88), I start the sunchokes in cold oil and heat everything together. Once they start frying, the sunchokes will turn light golden brown; this is when you should remove them from the oil, as they'll quickly go from golden brown to burnt. Once cooled, they should stay crispy for a day or two, stored in an airtight container at room temperature.

— ORANGE-GINGER PUREE —

MAKES ABOUT 1 CUP

Strips of zest (no pith) from 1 medium orange

2½ ounces fresh ginger (about one 5-inch piece), peeled and thinly shaved (use a mandoline if you have one)

¼ cup fresh lime juice

¼ cup champagne vinegar

¼ cup sugar

2 tablespoons plus ¾ teaspoon kosher salt

2 tablespoons extra-virgin olive oil

½ Thai chile, with seeds

PLACE THE zest strips in a small saucepan and cover with water. Bring the water to a boil, then drain. Repeat this process two more times (blanching the orange zest removes any bitter flavors). Place the ginger and orange zest in a jar or heatproof container. In a saucepan, bring the lime juice, vinegar, sugar, and ¾ teaspoon salt to a boil. Pour over the ginger and orange. Let cool to room temperature, then cover and refrigerate overnight. The pickled ginger can be refrigerated for a couple of months.

DRAIN THE pickled ginger and orange and save 3 tablespoons of the pickling liquid. Add both to a blender or mini food processor, along with the olive oil, chile, and remaining 2 tablespoons salt. Blend until very smooth, scraping down the side of the blender as needed. Transfer to a container and refrigerate until ready to use. The puree can be made a couple of days ahead.

CONTINUES ➡

ROASTED BEETS

1½ pounds beets (use a mix of colors if possible), about 5 medium

¼ cup extra-virgin olive oil

¼ cup white wine vinegar

¼ cup water

Kosher salt and freshly ground black pepper

PREHEAT THE oven to 375°F. Place the beets in a baking dish (if using a mix of red and golden beets, separate them into two smaller dishes and divide the oil, vinegar, and water between the two dishes). Drizzle with the oil and add the vinegar and water. Season with salt and pepper. Cover the pan with foil and roast until the beets are tender when pierced with a knife; this can take anywhere from 30 minutes to an hour, depending on the thickness of the beets. Let the beets cool, then peel and cut into 1-inch wedges. Place each color of beet, along with any accumulated juices, into a small mixing bowl.

TOASTED CASHEWS

1 tablespoon extra-virgin olive oil

½ cup roughly chopped cashews

IN A skillet, heat the oil over medium-low heat. Add the cashews and cook, stirring constantly, until golden brown. Transfer to a heatproof bowl.

SUNCHOKE CHIPS

MAKES ABOUT ½ CUP

Vegetable oil

4 large sunchokes, thinly shaved (use a mandoline if you have one)

Kosher salt

POUR 1 inch of oil into a small saucepan and add the sunchokes (there should be just enough oil to cover the sunchokes; add more oil if needed).

Turn the heat to medium and stir occasionally; when the sunchokes begin to sizzle and foam, increase the temperature to high and continue frying, stirring constantly, until the sunchokes are light golden brown. At this point the sunchokes will rapidly go from golden brown to burnt, so quickly transfer the chips to paper towels to drain. Lightly season with salt. The sunchoke chips can be stored in an airtight container at room temperature for a day or two, or until they start to soften.

FOR SERVING

1 medium orange

Roasted Beets

Extra-virgin olive oil

Kosher salt

¼ cup Orange-Ginger Puree

Freshly ground black pepper

Toasted Cashews

1 tablespoon roughly chopped tarragon

1 tablespoon roughly chopped dill fronds

Sunchoke Chips

USING A sharp knife, cut the peel and pith off the orange. Working over a bowl, cut the orange between the membranes to release the segments. Dice the segments, then return them to the bowl.

DRIZZLE THE beet wedges with a little bit of olive oil, season with salt, and toss.

SPREAD THE ginger puree on the bottom of a shallow serving bowl or plate. Arrange the beets over the puree. Sprinkle the chopped orange segments over the beets and grind some pepper over the dish. Top with the cashews, herbs, and sunchoke chips. Serve.

Roasted Beets and Grilled Fennel

WITH ORANGE VINAIGRETTE AND GOAT CHEESE

MAKES 4 SERVINGS

It's amazing how a vinaigrette can turn up the volume on other ingredients. Orange usually doesn't get to star in salad dressings—and it's not acidic enough to work alone—but it can really accentuate the sweetness of both beets and fennel. This dressing is probably too intense to use with a leafy lettuce-based salad, but it works well with chicories or shaved carrots. I like combining different colors of beets in the same dish, but it's important to cook them separately, lest their colors bleed together while they bake.

——— THE TAKEAWAY ———

I can't think of many vegetables where you can add the plant's own seed to boost its flavor—only fennel and celery. Here, roasting fennel with fennel seeds—and garnishing the dish with fennel fronds—combines all the flavors and textures the plant has to offer.

——— ROASTED BEETS ———

1½ pounds beets (use a mix of colors if possible), about 8 small or 5 medium

¼ cup extra-virgin olive oil

¼ cup white wine vinegar

¼ cup water

Kosher salt and freshly ground black pepper

PREHEAT THE oven to 375°F. Place the beets in a baking dish (if using a mix of red and golden beets, separate them into two smaller dishes and divide the oil, vinegar, and water between the two dishes). Drizzle with the oil and add the vinegar and water to the dish. Season with salt and pepper. Cover the pan with foil and roast until the beets are tender when pierced with a knife; this can take anywhere from 30 minutes to an hour, depending on the thickness of the beets. Let the beets cool, then peel and cut into 1-inch pieces. Place each color of beet, along with any accumulated juices, in a small mixing bowl.

——— GRILLED FENNEL ———

1 teaspoon fennel seeds, coarsely ground in a spice grinder or mortar and pestle

1 teaspoon sugar

1 teaspoon kosher salt

1 medium fennel bulb, halved, cored, and cut into ½-inch wedges

¼ cup extra-virgin olive oil

PREHEAT THE oven to 375°F. In a small bowl, combine the fennel seeds, sugar, and salt and stir until combined. In a medium bowl, toss the fennel wedges with the fennel sugar until well coated. Arrange the fennel in a single layer on a rimmed baking sheet (sprinkle with any remaining fennel sugar from the bowl) and drizzle with the olive oil. Cover with aluminum foil and roast for 10 minutes, then uncover and roast until just tender, about 10 minutes longer.

CONTINUES ➡

PREHEAT THE broiler, prepare a hot grill, or preheat a grill pan over high heat. Broil or grill the fennel until caramelized all over, a minute or two per side.

ORANGE VINAIGRETTE

MAKES ABOUT ¾ CUP

1 tablespoon finely grated orange zest (from 1 medium orange)

2 tablespoons plus 2 teaspoons fresh orange juice

2 tablespoons plus 2 teaspoons fresh lemon juice

1½ teaspoons honey

1 teaspoon champagne vinegar

1 teaspoon kosher salt

¼ teaspoon cayenne pepper

¼ cup extra-virgin olive oil

1½ tablespoons sunflower oil

COMBINE THE orange zest and juice, lemon juice, honey, vinegar, salt, and cayenne in a blender and puree until smooth. With the machine running, slowly drizzle in the oils until emulsified.

FOR SERVING

Roasted Beets

¼ cup plus 1 tablespoon Orange Vinaigrette

Kosher salt

Grilled Fennel

½ jalapeño chile, seeded and finely chopped (about 1 tablespoon)

Flaky sea salt

Extra-virgin olive oil

1 tablespoon chopped fennel fronds

1 tablespoon chopped dill fronds

1 tablespoon chopped tarragon

¼ cup crumbled goat cheese

TOSS THE beets with half of the dressing and season with kosher salt. On a serving platter, arrange the fennel wedges, fanning them out slightly. Scatter the beets over the fennel. Sprinkle the jalapeño over the salad. Drizzle the remaining dressing over the salad. Sprinkle with flaky salt and drizzle with olive oil. Top with the herbs and goat cheese and serve.

Celery and Celery Root Caesar Salad

MAKES 4 SERVINGS

There's no lettuce in this salad, but it's unmistakably Caesar-like in flavor. I love making the salad in the dead of winter, when fresh greens are scarce at the farmers market and crunchy, earthy celery root is in abundance. The dressing gets its heat from a splash of homemade Red Hot Sauce; if you don't want to make your own, you can swap in Tabasco or another vinegar-based sauce.

THE TAKEAWAY

My Caesar dressing is based on the classic recipe, with one twist: Instead of using raw egg yolks, I soft-boil an entire egg and blend that into the dressing, which creates a richer version. I also don't blend cheese into my dressing, which makes it a dairy-free option.

RED HOT SAUCE

MAKES ABOUT 2 CUPS

1 pasilla chile, stemmed and roughly chopped

2 guajillo chiles, stemmed and roughly chopped

3 red finger chiles, stemmed and roughly chopped

Finely grated zest of 3 oranges

2 large garlic cloves

2 medium carrots, peeled and roughly chopped

2 tablespoons plus 2 teaspoons kosher salt

1 tablespoon sugar

½ cup plus 2 tablespoons champagne vinegar

⅓ cup water

COMBINE THE chiles, zest, garlic, carrots, salt, and sugar in a food processor and process until finely chopped. Transfer to a very clean container and cover with cheesecloth. Let ferment at room temperature for 3 days. Transfer to a blender, add the vinegar and water, and blend until smooth. Transfer to a sterilized bottle or jar, seal, and refrigerate for up to 1 month.

CAESAR DRESSING

MAKES 1 CUP

1 egg

1 serrano chile

3 tablespoons red wine vinegar

1 tablespoon fresh lemon juice

1 tablespoon Dijon mustard

2 oil-packed anchovy fillets

1 teaspoon Worcestershire sauce

1 teaspoon Red Hot Sauce or Tabasco hot sauce

½ teaspoon kosher salt

¼ teaspoon freshly ground black pepper

¾ cup extra-virgin olive oil

BRING A small saucepan of water to a boil and prepare an ice bath. Add the egg, reduce the heat to a simmer, and cover the pot. Let the egg cook for 7 minutes, then transfer to the ice bath to cool. Peel the egg.

CUT ½ inch from the end of the serrano and roughly chop it (with the seeds). Thinly slice the rest of the chile and set aside for the salad.

ADD THE egg to a blender along with the chopped serrano, vinegar, lemon juice, mustard, anchovies, Worcestershire, hot sauce, salt, and pepper and blend until smooth. With the machine running, slowly drizzle in the olive oil until emulsified. The dressing can be made up to 1 day ahead and refrigerated until ready to use.

--------------------- FOR SERVING ---------------------

- 1 large celery root, peeled and cut into ¼-inch matchsticks (about 3 cups)
- 4 large celery stalks, thinly sliced on a sharp bias into ¼-inch pieces (about 3 cups)
- ¼ cup chopped celery leaves
- ¼ cup finely chopped mixed herbs (such as parsley, chives, tarragon, and chervil)
- Reserved serrano chile slices (from dressing above)
- 1 cup coarsely grated Parmesan cheese
- 1 teaspoon kosher salt
- Caesar Dressing
- Freshly ground black pepper
- Finely grated lemon zest

IN A large bowl, combine the celery root, celery, celery leaves, herbs, chile slices, ¾ cup of the Parmesan, and the salt. Toss well. Divide among four shallow bowls. Drizzle about 2 tablespoons dressing over each salad in a zigzag pattern. Top with the remaining Parmesan, freshly ground black pepper, and lemon zest. Serve.

Celery Root, Fennel, Pear, and Apple Salad
WITH MEYER LEMON VINAIGRETTE

MAKES 4 TO 6 SERVINGS

This salad is super crunchy and satisfying, thanks to a medley of shaved vegetables and candied walnuts. It's the kind of salad you want to assemble and eat right away, before the vegetables begin to oxidize. Tying it all together is a sharp Meyer lemon vinaigrette. When I can't find Meyer lemons, I use an equal-parts combination of regular lemon zest and juice and tangerine or mandarin orange zest and juice—they are a close approximation to the Meyer's fragrant, sweet-sour flavor profile.

THE TAKEAWAY

If you don't already own a mandoline, this recipe is a great excuse to buy one. You don't need to spend a fortune on one, either: I use the Japanese-made Benriner brand, which runs about $25. It's a worthy investment, as you'll save yourself hours of time (and frustration) of trying to cut perfectly thin slices with a knife.

MEYER LEMON VINAIGRETTE

MAKES 1 CUP

1 tablespoon finely grated Meyer lemon zest (from about 2 lemons)

½ cup plus 1 tablespoon fresh Meyer lemon juice

1 teaspoon Dijon mustard

¾ teaspoon kosher salt

½ cup extra-virgin olive oil

COMBINE THE lemon zest and juice, mustard, and salt in a blender and blend until smooth. With the machine running, slowly drizzle in the oil until emulsified.

FOR SERVING

1 medium bulb celery root, peeled, quartered, and thinly shaved on a mandoline (about 2 cups)

1 large or 2 small bulbs fennel, halved, cored, and thinly shaved on a mandoline (about 2 cups)

1 Asian pear, quartered, cored, and thinly shaved on a mandoline (about 1 cup)

1 Granny Smith apple, quartered, cored, and thinly shaved on a mandoline (about 1 cup)

1 jalapeño chile, finely chopped (with seeds)

¼ cup Candied Walnuts (page 160), finely chopped

3 tablespoons fines herbes (equal parts finely chopped chervil, chives, parsley, and tarragon)

1 tablespoon finely chopped mint

Meyer Lemon Vinaigrette

Kosher salt

Flaky sea salt

Freshly ground black pepper

IN A large bowl, combine the celery root, fennel, pear, apple, jalapeño, walnuts, and herbs. Add ¼ cup vinaigrette and toss. Season to taste with kosher salt and more vinaigrette, if needed. Transfer to a shallow serving bowl, season with flaky salt and pepper, and serve.

Mixed Greens and Citrus Salad
WITH FENNEL VINAIGRETTE AND SESAME CLUSTERS

MAKES 4 SERVINGS

I first made this dish for a midwinter dinner in Upstate New York, where I was cooking for my friend, the fashion designer Lela Rose. I wanted a salad to serve alongside a braised short rib, so it needed hearty greens and a boldly flavored dressing. I landed on a fennel vinaigrette, which carries a bit of heat from habanero and serrano chiles and has the chunky texture of a mignonette. Because of its chunkiness, be sure to give the dressing a good stir right before you dress the salad.

—————— **THE TAKEAWAY** ——————

These spiced sesame clusters were inspired by the Asian and Middle Eastern-style sesame candies that always found their way into my Halloween haul as a kid. Recreating them as a crunchy garnish wasn't hard, and they've proven to be quite versatile in all kinds of salads. When you're making these clusters yourself, it's helpful to think of the process as akin to making granola rather than a nut brittle: Stir the seeds often while they bake to keep the clusters light and airy, rather than one large clump that needs to be broken up. The clusters are a great vehicle for a variety of spices, so play around with different flavors to match whatever you're cooking.

—————— SESAME CLUSTERS ——————

MAKES ABOUT 1 CUP

1 large egg white
3 tablespoons sugar
½ teaspoon kosher salt
¼ teaspoon ground cinnamon
¼ teaspoon ground cloves
¼ teaspoon ground nutmeg
1 cup sesame seeds

PREHEAT THE oven to 350°F and line a baking sheet with parchment or a silicone mat. In a small bowl, whisk the egg white until slightly foamy. Whisk in the sugar, salt, cinnamon, cloves, and nutmeg. Add the sesame seeds and stir well to coat.

SPOON THE sesame mixture in clumps onto the lined baking sheet. Bake, stirring frequently (to avoid the seeds becoming one large mass), until golden brown, 10 to 15 minutes. Let cool; if the clusters are large, break them into bite-size pieces. The sesame clusters can be made a few days ahead; store in an airtight container.

—————— FENNEL VINAIGRETTE ——————

MAKES 1 CUP

½ cup extra-virgin olive oil
2 tablespoons finely chopped fennel bulb, plus 1 tablespoon chopped fennel fronds
2 tablespoons finely chopped shallot
2 tablespoons finely chopped ginger
⅛ teaspoon fennel seeds, lightly crushed
2 tablespoons honey
½ cup white wine vinegar
½ habanero chile, seeded and finely chopped
½ serrano chile, seeded and finely chopped
2 teaspoons chopped chervil or tarragon
Kosher salt

IN A medium skillet, heat the oil over medium-low heat. Add the fennel bulb, shallot, ginger, and fennel seeds and cook until the vegetables are soft, 7 to 10 minutes. Stir in the honey and turn off the heat. Whisk in the vinegar and let cool. Stir in the habanero, serrano, fennel fronds, and chervil. Season to taste with salt. The vinaigrette can be made up to 1 day ahead; shake or whisk well before using.

─────────── FOR SERVING ───────────

2 blood or navel
   oranges,
   or 1 grapefruit
5 ounces mixed greens
   (such as arugula,
   frisée, radicchio,
   and/or endive)

Fennel Vinaigrette,
   to taste
½ cup Sesame Clusters

USING A sharp knife, cut the peel and white pith from the oranges. Cut between the membranes to release the orange segments into a bowl.

PLACE THE greens in a serving bowl and spoon some of the fennel vinaigrette over. Sprinkle the sesame clusters and citrus segments over the top, toss gently, and serve.

Citrus and Chicory Salad

WITH SHERRY VINAIGRETTE AND GOAT'S MILK GOUDA

MAKES 4 SERVINGS

This salad is about highlighting a few key ingredients. It starts with finding some great chicories. At the grocery store you'll probably find radicchio and Belgian endive, but it's worth the trip to the farmers market to find heads of speckled Castelfranco, finger-shaped Tardivo, or the frisée-like Coraline. I also use multiple kinds of citrus to bring some sunshine onto your table in midwinter, when citrus from California is at its best.

--- THE TAKEAWAY ---

Cheese is often an afterthought with salad, but I like to carefully select what a cheese is going to bring to the dish. Here, I want the buttery flavors of an aged goat's milk Gouda to smooth out the bitterness of the greens and the acidity of the dressing. At my restaurant we use Consider Bardwell Farm's Danby cheese, but you can ask your cheesemonger for something similar.

--- SHERRY VINAIGRETTE ---

MAKES ½ CUP

⅓ cup sherry vinegar
2 teaspoons Dijon mustard
2 teaspoons sugar
1 teaspoon kosher salt
¼ cup extra-virgin olive oil

IN A small bowl, whisk together the vinegar, mustard, sugar, and salt. Slowly whisk in the olive oil until emulsified.

--- FOR SERVING ---

1 navel orange
1 blood orange
1 grapefruit
3 clementines
2 tangerines
4 cups roughly chopped mixed chicories (such as radicchio, endive, Castelfranco, Tardivo, or Coraline)
1 avocado, halved, pitted, and thinly sliced
2 ounces goat's milk Gouda
Sherry Vinaigrette
1 teaspoon finely chopped serrano chile
¼ cup thinly sliced mint
Extra-virgin olive oil
Flaky sea salt

USING A sharp knife, cut the skin and white pith from the oranges, grapefruit, clementines, and tangerines. Cut the oranges crosswise into ¼-inch slices and place in a medium bowl. Cut between the grapefruit membranes to release the segments onto a cutting board, then cut each segment into three pieces and add to the bowl. Separate the clementines and tangerines into segments and add to the bowl. Add the chicories and gently toss.

DIVIDE THE citrus and chicories evenly among four plates. Divide the avocado among the salads. Using a vegetable peeler, shave some cheese over each salad, and drizzle each with a tablespoon or two of the vinaigrette. Sprinkle with the chile and mint. Drizzle some olive oil over each salad, sprinkle with flaky salt, and serve.

136

Winter Chicories

WITH PERSIMMONS, GRILLED DATES, AND POMEGRANATE VINAIGRETTE

MAKES 4 SERVINGS

It's been a long time coming, but chicories are finally getting the attention they deserve in America. This family of hearty lettuces is my favorite thing to use in winter salads, as their slightly bitter flavor can stand up to pretty much anything you throw at them: raw and cooked preparations, punchy vinaigrettes, cheesy dressings, fruit, vegetables, you name it. They're also sturdier than their soft-leafed cousins, so they won't wilt if you dress them ahead of time—in many cases, they get better.

Another underappreciated ingredient in this salad is persimmon, a fruit that fascinates me and inspires me to come up with new dishes every winter (when they're in season). You'll likely encounter two kinds of persimmons at the market: Hachiya and Fuyu. Hachiyas are oblong (like a Roma tomato), custard-soft in texture, and mouth-puckeringly astringent when not perfectly ripe. I rarely use Hachiyas, but Fuyu persimmons are a joy: They're firmer and have a great flavor that I've heard described as "an apricot dusted with cinnamon."

You're probably familiar with Belgian endive, escarole, and radicchio, but I strongly encourage you to seek out some new varieties, such as Treviso, Tardivo, and Castelfranco.

THE TAKEAWAY

You'll find grilled dates in many of my dishes. Like other dried fruit, they add a chewy texture and an intense sweetness that pairs especially well with bitter greens. But dates are also large enough to throw on the grill, and doing so caramelizes some of their sugars and gives them a light crunch as well. I usually use Medjool, Halawi, or Khadrawy from California, but whatever you use, make sure they're not too dried out—the "fresher" the date, the better.

In the Brussels Sprout Salad on 120, we use fresh fruit and vegetable juice as the base for the dressing, but sometimes you need a more intense flavor, or a thicker, emulsified dressing that will adhere to heartier ingredients. In these cases, I reduce fruit juice down to a syrup, then blend that into a dressing. I do this often with cherry juice, grape juice, and citrus juices. Here we're using pomegranate juice, which you can buy bottled (make sure to get pure, unsweetened juice), or you can juice your own by pulsing pomegranate seeds in a food processor, then straining the juice.

CONTINUES ➡

137

POMEGRANATE VINAIGRETTE

MAKES ABOUT ½ CUP

½ cup 100% pomegranate juice

2 tablespoons liquid from Pickled Jalapeños (page 227), or 2 tablespoon white wine vinegar plus a pinch of cayenne pepper

1 tablespoon fresh lemon juice

1½ teaspoons Dijon mustard

¾ teaspoon Colman's mustard powder

½ teaspoon kosher salt, plus more to taste

¼ cup extra-virgin olive oil

IN A medium saucepan, bring the pomegranate juice to a boil and reduce until syrupy. Let cool, then pour the reduced juice into a bowl. Add the jalapeño liquid, lemon juice, Dijon mustard, mustard powder, and salt. Slowly whisk in the olive oil until emulsified and season to taste with salt.

FOR SERVING

1 cup Medjool, Halawi, or Khadrawy dates, halved lengthwise and pitted

1 head radicchio (or other chicory), cored and roughly chopped (about 2 cups)

1 Belgian endive (or other chicory), roughly chopped

1 tablespoon chopped tarragon

1 tablespoon chopped mint

2 tablespoons extra-virgin olive oil

Flaky sea salt

1 Fuyu persimmon, cut into ⅛-inch wedges

Pomegranate Vinaigrette

¼ cup pomegranate seeds

Lemon wedges

Freshly cracked black pepper

PREPARE A hot grill or preheat a grill pan over high heat. Grill the dates, turning once or twice, until some char develops, about 1 minute. Transfer to a cutting board and cut into strips.

IN A mixing bowl, toss the greens with the herbs, olive oil, and a couple pinches of flaky salt. Divide among salad plates or shallow bowls and top with the grilled dates and persimmon. Drizzle each salad with some of the pomegranate vinaigrette and sprinkle with the pomegranate seeds. Finish the salads with a squeeze of lemon juice and some freshly cracked pepper. Serve.

Vegetables

—

Grilled Asparagus
WITH BROKEN CHILE SAUCE AND POTATO RIBBONS

MAKES 4 SERVINGS

Usually when we make sauces, we want a consistent, homogenous texture. But sometimes you want a sauce to deliver two textures. In this case, I'll cook a puree until it "breaks" and separates into an intensely flavored oil and a thicker paste. The smoky broken chile sauce in this dish was inspired by harissa, the North African chile paste, as well as some of the chile-based sauces we made at Tabla. It's a great condiment to keep on hand; spoon it over grilled lamb, fried eggs, broccoli, green beans, or a rice bowl.

— THE TAKEAWAY —

I love the airy crispness of tempura flakes, which you'll often find surrounding elaborate sushi rolls. But I wanted to make a gluten-free version, so I grated some potatoes into hot oil and was thrilled with the result. The key to achieving the light, flaky texture is to use a ribbon-style grater (Microplane and other brands make these). If you don't have one, use the large holes on a box grater, but the final product will be a bit denser and chewier. The potato ribbons also make a great salad topper and garnish for soup and rice.

——— BROKEN CHILE SAUCE ———

MAKES ABOUT 2 CUPS

5 pasilla chiles, stems and seeds discarded

5 ancho chiles, stems and seeds discarded

5 guajillo chiles, stems and seeds discarded

1 cup extra-virgin oil

¼ cup annatto seeds

2 medium shallots, thinly sliced

4 garlic cloves, thinly sliced

⅔ cup white wine vinegar

½ cup sugar

2 tablespoons kosher salt

2 teaspoons brown mustard seeds

¼ cup coriander seeds, toasted and finely ground

1 tablespoon plus 2 teaspoons Aleppo pepper

¼ teaspoon red pepper flakes

PLACE THE chiles in a bowl and cover with 2 cups boiling water. Cover the bowl with plastic wrap and let sit for 1 hour. Strain and set the softened chiles aside, reserving the liquid.

MEANWHILE, IN a small saucepan, heat the oil and annatto seeds over medium heat until the oil reaches 180°F. Turn off the heat and let sit for 2 hours. Strain and return half the oil to the pot, reserving the other half to use later. Add the shallots and garlic to the pot and cook over low heat until both are soft and lightly golden brown, about 30 minutes. Transfer to a blender along with the softened chiles, vinegar, sugar, salt, and 1¼ cups of the chile soaking liquid. Puree until smooth, scraping down the side of the blender as needed.

IN A medium nonstick skillet, heat the remaining annatto oil over medium heat. Add the mustard seeds and cook until they've bloomed and begin to pop, then add the coriander, Aleppo, and red pepper flakes and cook for 1 minute. Add the chile puree and cook over medium heat, stirring constantly. After a few minutes, the oil will "break,"

CONTINUES ➡

and separate from the puree. Cook for 2 minutes longer, then transfer to a bowl and let cool. The sauce can be made up to 2 days ahead and refrigerated until ready to use; let warm to room temperature before using.

POTATO RIBBONS

Vegetable oil, for frying   Kosher salt

1 small russet potato,
  peeled

IN A medium saucepan, heat 1 inch of oil to 300°F. Use a Microplane ribbon grater to grate the potatoes into a bowl of cold water (to rinse off the starch), then drain and lay out on a clean kitchen towel. Gently squeeze the potatoes until dry. Working in batches, fry the potato ribbons until golden brown, about 1 minute. Transfer the fried potatoes to paper towels and season with salt. Continue until you have about ½ cup of crispy ribbons.

FOR SERVING

1 bunch asparagus,
  woody stems trimmed

⅓ cup Broken Chile
  Sauce

1 tablespoon extra-
  virgin olive oil

Potato Ribbons

½ cup Greek yogurt

1 tablespoon finely
  chopped parsley

2 tablespoons roughly
  chopped olives

1 tablespoon finely
  chopped tarragon

Lemon wedge

Flaky sea salt

PREPARE A hot grill or preheat a grill pan over high heat. Toss the asparagus with the olive oil and grill until lightly charred and just tender, 5 to 8 minutes (depending on the thickness of the asparagus).

SPREAD A stripe of yogurt on the bottom third of a serving platter and top with the asparagus, lined up in a row. Sprinkle the olives over the asparagus. Squeeze the lemon over. Spoon the broken chile sauce over the asparagus, and sprinkle with the potato ribbons, herbs, and flaky salt. Serve.

Grilled Carrots

WITH SWEET AND SOUR CARROT SAUCE

MAKES 4 SERVINGS

When's the last time you grilled a carrot? Maybe it's because they're not considered a "summer vegetable," but we don't think about carrots often enough when we're cooking over a live fire. This dish started out with me throwing some carrots on the wood-fired grill at my restaurant, and I let them go until they were very charred all over. They tasted like barbecued carrots, so I created a carrot-based barbecue sauce to double up on their sweet, earthy flavor. As with other vegetables and meats, I season carrots with both salt and sugar before they hit the grill to help them quickly pick up some char. To ensure even cooking, try to use carrots that are mostly uniform in thickness.

— THE TAKEAWAY —

Most barbecue sauces are based on tomatoes (or ketchup), but why not use another vegetable as the main ingredient? Carrots are certainly up to the task, as are beets, parsnips, red peppers, and other earthy vegetables that also have some inherent sweetness. This carrot sauce will go with anything you'd slather with regular barbecue sauce, from smoked ribs to grilled chicken and even fatty fish like salmon.

—— SWEET AND SOUR CARROT SAUCE ——

MAKES 2 CUPS

1 tablespoon sunflower or vegetable oil

1 medium shallot, thinly sliced

3 medium orange carrots, peeled and cut into ¼-inch rounds (about 1 cup)

1½ teaspoons kosher salt

½ teaspoon hot smoked paprika

1 tablespoon finely chopped red finger chile

⅓ cup sugar

⅓ cup fresh lime juice

½ cup champagne vinegar

⅔ cup extra-virgin olive oil

IN A medium skillet, heat the sunflower oil over medium heat. Add the shallots and cook, stirring, until they start to turn golden brown, 2 to 3 minutes. Add the carrots, salt, and paprika and cook until slightly tender, 3 to 4 minutes. Add the chile, sugar, lime juice, and vinegar, bring to a simmer, and cook until the carrots are just tender and the liquid has reduced by about half, 2 to 3 minutes longer. Scrape the contents of the skillet into a blender. With the machine running, slowly drizzle in the olive oil. Transfer to a container and reserve. The sauce can be made a day or two ahead of time and refrigerated until ready to use.

—— GRILLED CARROTS ——

1 pound medium carrots (or a mix of medium and baby carrots), peeled, leaving some greens attached

2 tablespoons extra-virgin olive oil

1 teaspoon kosher salt

1 teaspoon sugar

Sweet and Sour Carrot Sauce

BRING A large saucepan of salted water to a boil. If any of the carrots are thicker than 1 inch, cut them on the bias into ½-inch slices. Working in batches, blanch the carrots until crisp-tender, about 4 minutes. Transfer to paper towels and pat dry.

CONTINUES ➡

PREPARE A hot grill or preheat a grill pan over high heat. On a rimmed baking sheet, toss the carrots with the olive oil and season with the salt and sugar. Grill the carrots until well charred and just tender, 3 to 4 minutes. Return them to the baking sheet and toss with about ½ cup of the carrot sauce, or more as needed to coat them completely.

FOR SERVING

¼ cup roasted sunflower seeds

¼ cup roasted pumpkin seeds

Grilled Carrots

1 lemon

2 tablespoons roughly chopped parsley

2 tablespoons roughly chopped mint

Flaky sea salt

Freshly ground black pepper

Extra-virgin olive oil

PULSE THE sunflower and pumpkin seeds in a food processor until roughly chopped (you can also do this with a knife).

ARRANGE THE carrots on a platter or large, shallow bowl and sprinkle with the chopped seeds. Finely grate some lemon zest over, then cut the lemon into wedges and squeeze one or two over the carrots. Sprinkle the parsley and mint over and season with flaky salt and pepper. Drizzle with olive oil and serve.

Pan-Roasted Asparagus
WITH SPRING ONIONS AND LEMON-MAYO DRESSING

MAKES 4 SERVINGS

This is a simple side dish you should make as soon as spring's first asparagus comes to market. It was inspired by the classic pairing of asparagus and hollandaise sauce, but I didn't want to deal with the challenges of making hollandaise. Instead, I use a mayonnaise-thickened vinaigrette, which falls midway between an aioli and a creamy dressing in thickness. It's also a great dressing to keep in mind for other green vegetables, and it's just thick enough to spread on sandwiches as well. Add a poached or fried egg to this dish, and you have an elegant brunch course.

THE TAKEAWAY

Quickly sautéing the spring onions in a small amount of oil will give them a similar charred flavor you'd get from a grill, without having to figure out how to grill the tiny vegetables. This isn't quite "dry roasting," but it's close. Keep this technique in mind when you want to develop some smoky charred flavor with alliums (onions, shallots, scallions, etc.) while retaining some of their crunch.

HOUSE MAYONNAISE

MAKES ABOUT 1½ CUPS

1 large egg

1 tablespoon champagne or white wine vinegar

1½ teaspoons fresh lemon juice

1 teaspoon Dijon mustard

½ teaspoon kosher salt

1 cup canola oil

IN A blender, combine the egg, vinegar, lemon juice, mustard, and salt. Blend until combined. With the machine running, very slowly add the oil in a thin stream until the mixture is thickened. Transfer to a storage container and refrigerate for up to 1 week.

LEMON-MAYO DRESSING

MAKES ABOUT ¾ CUP

½ cup House Mayonnaise, or other mayonnaise

Finely grated zest of 1 lemon

2 tablespoons fresh lemon juice

1 tablespoon Dijon mustard

1 teaspoon honey

¾ teaspoon kosher salt

½ teaspoon freshly ground black pepper

¼ cup chopped parsley

COMBINE ALL ingredients in a bowl and whisk until combined.

150

──────── FOR SERVING ────────

4 spring onions, roots trimmed

2 tablespoons extra-virgin olive oil

Kosher salt

1 bunch asparagus, woody stems trimmed, cut on the bias into 1½-inch pieces

¼ cup thinly sliced basil

Freshly ground black pepper

Lemon-Mayo Dressing

SEPARATE THE onion bulbs from the greens. Cut the bulbs into ⅛-inch wedges and thinly slice the greens. In a skillet, heat 1 tablespoon of the olive oil over high heat. When the oil shimmers, add the onion bulbs and sauté until lightly charred but still crunchy, 3 to 4 minutes. Season to taste with salt and set aside.

BRING A saucepan of well-salted water to a boil and prepare an ice bath. Blanch the asparagus until crisp-tender, 1 to 3 minutes depending on the thickness of the stalks. Transfer to the ice bath to cool, then drain and pat dry.

IN A large skillet, heat the remaining 1 tablespoon olive oil over medium-high heat. Add the asparagus and cook until lightly charred, 1 to 2 minutes. Turn off the heat and add the onion bulbs and greens and the basil and toss well. Season to taste with salt and pepper.

ADD ENOUGH dressing to cover the bottom of a platter or shallow bowl. Arrange the asparagus mixture over the top in an even layer and serve.

Roasted Portobello Mushrooms
WITH LEMON-PECORINO DRESSING

MAKES 4 SERVINGS

You could easily move this dish to the grill (by grilling the mushrooms rather than roasting them) and serve it as a side with some steak, or add a side salad and call it a meat-free meal. If you can find meaty king trumpet mushrooms or maitakes, feel free to use those in place of the portobellos.

——— THE TAKEAWAY ———

We often use Dijon or eggs to help thicken and emulsify vinaigrettes, but keep miso in mind whenever you want a creamy dressing. It's basically umami paste, so it will add loads of savory flavor and plays especially well with cheese. Over the years, I've found myself using less Dijon (which is great but adds a spicy acidity you don't always want) and more miso in dressings, and you will likely find yourself doing the same once you start playing around with it.

——— LEMON-PECORINO DRESSING ———

MAKES ABOUT ¾ CUP

½ cup extra-virgin olive oil

¼ cup plus 2 tablespoons champagne vinegar

Finely grated zest of 2 lemons

¼ cup fresh lemon juice

3 tablespoons white miso

3 ounces Pecorino cheese, broken into chunks

2 teaspoons thyme leaves

1 tablespoon kosher salt

½ teaspoon freshly ground black pepper

COMBINE ALL of the ingredients in a blender and blend until very smooth, scraping down the side of the blender as needed. The dressing can be made up to 2 days ahead and refrigerated until ready to use.

——— ROASTED PORTOBELLO MUSHROOMS ———

1 pound portobello mushrooms (about 4 large), each cut into 8 wedges

¼ cup extra-virgin olive oil

2 teaspoons kosher salt

1 teaspoon freshly ground black pepper

PREHEAT THE oven to 450°F and place a wire rack inside a large rimmed baking sheet. In a bowl, toss the mushrooms with the olive oil, salt, and pepper. Let stand for 20 minutes. Arrange the mushrooms in a single layer on the rack and roast until well browned all over and crispy around the edges, 10 to 15 minutes.

——— FOR SERVING ———

6 scallions, roots trimmed

2 tablespoons extra-virgin olive oil

Kosher salt and freshly ground black pepper

Lemon-Pecorino Dressing

Roasted Portobello Mushrooms

3 tablespoons chopped parsley

Flaky sea salt

WHILE THE mushrooms roast, grill the scallions. Prepare a medium-hot grill or preheat a grill pan over medium-high heat. Brush the scallions with olive oil and season with kosher salt and pepper. Grill the scallions, turning frequently, until softened and charred, 2 to 3 minutes.

SPREAD THE dressing on a serving platter. Scatter the scallions and mushrooms over the dressing. Sprinkle with parsley and flaky salt and serve.

Pan-Roasted Summer Squash
WITH GRILLED LETTUCE AND HERBED GOAT CHEESE

MAKES 4 SERVINGS

I grew up eating garlicky Alouette cheese spread by the tub, so I wanted to re-create (and slightly elevate) those flavors. My herbed goat cheese spread forms the creamy base for grilled lettuce and caramelized squash. If you're stationed at the grill and don't want to cook the squash indoors, you can cut them lengthwise into quarters, grill until charred and tender, then slice into ½-inch pieces.

THE TAKEAWAY

If you are a proud Alouette (or Boursin) fan, I probably don't need to tell you that the herbed goat cheese makes an excellent dip for crudités and crackers, as well as a fine sandwich spread. But you can also use it as the base for a white pizza, or stuff it into pasta shells or ravioli. It also makes a great layer in vegetable lasagna.

PICKLED RAMPS

MAKES 2 CUPS

- 1 pound ramps, roots trimmed
- 1 teaspoon brown or red mustard seeds
- 1 teaspoon coriander seeds
- Pinch of red pepper flakes
- 1½ cups white wine vinegar
- ¼ cup sugar
- 2 tablespoons kosher salt

WASH THE ramps well. Separate the bulbs from the leaves, trimming the ramps before the red end of the bulb turns into the leaf. Place the ramp bulbs in a clean pint-size jar and add the mustard seeds, coriander seeds, and red pepper flakes.

IN A small saucepan, combine the vinegar, sugar, and salt and bring to a boil. Pour the hot brine over the ramps, leaving about ½ inch of room at the top of the jar. Tap the jar to release any air bubbles, and add more brine if necessary. Seal the jar and let cool to room temperature, then refrigerate for at least 24 hours before using. The pickles can be refrigerated for up to 1 month.

HERBED GOAT CHEESE

- 8 ounces goat cheese
- ¼ cup buttermilk, shaken
- ¼ cup thinly sliced mint
- ¼ cup finely chopped parsley
- 2 tablespoons chopped Pickled Ramps
- 2 teaspoons finely chopped oregano
- ½ teaspoon red pepper flakes
- 1 teaspoon kosher salt
- 4 teaspoons fresh lemon juice

IN A bowl, blend all ingredients with a fork until well mixed. The herbed goat cheese can be made a few days ahead; refrigerate until ready to use.

——————— FOR SERVING ———————

1 small zucchini

1 small yellow summer squash

2 heads Little Gem lettuce, cut into quarters through the root end

Extra-virgin olive oil

Kosher salt

Herbed Goat Cheese

2 teaspoons balsamic vinegar mixed with 2 pinches of sugar

2 tablespoons chopped parsley

2 tablespoons chopped mint

2 teaspoons chopped oregano

Flaky sea salt

CUT THE zucchini and squash lengthwise into quarters, then cut out the seeds. Cut both on the bias into ½-inch pieces.

PREPARE A hot grill or preheat a grill pan over high heat. Drizzle the lettuce with olive oil and season with kosher salt. Grill until the cut sides are charred, about 2 minutes. Set aside.

IN A large skillet, heat 2 tablespoons olive oil over high heat until it shimmers. Add the squash and cook, stirring occasionally, until just tender and browned in spots, 3 to 4 minutes.

SPREAD THE herbed goat cheese on a serving platter. Scatter the squash and lettuce wedges over. Drizzle with the vinegar mixture and sprinkle with the herbs and flaky salt. Serve.

Fresh-Corn Polenta
WITH BUTTER AND HERBS

MAKES 4 SERVINGS

I first saw this technique of cooking fresh corn into a porridge-like consistency while working for Jean-Georges Vongerichten. We were opening a restaurant in Washington, D.C., and needed an accompaniment for a salmon dish. He grabbed a few corn cobs and started grating the kernels into a pan, then cooked the fresh corn down until it was a chunky puree. I was blown away by the result. I've adapted the technique over the years, opting to puree the corn in a food processor (for a smoother texture) with a pinch of turmeric (to help boost the yellow color), then cooking it down in a sauce-pan until it's thick enough to hold its shape when spooned onto a plate.

This summery side dish can be served alongside anything you'd eat with polenta, but it's also lighter than its cornmeal-based counterpart (which is usually enriched with butter and/or cheese), so it works well with lighter fare like seafood as well.

THE TAKEAWAY

The technique at the heart of this recipe is a primer on how to get the most out of an ear of corn. Make sure you use a sharp knife to cut the kernels from the cob, and work over a bowl so you aren't chasing corn around the kitchen. When you've finished shaving off the kernels, turn the knife over and use the blunt side of the blade to scrape any milk left on the cob into the bowl as well—this tiny bit of liquid will add a lot of flavor.

FRESH-CORN POLENTA

8 ears corn, shucked	¼ teaspoon turmeric
3 tablespoons extra-virgin olive oil	1 tablespoon kosher salt

WORKING OVER a large bowl, cut the kernels from the corn, then use the blunt end of the knife to scrape any milk from the cob into the bowl. Discard the cobs or save for making Corn Stock (page 48). Add the contents of the bowl to a food processor and puree until as smooth as possible.

IN A medium saucepan, heat the oil over medium heat. Add the pureed corn, turmeric, and salt and cook, stirring constantly, until the corn has thickened into a polenta-like consistency, 8 to 10 minutes (the corn should be thick enough to hold its shape when spooned onto a plate). Season to taste with salt and keep warm.

FOR SERVING

2 ears corn, shucked	1 tablespoon chopped chives
1 tablespoon extra-virgin olive oil	1 tablespoon roughly chopped mint
Kosher salt	1 tablespoon roughly chopped basil
4 tablespoons unsalted butter	Lemon wedge
1 tablespoon finely chopped jalapeño chile	Fresh-Corn Polenta

CUT THE kernels from the corn into a bowl. In a large skillet (preferable cast-iron or nonstick), heat the olive oil over medium-high heat. Add the corn and cook, stirring, until well browned, about 5 minutes. Season with salt. Add the butter and cook until it begins to brown, about 4 minutes. Add the jalapeño and cook for 2 minutes. Turn off the heat and stir in the herbs. Squeeze the lemon over and stir to combine.

TRANSFER THE corn polenta to a serving bowl. Top with the charred corn mixture and serve.

Grilled Broccoli

WITH ORANGE AIOLI AND PISTACHIO VINAIGRETTE

MAKES 4 TO 6 SERVINGS

I was staying at a friend's beach house one weekend and found some gorgeous broccoli at the local farm stand. I wanted to turn the broccoli into something as satisfying as grilled meat, so I cut it into big pieces and cooked them over a fire until they were deeply charred. We now serve this version of the dish at Loring Place, and our guests often tell us that if they could eat vegetables like this all the time, they wouldn't need meat. Because the broccoli has such a big flavor, it needs an equally intense dressing to balance it out. Infusing olive oil with toasted pistachios and mint makes the base for a deeply flavored vinaigrette, while miso adds umami to the orange aioli.

——— ORANGE AIOLI ———

MAKES 1½ CUPS

1 large egg	½ teaspoon kosher salt
2 tablespoons orange marmalade	1 medium garlic clove, finely grated
1 teaspoon finely grated orange zest	1 cup sunflower oil
1 tablespoon Dijon mustard	1 tablespoon fresh lemon juice
1 teaspoon yellow miso	1 tablespoon white wine vinegar

CRACK THE egg into a tall mixing cup. Add the marmalade, orange zest, mustard, miso, salt, and garlic. Pour half of the oil on top and wait 15 seconds. Insert an immersion blender to the bottom of the cup, turn it on, and blend until emulsified. Transfer the aioli to a bowl and slowly whisk in the remaining oil, followed by the lemon juice and vinegar. The aioli can be made up to 2 days in advance and refrigerated.

——— PISTACHIO VINAIGRETTE ———

MAKES ABOUT ½ CUP

½ cup roughly chopped unsalted raw pistachios	Kosher salt
	2 teaspoons fresh lemon juice
7 tablespoons extra-virgin olive oil	2 tablespoons chopped mint

IN A small saucepan, combine the nuts, 1 tablespoon of the olive oil, and 1 teaspoon salt and cook over medium heat until the nuts are toasted, about 5 minutes. Transfer to a bowl and whisk in the remaining olive oil, lemon juice, and mint. Season to taste with salt.

——— FOR SERVING ———

1 pound broccoli, stems peeled, cut into long, thick spears	½ jalapeño chile, finely diced (include some seeds if you like the heat)
2 tablespoons extra-virgin olive oil	4 radishes, thinly sliced
Kosher salt	2 tablespoons thinly sliced mint leaves
Orange Aioli	Freshly grated orange zest
Pistachio Vinaigrette	

BRING A large saucepan of salted water to a boil. Blanch the broccoli until crisp-tender (but not soft), 1 to 2 minutes. Transfer to a wire rack to drain and let cool to room temperature.

PREPARE A hot grill or preheat a grill pan over high heat. Toss the broccoli with the olive oil and season with salt. Grill the broccoli, turning once, until charred, about 2 minutes per side.

TO SERVE, spread a thin layer of the orange aioli in a large, shallow bowl or platter. Arrange a pile of broccoli on top, then spoon some of the pistachio vinaigrette over the top. Garnish with the diced jalapeño, sliced radishes, mint, and some freshly grated orange zest, and serve.

A ripping-hot grill is my favorite tool for coaxing the best flavor out of broccoli, but if you throw a dense vegetable like this on the grill, you'll dry it out before it's tender. To keep broccoli (and other hearty vegetables like carrots) moist, I'll first blanch them until they're crisp-tender, then throw them on the hottest grill possible. That way I can concentrate on giving them a good char without worrying about cooking them through.

Leeks and Pears
WITH CANDIED WALNUTS, YOGURT, AND SHERRY VINAIGRETTE

MAKES 4 TO 6 SERVINGS

This salad is like a cross between a classic French side, leeks vinaigrette, and an American salad made with pears and walnuts. You can serve it as an elegant winter side, or a pretty starter for a dinner party. I first made it at a Long Island summer house after picking up some leeks from a farm stand, which I blanched in some pasta water and threw on the grill until they were deeply charred and infused with a smoky flavor. I love the contrast between the tender leeks, creamy yogurt, and crunchy pears and walnuts.

--- CANDIED WALNUTS ---

MAKES 2 CUPS

2 cups walnuts	¾ cup sugar
2 tablespoons water	1 tablespoon kosher salt

PREHEAT THE oven to 350°F. Scatter the walnuts on a rimmed baking sheet and bake until lightly toasted, about 5 minutes. Transfer to a cutting board and coarsely chop.

IN A medium saucepan, bring the water and sugar to a boil. Add the walnuts and cook, stirring constantly, until the water evaporates and the sugar crystallizes around the walnuts, about 2 minutes. Stir in the salt and spread the walnuts on a baking sheet to cool. Store the walnuts in an airtight container for a few days, or until they begin to lose their crunch.

--- SHERRY VINAIGRETTE ---

MAKES ½ CUP

2 tablespoons finely chopped shallot	1 teaspoon organic sugar
2 tablespoons sherry vinegar	3 tablespoons extra-virgin olive oil
1 teaspoon Dijon mustard	Kosher salt

IN A medium bowl, whisk together the shallot, vinegar, mustard, and sugar until combined. Slowly whisk in the oil until emulsified. Season with salt and let sit 30 minutes to lightly pickle the shallots. The dressing can be made up to 2 days ahead and refrigerated until ready to use.

--- FOR SERVING ---

1 firm ripe pear (8 ounces), such as Bartlett or Bosc, quartered, cored, and very thinly sliced (use a mandoline if you have one)	½ small celery stalk, thinly sliced on a bias (about ¼ cup), plus ¼ cup roughly chopped celery leaves
1 tablespoon fresh lemon juice	1 tablespoon finely diced jalapeño chile (with seeds)
4 leeks, each about ¾ to 1 inch in diameter, whites and light green parts only, roots trimmed	Extra-virgin olive oil
	1 cup Candied Walnuts
½ cup Greek yogurt	1 tablespoon chopped parsley
Sherry Vinaigrette	1 tablespoon chopped tarragon leaves
	Flaky sea salt

IN A bowl, toss the pear with the lemon juice.

BRING A large pot of salted water to a boil. Add the leeks and blanch until just tender, 3 to 5 minutes. Transfer to paper towels to drain, then cut in half lengthwise.

HEAT A large skillet (preferably cast-iron) over high heat. Working in batches, add the leeks, cut

CONTINUES ➡

160

THE TAKEAWAY

The technique for making candied walnuts almost seems like magic. As you cook them with sugar and a splash of water, a crystalline coating will start to cover the nuts. I picked up this trick not from a chef or cookbook, but from the vendors who make candied nuts on the streets of Manhattan. You can apply this technique to almost any kind of nut; just make sure you keep stirring and stirring until the nuts are covered with their sugary coating. In addition to topping salads, you can sprinkle the candied nuts on ice cream or serve them as part of a cheese board.

CONTINUED FROM PAGE 160

side down, and cook until charred on the bottom, about 3 minutes. Turn the leeks over and continue cooking until charred all over, about 4 minutes longer. Transfer to a plate, let cool slightly, then peel the outer charred layer from the leeks and discard.

SPREAD A thin layer of yogurt on the bottom of four to six shallow bowls. Arrange the leeks on top. Drizzle with the sherry vinaigrette and top with the sliced celery, jalapeño, and pear slices. Drizzle with olive oil. Sprinkle with the celery leaves, walnuts, parsley, tarragon, and flaky salt. Serve.

Roasted Summer Squash
WITH MISO-HERB SAUCE

MAKES 4 SERVINGS

Although it doesn't taste like much on its own, summer squash is like a flavor sponge, which is why I often apply a spice paste—or in this case, a garlic and herb–infused oil—before roasting it. This side comes together rather quickly, and is a great way to use up your squash harvest in those late-summer weeks when our markets and gardens are suddenly overrun with green and yellow vegetables. Feel free to combine as many squash varieties as you can find.

—— THE TAKEAWAY ——

This boldly flavored miso-herb sauce is like a cheese-free pesto, with flavors that remind me of a green Indian chutney. It's a great year-round accompaniment for grilled shrimp and fish, roast chicken, winter squash, beets, and tomatoes.

———— ROASTED SQUASH ————

¼ cup rosemary needles, finely chopped

3 tablespoons oregano leaves, finely chopped

1 large clove Garlic Confit (page 112); or 1 large garlic clove, blanched and finely grated

1 teaspoon kosher salt

3 tablespoons extra-virgin olive oil

2 pounds zucchini and/ or summer squash, cut crosswise into 1-inch-thick rounds

PREHEAT THE oven to 425°F. In a large bowl, stir the rosemary, oregano, garlic, and salt into the oil, smashing the garlic clove with a fork to break it up. Add the squash, toss to coat, and scrape onto a baking sheet in a single layer. Bake until the squash is golden brown and knife-tender, 15 to 20 minutes.

———— MISO-HERB SAUCE ————

MAKES ABOUT ¾ CUP

½ cup roughly chopped chives

½ cup roughly chopped cilantro

¼ cup toasted cashews, roughly chopped

¼ cup white miso

2 tablespoons extra-virgin olive oil

1 tablespoon honey

One 1-inch piece ginger, peeled and chopped

½ small jalapeño chile, chopped (with seeds)

¼ teaspoon ground coriander

¼ cup fresh lime juice

Kosher salt

IN A blender, combine all the ingredients. Blend until very smooth. Transfer to a small bowl and season with salt. The sauce is best made right before using, but if you want to make it a few hours ahead of time, leave the lime juice out and stir it in right before serving.

———— FOR SERVING ————

Miso-Herb Sauce

Roasted Squash

½ cup toasted cashews, roughly chopped

1 tablespoon whole brown flaxseeds

2 teaspoons Aleppo pepper

Extra-virgin olive oil

SPREAD THE miso-herb sauce on the bottom of four plates or a serving platter. Arrange the roasted squash on top and sprinkle with the cashews, flaxseeds, and Aleppo pepper. Drizzle with olive oil and serve.

164

Parmesan-Crusted Butternut Squash
WITH MEYER LEMON GREMOLATA

MAKES 4 SERVINGS

I originally made a version of this recipe with summer squash at ABC Kitchen, but I've found that it works even better with winter squash, best of all butternut squash, which becomes perfectly soft when roasted. If you take the care to completely coat the squash in cheese (more on that below), you'll be rewarded with cubes of warm, creamy squash covered in a crunchy, nutty, caramelized cheese shell. These cheesy bites are so snackable that this dish also makes a great appetizer or part of a fancy snack spread.

THE TAKEAWAY

You need to completely coat the squash in cheese in order to build a crispy encasement. I think of it like battering a piece of chicken in breadcrumbs. To get complete cheese coverage, I like to grate fine ribbons of Parmesan right over a sheet pan using a Microplane (or similar) grater, then roll each cube of squash in the cheese until all six sides are well coated. You can apply this technique to baby or fingerling potatoes (leave the skin on), or other cheese-loving vegetables such as carrots or parsnips.

PARMESAN-CRUSTED BUTTERNUT SQUASH

One 2- to 2½-pound butternut squash, peeled, seeded, and cut into 1-inch pieces

¼ cup extra-virgin olive oil

1 tablespoon kosher salt

1 teaspoon freshly ground black pepper

1½ cups finely grated Parmesan cheese (grated on a Microplane or similar grater)

PREHEAT THE oven to 450°F and place a wire rack inside a rimmed baking sheet. Brush the rack with olive oil or grease with nonstick cooking spray. In a bowl, toss the squash with the olive oil until well coated, then season with the salt and pepper. Scatter the cheese on a plate or baking sheet and roll the squash, one piece at a time, in the cheese until well coated on all sides. Transfer

CONTINUES ➡

165

to the wire rack. Roast the squash, flipping the pieces over with a metal spatula about halfway through cooking, until the squash is tender throughout and the cheese has formed a light brown crust, 25 to 30 minutes. Remove from the oven and let cool on the rack, then release with the spatula. You can roast the squash a couple hours ahead and rewarm in a 300°F oven.

FRIED PUMPKIN SEEDS

½ cup plus 2 tablespoons extra-virgin olive oil

½ cup raw pumpkin seeds

Kosher salt

IN A medium skillet, heat the olive oil over medium heat. Add the pumpkin seeds and cook, stirring constantly, until golden brown (they might start to sizzle and pop), 3 to 5 minutes. Drain in a sieve, saving the oil for another use; transfer the seeds to paper towels to drain completely, then season with salt.

FOR SERVING

1 Meyer lemon

1 red finger chile, finely chopped (no seeds)

2 tablespoons chopped parsley

2 tablespoons chopped mint

Parmesan-Crusted Butternut Squash

Extra-virgin olive oil

Fried Pumpkin Seeds

Coarsely ground black pepper

Flaky sea salt

FINELY GRATE the zest from the lemon into a bowl. Using a sharp knife, cut the peel and pith off the lemon. Working over the same bowl, cut the lemon between the membranes to release the segments. Dice the segments, then return them to the bowl. Add the chile, parsley, and mint and toss the gremolata well.

ARRANGE THE squash on a serving plate or in a shallow bowl. Drizzle with olive oil and spoon some of the gremolata over. Sprinkle with pumpkin seeds, season with black pepper and flaky salt, and serve.

167

Crispy Potatoes and Sunchokes
WITH CARROT-HAZELNUT ROMESCO

MAKES 4 SERVINGS

My favorite sauce—chunky carrot-hazelnut romesco—makes another appearance here, complementing a duo of root vegetables. You only need to add a piece of protein to turn this side into a meal; the romesco tastes great with pretty much anything.

--- **THE TAKEAWAY** ---

Air circulation is the key to both evenly browning and crisping vegetables, so I almost always use a wire rack when roasting vegetables. When you roast vegetables directly on the pan, you end up roasting the top half of the vegetable and steaming the bottom half (and you risk burning the bottom of the vegetable before it's finished cooking as well). Yes, you can always stir ingredients to help them brown more evenly, but a rack will save you from going through the trouble.

— CRISPY POTATOES AND SUNCHOKES —

8 ounces Butterball or baby potatoes

Kosher salt

8 ounces sunchokes, scrubbed and cut into 1-inch obliques

2 tablespoons extra-virgin olive oil

¼ teaspoon freshly ground black pepper

Vegetable oil

PREHEAT THE oven to 450°F and place a wire rack inside a rimmed baking sheet. In a medium saucepan, cover the potatoes with 1 inch of water and salt the water. Bring to a boil, then reduce the heat and simmer the potatoes until tender. Drain and let dry. When cool enough to handle, break the potatoes apart with your hands into 1-inch chunks.

MEANWHILE, IN a medium bowl, toss the sunchokes with the olive oil, 1¼ teaspoons salt, and the pepper. Spread on the rack and roast until just tender and lightly browned, 20 to 25 minutes.

IN A medium saucepan, heat 2 inches of vegetable oil to 360°F. Add the potatoes and fry until golden brown and crispy, 4 to 5 minutes. Transfer to paper towels to drain. Return the oil to 360°F and fry the sunchokes until golden brown and crispy, 1 to 2 minutes.

—————— FOR SERVING ——————

⅓ cup Carrot-Hazelnut Romesco (page 54)

Crispy Potatoes and Sunchokes

4 teaspoons chopped Pickled Red Onions (page 55)

Extra-virgin olive oil

Lemon wedge

1 tablespoon thinly sliced scallion greens

1 tablespoon chopped mint

1 tablespoon chopped parsley

Flaky sea salt

SPREAD THE romesco on the bottom of a serving plate or shallow bowl. Top with the potatoes, sunchokes, and pickled onion. Drizzle with olive oil and squeeze a lemon wedge over the top. Sprinkle with the scallions, mint, parsley, and flaky salt and serve.

168

Grilled Chard Stems
WITH LEMON-BALSAMIC VINAIGRETTE

MAKES 4 SERVINGS

We use a lot of Swiss chard greens at the restaurant, so we always have a mess of leftover stems. To be honest, chard stems are not the most exciting ingredient, but a quick turn on the grill and a chunky, powerfully flavored vinaigrette turns them into an intriguing side dish that you can serve with grilled lamb, roast chicken, steak, fish, and anything that would taste great with a lemony sauce.

LEMON-BALSAMIC VINAIGRETTE

MAKES ½ CUP

1 medium lemon

2 tablespoons fresh lemon juice

2 tablespoons balsamic vinegar

1½ teaspoons finely chopped peel from Quick Preserved Lemons (page 249)

2 teaspoons finely chopped serrano chile, seeds removed

½ teaspoon red pepper flakes

½ teaspoon kosher salt

2 tablespoons extra-virgin olive oil

1 tablespoon coarsely chopped parsley

USING A sharp knife, cut the peel and pith off the lemon. Working over a bowl, cut the lemon between the membranes to release the segments. Dice the segments, then return them to the bowl.

IN ANOTHER bowl, whisk the lemon juice with the vinegar, preserved lemon peel, serrano chile, red pepper flakes, and salt. Slowly whisk in the olive oil until emulsified, then stir in the lemon segments and parsley.

FOR SERVING

8 cups water

½ cup kosher salt, plus more for seasoning

½ teaspoon baking soda

Stems from 2 bunches Swiss chard

Extra-virgin olive oil

Lemon-Balsamic Vinaigrette

Flaky salt

Coarsely ground black pepper

IN A medium saucepan, bring the water, kosher salt, and baking soda to a boil. Add the chard stems and cook until crisp-tender, 1 to 2 minutes. Transfer to a paper towel–lined baking sheet and pat dry. Let cool for a few minutes.

PREPARE A medium-hot grill or preheat a grill pan over medium-high heat. Brush the chard stems with olive oil and season with kosher salt. Grill the stems, turning once or twice, until lightly charred, 2 to 4 minutes. Transfer to a serving platter and drizzle with some of the vinaigrette. Sprinkle with flaky salt, season with black pepper, and serve.

THE TAKEAWAY

Sometimes a dressing is the most interesting thing about a dish. When I want a vinaigrette to add more than just flavor, I'll add diced citrus segments, which gives you pops of bright acidity. You'll find this approach in several dressings throughout this cookbook, but you can use it anytime you want to add some texture to a dressing—just hold back on the acid a little bit.

Broccoli Rabe
WITH TOMATO COMPOTE AND CRISPY ONIONS

MAKES 4 SERVINGS

This is a great side dish for lamb or other roasted meats. When I was cooking Indian-influenced food at Tabla, I fell in love with pairing spicy condiments with yogurt, which both cools down the heat and adds an acidic tang to the dish. If you swap out the broccoli rabe, the combination of a sweet and smoky tomato compote and creamy yogurt could bookend all sorts of other vegetables—pretty much anything would work here.

THE TAKEAWAY

This sweet and spicy tomato compote is a versatile pantry staple that will keep for several days in the refrigerator, and it also freezes well. In addition to vegetable dishes, it can be a chunky companion to lamb and beef, a bold condiment for burgers and sandwiches, or a slightly smoky pasta sauce.

TOMATO COMPOTE

MAKES ABOUT 2 CUPS

Two 14.5-ounce cans diced tomatoes (I prefer Muir Glen brand)

¼ cup extra-virgin olive oil

4 large garlic cloves, thinly sliced

1 tablespoon plus ½ teaspoon kosher salt, plus more for seasoning

1 cup sugar

¾ cup plus 2 tablespoons white wine vinegar

¾ teaspoon chipotle powder

¼ teaspoon red pepper flakes

8 scallions, thinly sliced

DRAIN THE tomatoes in a fine-mesh strainer and reserve the liquid. In a medium saucepan, combine the olive oil, garlic, and salt and cook over medium-low heat, stirring, until the garlic is softened, about 3 minutes. Add the juice from the tomatoes, the sugar, and vinegar, bring the liquid to a simmer, and cook until syrupy. Add the tomatoes, chipotle powder, red pepper flakes, and scallions, bring to a simmer, and cook until the tomatoes begin to break down, 5 to 7 minutes. Season to taste with salt and keep warm until ready to serve. The compote can be made several days ahead and refrigerated until ready to use.

CRISPY ONIONS

1 medium white onion, thinly sliced (use a mandoline if you have one)

Vegetable or sunflower oil

Kosher salt

PLACE THE onions in a medium saucepan and add enough oil to cover. Place over medium-high heat and cook, stirring every couple of minutes, until light golden brown (they will continue to cook and crisp up as they cool). Pour the onion and oil through a fine-mesh strainer and gently press with a spoon or ladle to squeeze out all of the oil (you can save the onion-infused oil for another use, if you like). Spread out on paper towels and season with salt. You can make the onions a day or two ahead of time and re-crisp them in a 200°F oven.

─────────── FOR SERVING ───────────

1 pound broccoli rabe, trimmed

1 cup Tomato Compote

1 teaspoon chopped thyme

2 tablespoons Greek yogurt

Crispy Onions

Flaky salt

BRING A large saucepan of salted water to a boil and prepare an ice bath. Trim the bottom inch or so off the end of the broccoli rabe stems. Working in batches, blanch the broccoli rabe until bright green and crisp-tender, 2 to 3 minutes. Transfer to the ice bath to cool, then drain and lightly squeeze dry.

IN A saucepan, heat the tomato compote until simmering. Add the broccoli rabe and cook until warmed through. Transfer the broccoli rabe to a serving plate and spoon the tomato compote over. Sprinkle with the thyme and dollop the yogurt on top. Sprinkle with the crispy onions and flaky salt and serve.

Roasted Broccolini
WITH GINGER-SCALLION TOPPING

MAKES 4 SERVINGS

One of my favorite late-night, post-work dinners is at the Great N.Y. Noodletown in Manhattan's Chinatown. There, they serve a poached chicken with a ginger-scallion sauce that I love. I played with this idea and made it my own, and it's become a versatile condiment in my repertoire. Here it dresses a simple side dish of roasted broccolini, but it works very well with chicken, fish, steak, and other green things, especially spinach.

— THE TAKEAWAY —

To make the topping, I pour hot oil over raw chopped ginger, scallions, and jalapeño. This is a common technique in Asian cooking, and works well whenever you want to lightly cook a dressing but retain some texture. The result is similar to the Broken Chile Sauce on page 145, where you have both a chunky component and a deeply flavored oil.

— GINGER-SCALLION TOPPING —

MAKES ABOUT 1 CUP

1 bunch scallions, white and green parts, thinly sliced (about 1 cup)

¼ cup finely chopped ginger

1 tablespoon finely diced jalapeño chile (with seeds)

2 tablespoons yellow miso

1 teaspoon kosher salt

½ cup extra-virgin olive oil

IN A heatproof bowl, combine the scallions, ginger, jalapeño, miso, and salt. In a small saucepan, heat the oil to 370°F. Pour the oil into the bowl with the scallion mixture and let sit until cool. It's best to make the topping at least a couple of hours in advance so the flavors can meld. Once cool, refrigerate until ready to use, up to 1 week.

— FOR SERVING —

1½ pounds (3 bunches) broccolini

¼ cup extra-virgin olive oil

Kosher salt and freshly ground black pepper

Ginger-Scallion Topping

2 tablespoons roughly chopped cilantro

2 lemon wedges

PREHEAT THE oven to 425°F. Scatter the broccolini on a rimmed baking sheet and drizzle with the olive oil. Toss well to coat with the oil, then season with salt and pepper. Roast the broccolini until just tender, about 15 minutes.

TRANSFER THE broccolini to a serving bowl. Spoon some of the ginger-scallion topping over and sprinkle the cilantro on top. Serve with lemon wedges.

Roasted Brussels Sprouts
WITH AVOCADO AND APPLE

MAKES 4 SERVINGS

This a healthier (and vegan) take on the typical roasted Brussels sprout side dish, which often involves cured pork and/or cheese. I dress it with a quick honey-mustard vinaigrette, which should also become part of your regular salad-dressing rotation.

THE TAKEAWAY

We talk a lot about balancing flavor and texture when creating new dishes, but I also like to consider temperature, specifically contrasting temperatures. There's something exciting about pairing hot and cold in a dish, like a drizzle of cool yogurt on a hot soup. Here, I pair roasted sprouts with cool, crisp apple and creamy avocado.

HONEY-MUSTARD VINAIGRETTE

MAKES ABOUT ¾ CUP

2 tablespoons fresh lime juice

2 tablespoons fresh lemon juice

2 tablespoons champagne vinegar

1 teaspoon honey

1½ teaspoons Dijon mustard

½ teaspoon whole-grain mustard, store-bought or homemade (page 62)

¾ teaspoon Tabasco hot sauce (or Red Hot Sauce, page 130)

1 teaspoon kosher salt

2 tablespoons extra-virgin olive oil

IN A mixing bowl, combine all the ingredients except the olive oil and whisk to combine. Slowly whisk in the olive oil until emulsified.

ROASTED BRUSSELS SPROUTS
---

1 pound Brussels sprouts, trimmed

¼ cup extra-virgin olive oil

1 tablespoon kosher salt

Freshly ground black pepper

PREHEAT THE oven to 400°F. Bring a large saucepan of salted water to a boil and prepare an ice bath. Working in batches, blanch the Brussels sprouts until almost tender, about 2 minutes. Transfer to the ice bath to cool, then transfer to paper towels and pat dry. Cut the Brussels sprouts in half.

IN A large ovenproof skillet, heat the oil over high heat until it shimmers. Add the Brussels sprouts, salt, and pepper and stir. Transfer to the oven and roast, stirring a few times, until the sprouts are well browned, 15 to 20 minutes.

FOR SERVING

Roasted Brussels Sprouts

2 tablespoons toasted sunflower seeds

½ red finger chile, thinly sliced (with seeds)

½ large avocado, cut into ½-inch cubes

½ Mutsu (aka Crispin) or Golden Delicious apple (with skin), cored and cut into ½-inch cubes

¼ cup Honey-Mustard Vinaigrette

½ cup roughly chopped basil

¼ cup roughly chopped mint

1 lime, for zesting

Flaky salt

Freshly ground black pepper

AS SOON as the Brussels sprouts come out of the oven, add the sunflower seeds and chile slices to the skillet and stir for a minute or so. Transfer to a serving platter or bowl. Top with the avocado and apple. Drizzle with the vinaigrette and top with the basil, mint, and some freshly grated lime zest. Season with flaky salt and pepper and serve.

Roasted Cauliflower
WITH PEACH-APRICOT PUREE AND NUT VINAIGRETTE

MAKES 4 TO 6 SERVINGS

This recipe started in a roundabout way as a dish I cooked for a friend's Passover Seder. I wanted to incorporate some of the traditional Seder ingredients, so I made a puree with dates, walnuts, and spices, and served it with thick slices of roasted cauliflower. I've since adapted this recipe for other seasons, even as cauliflower "steaks" have become trendy. This recipe is the summertime version, with a sweet and sour peach-based puree that accentuates the sweetness of the deeply caramelized cauliflower, and a nut-laden dressing to give the dish some crunchy texture. To get as much color on the cauliflower as possible, I treat it like a pan-roasted steak, first searing it in a hot skillet until it's deeply browned, then transferring it to the oven to finish cooking.

THE TAKEAWAY

Both the peach-apricot puree and nut vinaigrette can live beyond this recipe: The puree is great with roast pork (like the Raisin-Stuffed Pork Loin on page 285), as well as chicken, duck, and root vegetables. And the nut vinaigrette is excellent with chicories and other hearty greens, as well as fish.

PEACH-APRICOT PUREE

MAKES 1 CUP

4 teaspoons sunflower or vegetable oil

¾ teaspoon yellow mustard seeds

One 1-inch piece ginger, peeled and thinly sliced

½ Thai chile (with seeds)

1 large peach, peeled and diced

7 dried apricots, chopped

3 tablespoons fresh grapefruit juice

4 teaspoons white wine vinegar

1¼ teaspoons kosher salt

2 tablespoons plus 2 teaspoons fresh lime juice

1½ teaspoons elderflower syrup or ¾ teaspoon light honey

IN A small saucepan, heat the sunflower oil over medium-low heat. Add the mustard seeds and cook, stirring, for 2 minutes. Add the ginger, chile, peaches, apricots, grapefruit juice, vinegar, and salt. Bring to a simmer over low heat, cover, and cook until the peaches are tender, 10 to 12 minutes. Transfer to a blender or mini food processor and add the lime juice and elderflower syrup. Puree until smooth. The puree can be made up to 1 day ahead and refrigerated until ready to use.

NUT VINAIGRETTE

MAKES 1 CUP

½ cup extra-virgin olive oil

1½ teaspoons coriander seeds, crushed

¼ cup pistachios, roughly chopped

3 tablespoons sunflower seeds

½ teaspoon kosher salt

4 dried apricots, cut into ⅛-inch dice

2 tablespoons fresh orange juice

1 tablespoon fresh lemon juice

IN A medium skillet, heat the oil over medium-high heat. Add the coriander and toast until fragrant, about 2 minutes. Add the pistachios, sunflower seeds, and salt and cook, stirring, until

CONTINUES ➡

golden brown, about 2 minutes. Transfer the contents of the skillet to a food processor and pulse a few times, until the nuts are roughly chopped. Transfer to a bowl and stir in the apricots, orange juice, and lemon juice. The nut vinaigrette can be made up to 1 day ahead and refrigerated until ready to use.

—————— FOR SERVING ——————

1 medium head cauliflower	2 tablespoons finely chopped tarragon
¼ cup extra-virgin olive oil, plus more for drizzling	2 tablespoons thinly sliced mint
Kosher salt and freshly ground black pepper	½ red finger chile, thinly sliced into half moons
½ cup Peach-Apricot Puree	1 orange, for zesting
Nut Vinaigrette	Flaky sea salt

PREHEAT THE oven to 400°F. Remove the outer leaves from the cauliflower and set the head, stem side down, on a cutting board. Cut the cauliflower from top to bottom into ¾-inch-thick slices. You should be able to get a couple of large steaks out of the middle of the cauliflower and some smaller pieces from the outsides.

HEAT THE olive oil in a large skillet over medium-high heat. Working in batches if necessary, season the cauliflower with salt and pepper and add to the skillet. Sear on one side until deeply golden brown, about 5 minutes, then flip and continue cooking until the other side is well browned, about 5 minutes longer. Transfer to a rimmed baking sheet. Roast until the cauliflower is tender, 15 to 20 minutes.

SPREAD THE peach-apricot puree on the bottom of a serving platter. Arrange the cauliflower pieces over, and drizzle with the nut vinaigrette. Sprinkle with the tarragon, mint, and chile, drizzle with olive oil, and grate some orange zest over the top. Season with flaky salt and serve.

Roasted Sweet Potatoes
WITH CHARRED SHALLOTS AND CASHEWS

MAKES 4 SERVINGS

As with many vegetable-forward recipes, you can take this easy fall side dish in either of two directions. The ingredients are all easy to find at any supermarket, or you could take a trip to the farmers market to buy a colorful mix of local sweet potatoes, as well as various alliums to combine with the charred shallots (I especially like cipollini onions). Both the shallots and potatoes get covered in a maple-vinegar glaze, which makes the whole thing taste like fall.

— THE TAKEAWAY —

Here's a great trick for getting ahead on dinner party or holiday feast prep: Roast a bunch of vegetables ahead of time, then pan-glaze them just before serving to bring them back to life. Here, the glaze is a simple mixture of maple syrup and vinegar, but you can play around with other sweeteners and acids. You'll see this technique applied to roasted and braised meat later in the book as well.

PREHEAT THE oven to 500°F. In a large bowl, toss the potatoes with olive oil and season with salt and pepper. Scatter the potatoes on a rimmed baking sheet and roast until tender and caramelized in spots, 15 to 20 minutes. The potatoes can be roasted a few hours ahead of time and rewarmed in a skillet before adding the glaze.

— CHARRED SHALLOTS —

2 medium shallots, cut lengthwise into ¼-inch slices (about ½ cup)

1 tablespoon extra-virgin olive oil

½ teaspoon kosher salt

¼ teaspoon freshly ground black pepper

IN A bowl, toss the shallots with the olive oil and season with salt and pepper. Heat a skillet over high heat until very hot, then add the shallots and cook, stirring frequently, until deeply browned and slightly softened (they should still have some crunch), 2 to 4 minutes.

— FOR SERVING —

2 tablespoons maple syrup

¼ cup champagne vinegar

2 tablespoons extra-virgin olive oil

Roasted Sweet Potatoes

Charred Shallots

½ cup toasted cashews, roughly chopped

¼ cup chopped parsley

¼ cup chopped chives

Pinch of red pepper flakes

Freshly ground black pepper

Flaky sea salt

IN A bowl, whisk together the maple syrup and vinegar until combined. In a large skillet, heat the olive oil over high heat. Add the sweet potatoes and cook until warmed through. Add the maple-vinegar mixture and cook, stirring frequently, until most of the liquid has evaporated and the potatoes are glazed. Add the shallots and cashews and toss. Transfer to a platter and sprinkle with the parsley and chives. Season with red pepper flakes, black pepper, and flaky salt. Serve.

— ROASTED SWEET POTATOES —

1½ pounds sweet potatoes (2 to 3 medium), peeled and cut into irregular 1½-inch pieces (about 4 cups)

2 tablespoons extra-virgin olive oil

2 teaspoons kosher salt

½ teaspoon freshly ground black pepper

THE TAKEAWAY

The technique I use to quickly cook spring onions in the Asparagus with Spring Onions (page 150) can be applied to thicker slices of onions as well, as it is here. These jammy, spicy onions that smother the roasted squash are a recipe in their own right and great with burgers, steaks, and grilled chicken. Make sure you get the pan nice and hot before you add them, and stop cooking before they get soft—these aren't caramelized onions, and you want a bit of crunch to them.

Roasted Delicata Squash
WITH HAZELNUTS, SPICY ONIONS, AND GOAT CHEESE

MAKES 4 SERVINGS

Delicata is a great in-a-hurry squash because it's small, cooks quickly, and has tasty edible skin—and you can even roast the squash with the seeds intact, and they'll be crispy by the time the squash is finished cooking. It's a versatile side dish that can round out roast chicken or grilled steaks, or add a simple arugula salad to turn it into a vegetarian main course.

--------------- SPICY ONIONS ---------------

MAKES ABOUT 2 CUPS

1 large red onion, halved and cut into ⅛-inch rings	1½ teaspoons red pepper flakes
2 tablespoons extra-virgin olive oil	1 tablespoon honey
1 teaspoon kosher salt	2 tablespoons fresh lime juice
¼ teaspoon freshly ground black pepper	1 teaspoon finely grated lime zest

IN A medium bowl, toss the onions with the olive oil, salt, and pepper. Heat a large skillet over high heat. When the pan is hot, add the onions and cook, stirring occasionally, until they're lightly charred and starting to soften, about 5 minutes. Stir in the pepper flakes, then add the honey and lime juice and stir until well combined. Transfer to a bowl and let cool, then stir in the lime zest. The onions can be made up to 1 day ahead of time; refrigerate until ready to use.

--------------- FOR SERVING ---------------

2 delicata squash	1 tablespoon thinly sliced mint
¼ cup extra-virgin olive oil, plus more for drizzling	1 tablespoon chopped marjoram
1 teaspoon kosher salt	1 tablespoon chopped parsley
¼ teaspoon freshly ground black pepper, plus more for serving	½ cup crumbled goat cheese
½ cup Spicy Onions	Flaky salt
½ cup roughly chopped toasted hazelnuts	

PREHEAT THE oven to 425°F and place a wire rack inside a rimmed baking sheet. Cut the squash in half lengthwise and scoop out the seeds, then cut the squash crosswise into ¼-inch half-moons. In a large bowl, toss the squash with the olive oil and season with the salt and pepper. Arrange the squash in a single layer on the rack, then roast until browned and tender, 20 to 25 minutes.

TRANSFER THE squash to a bowl and gently toss with the onions and hazelnuts. Add the mint, marjoram, and parsley and toss again. Transfer to a serving bowl or platter and sprinkle the cheese on top. Drizzle with olive oil, season with flaky salt and pepper, and serve.

Brussels Sprouts

WITH MUSTARD VINAIGRETTE

MAKES 4 SERVINGS

As simple as it seems today, this is the kind of dish that put my cooking on the map at ABC Kitchen: a single vegetable in the spotlight. Thanks to the tangy vinaigrette that dresses these sprouts (I swear it makes this dish taste like a burger with pickles and mustard), this might become your favorite Brussels sprout dish—and one you'll want to remember come Thanksgiving time. The mustard vinaigrette is also amazing with roasted pork.

——— THE TAKEAWAY ———

When I cook Brussels sprouts (and I cook a lot of sprouts), I want them to be juicy and tender on the inside and crispy on the outside—it's those contrasting textures that make them so fun to eat. But so many roasted sprouts recipes have you do all of the cooking in the oven, which will give you plenty of caramelization, but usually dries up the inside of the sprouts as well. The best way to get the right texture on your sprouts is to first blanch them until they're not quite tender, then cut them in half and finish them in a skillet, which gives you more control over the browning process.

——— MUSTARD VINAIGRETTE ———

MAKES 1 CUP

2 tablespoons honey

2¼ teaspoons Colman's mustard powder

3 tablespoons fresh lemon juice

1 tablespoon whole-grain mustard, store-bought or homemade (page 62)

1½ teaspoons Dijon mustard

1 tablespoon kosher salt

¼ cup extra-virgin olive oil

IN A medium bowl, combine the honey and mustard powder. Blend with a fork until well mixed, then let stand for 10 minutes to bloom the mustard. Whisk in the lemon juice, whole-grain mustard, Dijon mustard, and salt. Slowly whisk in the olive oil until emulsified. The dressing can be made up to 2 days ahead and refrigerated until ready to use.

——— PICKLED RED FINGER CHILES ———

MAKES ABOUT ½ CUP

4 red finger chiles

Red wine vinegar

THINLY SLICE the chiles crosswise and discard the stems. Place in a small sterilized jar or storage container and cover with red wine vinegar. Cover and refrigerate for at least 12 hours before using. The pickled chiles will keep for about 2 weeks.

——— FOR SERVING ———

1 pound Brussels sprouts

¼ cup extra-virgin olive oil

2 tablespoons unsalted butter

1 teaspoon finely chopped rosemary

Mustard Vinaigrette

2 tablespoons finely chopped Pickled Red Onions (page 55)

1 tablespoon finely chopped Pickled Red Finger Chiles

Flaky salt

BRING A large saucepan of salted water to a boil and prepare an ice bath. Working in batches, add the Brussels sprouts and blanch until slightly tender, 2 to 3 minutes. Transfer to the ice bath to cool, then transfer to paper towels to drain. Once all of the sprouts have been blanched, cut them in half lengthwise and pat dry with paper towels.

IN A large skillet, heat the oil over medium-high heat. Working in batches if necessary (don't crowd the pan), add the sprouts, cut side down, and cook until well browned on the bottom, 5 to 7 minutes. Stir and continue cooking until tender and caramelized all over, about 5 minutes longer. Return all of the sprouts to the pan and add the butter and rosemary, tossing until the butter has melted and coated the sprouts.

ADD ENOUGH mustard vinaigrette to cover the bottom of a serving bowl (about ⅓ cup). Top with the sprouts and sprinkle with the pickled onions and chiles. Season with flaky salt and serve.

Glazed Sweet Potatoes
WITH YOGURT AND DILL

MAKES 4 SERVINGS

Here's another side dish that looks way more complicated than it actually is. I usually cook with orange sweet potatoes, which have a big flavor and caramelize easily, but this is one recipe where I prefer white- or yellow-fleshed Japanese sweet potatoes, which have a lovely chestnut flavor and a more crumbly texture when cooked. Roughly breaking the potatoes apart makes all sorts of craters and crevices that caramelize under the broiler and catch the sweet-sour glaze.

THE TAKEAWAY

I love the flavor of charred potatoes, but they're harder to deeply caramelize than other vegetables. That's when the broiler can be your friend. It doesn't matter if you're first boiling or roasting sweet potatoes; a couple of minutes under the broiler before serving will add an exciting new flavor. Take a cue from this recipe and try to give the potatoes as much texture as possible before broiling them: You can break them up into rough chunks, scratch their surface with a fork, or, in the case of mashed potatoes, shape the top into peaks and valleys with a spatula.

MAPLE-LIME GLAZE

Finely grated zest of 1 medium orange
½ cup fresh orange juice
¼ cup fresh lime juice
¼ cup champagne vinegar
¼ cup maple syrup
1 teaspoon kosher salt

BRING ALL of the ingredients to a simmer in a small saucepan and reduce until thick enough to coat the back of a spoon. The glaze can be made a day or so ahead of time and refrigerated until ready to use.

FOR SERVING

1 pound sweet potatoes (preferably Japanese), 1 to 1½ inches thick
⅓ cup Greek yogurt
Maple-Lime Glaze
Extra-virgin olive oil
2 tablespoons chopped dill fronds
2 tablespoons thinly sliced mint
1 tablespoon finely chopped jalapeño chile (no seeds)
Flaky sea salt

PREHEAT THE oven to 500°F. Place the potatoes on a rimmed baking sheet and roast just until tender, 30 to 40 minutes. When cool enough to handle, break the potatoes into large pieces. Preheat the broiler. Return the potatoes to the baking sheet and broil until they start to caramelize and char in spots, 2 to 4 minutes.

SPREAD THE yogurt on a serving platter. Scatter the potatoes on top and drizzle with the maple-lime glaze and olive oil. Scatter the dill, mint, and jalapeño over the top, sprinkle with flaky salt, and serve.

Roasted Sunchokes

WITH PAPRIKA OIL AND LEMON-OREGANO VINAIGRETTE

MAKES 4 SERVINGS

I love the contrasting textures of roasted sunchokes: crunchy on the outside and soft on the inside, like creamy mashed potatoes. I've been making variations of this dish for several years, and in that time sunchokes (aka Jerusalem artichokes) have gone from obscure root vegetable to trendy darling. You can serve this dish as a starter or part of a tapas spread, and if you omit the cheese it makes a great side for fish.

PAPRIKA OIL

MAKES 1 CUP

1 teaspoon sweet smoked paprika	1 cup extra-virgin olive oil

IN A small saucepan, combine the paprika and olive oil. Bring the mixture to 180°F and turn off the heat. Let sit for 2 hours, then strain through a coffee strainer into a storage container. The oil can be refrigerated for up to 2 weeks.

LEMON-OREGANO VINAIGRETTE

MAKES ABOUT ¾ CUP

¼ cup fresh lemon juice	¼ teaspoon freshly ground black pepper
2 teaspoons Dijon mustard	½ cup plus 2 tablespoons extra-virgin olive oil
1½ teaspoons sugar	1 tablespoon chopped oregano
2 teaspoons kosher salt	

IN A small bowl, whisk the lemon juice with the mustard, sugar, salt, and pepper until the sugar is dissolved. Slowly whisk in the olive oil until emulsified. Stir in the oregano.

ROASTED SUNCHOKES

1 pound sunchokes, scrubbed well and cut crosswise into ¾-inch pieces	2 teaspoons finely chopped rosemary
	1 teaspoon kosher salt
3 tablespoons extra-virgin olive oil	¼ teaspoon freshly ground black pepper

PREHEAT THE oven to 400°F and place a wire rack inside a rimmed baking sheet. In a bowl, toss the sunchokes with the oil and season with the rosemary, salt, and pepper. Arrange the sunchokes in a single layer on the rack and roast until golden brown and just tender, 30 to 40 minutes.

FOR SERVING

Roasted Sunchokes	2 radishes, thinly sliced
2 tablespoons Lemon-Oregano Vinaigrette	¼ cup curly parsley leaves
2 tablespoons Paprika Oil	¼ cup crumbled goat cheese

PLACE THE warm sunchokes in a serving bowl. Drizzle the vinaigrette and paprika oil over. Scatter the radishes and parsley leaves over the salad and sprinkle the goat cheese over the top. Serve.

THE TAKEAWAY

The paprika oil that gets drizzled over the sunchokes is ever-present in my kitchen. It's vital to three of my most-used condiments: Fermented Chile Sauce (page 252), Sesame-Chile Condiment (page 52), and Broken Chile Sauce (page 145). I infuse the oil with sweet smoked paprika instead of hot so I can add heat with other ingredients, so its flavor is rather subtle. This means you can use it instead of olive oil in most applications, and it's a great finishing oil as well whenever you want to add some color—and a hint of smokiness—to the plate. Smoked paprika comes in a wide range of qualities, so get the best you can find or your oil won't taste like much. I like the La Chinata and Safinter brands, which are widely available.

Roasted Acorn Squash
WITH SPICY GRANOLA AND APPLE GASTRIQUE

MAKES 4 SERVINGS

Granola: It's not just for breakfast anymore! While you could spoon this spicy granola on top of yogurt, it makes a great topping for any dish, like the roasted squash here, that needs some crunch, including salads, vegetable sides (especially sweet potatoes and root vegetables), or roast pork loin. Add a schmear of yogurt or an arugula salad and this dish will make a satisfying vegetarian main course.

THE TAKEAWAY

Although a traditional gastrique starts by caramelizing sugar then adding vinegar, this simplified version achieves the same result. You can drizzle it over anything that needs some sweet-sour punch, from roasted vegetables to duck and pork, or turn it into a vinaigrette by whisking in more acid (vinegar or citrus) and olive oil.

SPICY GRANOLA

MAKES ABOUT 6 CUPS

1¼ cups old-fashioned rolled oats

½ cup raw pumpkin seeds

½ cup coarsely chopped cashews

¼ cup coconut oil, warmed until fluid

¼ cup packed light brown sugar

¼ cup sunflower seeds

3 tablespoons flaxseeds

2 tablespoons sesame seeds

2 tablespoons chia seeds

1 teaspoon kosher salt

1½ teaspoons red pepper flakes

¾ teaspoon ground cinnamon

½ teaspoon sweet smoked paprika

¼ cup maple syrup

¼ cup diced candied ginger

PREHEAT THE oven to 275°F and line a rimmed baking sheet with parchment or a silicone baking mat. In a large bowl, combine all of the ingredients except the maple syrup and ginger. Stir to combine, then stir in the maple syrup. Spread the granola on the baking sheet and bake, stirring every 10 minutes, until the oats, nuts, and seeds are golden brown, 25 to 35 minutes. Transfer to a bowl and stir in the ginger. The granola can be made several days ahead and stored in an airtight container at room temperature.

APPLE GASTRIQUE

MAKES ½ CUP

2 cups apple cider

1 cup apple cider vinegar

1 cup sugar

Pinch of kosher salt

IN A medium saucepan, bring all the ingredients to a boil. Cook until reduced and glazy, like maple syrup. The gastrique can be made a few days ahead and refrigerated until ready to use.

FOR SERVING

One acorn squash, seeded and cut into 1½-inch-thick wedges

¼ cup extra-virgin olive oil

Kosher salt

¼ cup Apple Gastrique

1 cup Spicy Granola

¼ cup chopped parsley

PREHEAT THE oven to 475°F and place a wire rack inside a rimmed baking sheet. In a bowl, toss the squash with the olive oil and season with salt. Arrange the squash, skin side down, on the rack and roast until tender and well browned in spots, about 30 minutes. Transfer the squash to a serving platter and drizzle with the gastrique. Sprinkle the granola and parsley over and serve.

Crispy Salt and Pepper Potatoes

MAKES 4 SERVINGS

These potatoes are like little starch balloons that pop when you bite into them. It's a quick side dish you can serve with any kind of protein, or add an aioli or creamy dressing and it becomes a snacky starter.

2 large egg whites

1 pound new potatoes (about 1 inch in diameter)

2 teaspoons kosher salt

¾ teaspoon finely ground black pepper

1 teaspoon finely chopped rosemary

1 teaspoon finely chopped thyme

1 teaspoon finely chopped parsley

THE TAKEAWAY

The trick for getting a crackling-crispy skin on the potatoes is egg whites, a technique I started using back at ABC Kitchen. You want to whip the whites until they're foamy and no liquid remains in the bowl, then add the potatoes, toss them until well coated, and strain away any excess before adding any seasoning. This technique works best with young "new" potatoes, which have a thin skin that crisps up easily. If you can't find new potatoes, grab the smallest fingerlings or baby russets you can find.

PREHEAT THE oven to 400°F and line a rimmed baking sheet with parchment. In a large bowl, whisk the egg whites until foamy (there shouldn't be any liquid whites in the bowl). Add the potatoes and toss until they're well coated with the egg whites, then transfer to a strainer or colander and let the excess whites drain. Season the potatoes with the salt, pepper, and herbs. Scatter the potatoes on the baking sheet (make sure they're not touching) and roast until the potatoes are very crispy and tender when poked with a knife, 15 to 20 minutes (depending on the size of the potatoes).

TRANSFER TO a bowl and serve.

Spiced Acorn Squash and Roasted Maitakes
WITH GOAT CHEESE DRESSING

MAKES 4 TO 6 SERVINGS

This extra-savory squash dish is substantial enough to serve as a vegetarian main course, or as a vegetable course alongside some roast pork or beef. I use a lot of spices and brown sugar to give the squash an intensely flavored, crunchy coating, which is balanced out by the richness of the goat cheese dressing. I also use two contrasting dressings: a bright lemon vinaigrette and a creamy, rich goat cheese dressing. Whenever I roast mushrooms, my intention is to use the oven's convective heat to crisp them up around the edges, which gives you a nice contrast in texture.

THE TAKEAWAY

Brown butter is a magical ingredient, adding both richness and a deep, roasted-nut flavor to vinaigrettes, sauces, and more. I especially love blending it with soft cheeses like goat cheese. It's good practice to make a large batch and keep it refrigerated for quick access. Just make sure you keep all of the browned milk solids that sink to the bottom of the butter as it cooks—those are where most of that great nutty flavor comes from.

LEMON VINAIGRETTE

MAKES ½ CUP

¼ cup fresh lemon juice
¾ teaspoon sugar
¾ teaspoon kosher salt
⅓ cup extra-virgin olive oil

IN A small bowl, whisk the lemon juice with the sugar and salt. Slowly whisk in the olive oil until emulsified. The vinaigrette can be made ahead and refrigerated for up to 2 days.

GOAT CHEESE DRESSING

MAKES ABOUT 1½ CUPS

4 tablespoons unsalted butter
8 ounces goat cheese
1 tablespoon finely grated lemon zest
¼ cup fresh lemon juice
3 tablespoons fresh orange juice
2 tablespoons maple syrup
1½ teaspoons kosher salt
2 tablespoons sunflower oil

IN A small skillet, cook the butter over medium heat until it turns brown and smells nutty (be careful not to let it burn), about 5 minutes. Transfer to a blender and add the goat cheese, lemon zest and juice, orange juice, maple syrup, and salt. Blend until smooth, then, with the machine running, slowly stream in the sunflower oil until emulsified. Refrigerate until ready to use. The dressing can be made a few hours ahead; stir well before using.

WINTER SPICE MIX

2½ teaspoons ground ginger
2½ teaspoons ground allspice
1 teaspoon ground star anise
1 teaspoon ground cinnamon
1 teaspoon light brown sugar
1 teaspoon red pepper flakes
¾ teaspoon kosher salt
1 teaspoon freshly ground black pepper

PLACE ALL of the ingredients in a small jar and shake until combined.

SPICED ACORN SQUASH AND ROASTED MAITAKES

1 medium acorn squash, halved, seeded, and cut into 1-inch wedges (with skin)

¼ cup extra-virgin olive oil

Winter Spice Mix

3 tablespoons oil from Garlic Confit (page 112) or extra-virgin olive oil

4 ounces maitake mushrooms, stems removed, cut into 1- to 1½-inch clusters

1 large shallot, finely chopped

PREHEAT THE oven to 425°F and line a large rimmed baking sheet with parchment paper. In a large bowl, toss the squash wedges with the olive oil. Add the spice mix, a pinch or two at a time, and toss well, making sure the squash is evenly coated. Arrange the squash on the prepared baking sheet. Roast, flipping halfway through, until tender and browned in spots, about 25 minutes.

MEANWHILE, HEAT the garlic oil in large skillet over high heat. Add the mushrooms in one layer and transfer to the oven. Roast for 10 minutes, then add the shallot and stir. Continue roasting until the mushrooms are golden brown and crispy around the edges, 5 to 10 minutes longer.

FOR SERVING

Goat Cheese Dressing

Spiced Acorn Squash and Roasted Maitakes

3 tablespoons Lemon Vinaigrette

3 tablespoons fines herbes (equal parts finely chopped chervil, chives, parsley, and tarragon)

Flaky sea salt

1 lemon, for zesting

SPREAD A thin layer of dressing (about ⅓ cup) over the bottom of a serving platter. In a large bowl, toss the squash and mushrooms with the lemon vinaigrette. Arrange the squash and mushrooms on the platter. Sprinkle with the herbs and season with flaky salt. Grate some lemon zest over and serve.

193

Citrus-Glazed Carrots
WITH PICKLED CHILES AND LIME

MAKES 4 TO 6 SERVINGS

Here's a great all-purpose side dish that works in every season and with every protein I can think of. The key to making the sweet-sour glaze extra tasty is to remove the carrots from the pot when they're tender, then reduce their braising liquid down until it's the thickness of maple syrup.

- 2 pounds medium or baby carrots, peeled and cut into ¾-inch obliques
- 2 cups water
- 3 tablespoons sugar
- 1 cup fresh orange juice, strained
- ¼ cup fresh lime juice, strained
- ¼ cup white wine vinegar
- ½ teaspoon kosher salt
- 2 tablespoons unsalted butter
- 2 tablespoons chopped chervil or tarragon
- 2 tablespoons Pickled Red Finger Chiles (page 182) cut into half-moons
- Flaky sea salt
- Lime wedges

IN A medium saucepan, combine the carrots, water, sugar, orange and lime juices, vinegar, and salt. Bring to a simmer and cook until the carrots are just tender, 15 to 20 minutes. Transfer the carrots to a parchment-lined baking sheet. Bring the cooking liquid to a boil and reduce until syrupy. Stir in the butter until it's melted into the glaze, then return the carrots to the pot and stir to coat in the glaze.

TRANSFER THE carrots to a serving bowl and sprinkle with the chervil and chiles. Sprinkle with flaky salt and serve with lime wedges.

—— THE TAKEAWAY ——

You'll notice that I call for some of the vegetables in my recipes (especially long, cylindrical veggies like carrots, cucumbers, parsnips, and squash) to be cut into "obliques." There are a couple of reasons why you should master this knife skill, which is called the "roll cut," or "faux tourné," in French. First, you're giving each piece of vegetable two angled sides, which means more surface area for caramelizing or glazing. I also like how rustic they look on the plate, and show attention to detail without being fussy. To do the roll cut, start by cutting one end of the vegetable at a 45-degree angle. Rotate the vegetable a quarter turn and cut again at a 45-degree angle, starting at the edge of your previous cut. Continue down the length of the vegetable. See pages 14 and 17 for a photo guide.

Pasta, Grains & Pizza

Delicata Squash Pizza

MAKES ONE 14-INCH PIZZA

While some vegetables (like the zucchini on the Zucchini Pizza on page 216) can be thinly sliced and cooked directly on top of the pizza, others need to be prebaked, like the sweet delicata squash here. Although I wouldn't tag it as health food, the combination of a whole-wheat crust, sweet squash, and crispy kale makes this about as wholesome as a pizza gets.

THE TAKEAWAY

This pizza also gifts you a great mini recipe for roasted squash. Coating squash with brown butter (instead of the usual olive oil) before roasting will intensify the nutty, caramelized flavor you get from a hot oven. This trick works with pretty much any kind of vegetable, so keep it in mind anytime you want your roasted vegetables to wow.

BROWN BUTTER–ROASTED DELICATA SQUASH

3 tablespoons unsalted butter

10 sage leaves

1 delicata squash

1 teaspoon kosher salt

1 teaspoon Aleppo pepper

IN A small saucepan, melt the butter over medium heat. Cook, stirring, until the butter turns dark amber and smells nutty, 5 to 6 minutes. Turn off the heat and add the sage leaves. Let sit for 30 minutes, then use tongs to remove and discard the sage.

PREHEAT THE oven to 475°F and place a wire rack inside a rimmed baking sheet. Cut the squash lengthwise into quarters and discard the seeds. Cut the squash pieces crosswise into ¼-inch pieces. In a large bowl, toss the squash with the brown butter, salt, and Aleppo pepper. Arrange the squash in a single layer on the rack and roast until just tender and browned in spots, 15 to 20 minutes.

FOR SERVING

One 250-gram portion Whole-Wheat Pizza Dough (page 200)

½ cup ricotta

4 ounces fresh mozzarella, torn or cut into 1-inch pieces

½ teaspoon dried oregano

1 cup Brown Butter–Roasted Delicata Squash

½ cup roughly chopped Tuscan kale

1 tablespoon oil from Garlic Confit (page 112) or extra-virgin olive oil

Kosher salt

Red pepper flakes

1 lemon wedge

1 lemon, for zesting

1 tablespoon honey

2 tablespoons freshly grated Parmesan cheese

¼ cup crumbled goat cheese

PREHEAT THE oven to 500°F. Place a pizza stone, pizza steel, or baking sheet in the oven to preheat. Stretch the dough into a 14-inch round and place on a floured pizza peel. Spread the ricotta evenly over the dough and top with the mozzarella. Sprinkle with the oregano. Arrange the roasted squash over the cheese and sprinkle the kale over. Drizzle with the garlic oil and season with salt. Bake on the preheated pizza stone, steel, or baking sheet until crispy on the bottom, 10 to 15 minutes. Remove from the oven, sprinkle a pinch of red pepper flakes over the pie, and squeeze a lemon wedge over. Grate some lemon zest over the pie, drizzle with the honey, and scatter the Parmesan and goat cheese over. Serve.

199

Bacon and Egg Pizza

MAKES ONE 14-INCH PIZZA

"Breakfast pizza" usually consists of reheated slices of whatever you ate the night before, but you can also make a start-your-day pie in the time it takes to make bacon and eggs. Cooking eggs on top of pizza is super easy and gives you a dramatic presentation, but you want to crack them into little wells of cheese and sauce, so they don't spread out too much as they bake.

—— THE TAKEAWAY ——

Most people put too much sauce on their pizza, which makes it nearly impossible to get a properly baked pie with a crispy crust. When I sauce a pie, I start with a small amount and add more as needed, just enough to cover the dough. And when I'm combining tomato sauce and a moist cheese like ricotta on the same pie, I'll put a layer of cheese down first, then top it with the sauce, as it protects the crust better from the juicy tomatoes and prevents the cheese from sliding around on top of the sauce.

—— WHOLE-WHEAT PIZZA DOUGH ——

MAKES ABOUT 3 POUNDS DOUGH (ENOUGH FOR 4 TO 5 PIZZAS, OR 7 CALZONES)

594 grams all-purpose flour

291 grams whole-wheat flour

3 grams active dry yeast

18 grams kosher salt

525 ml water, slightly cooler than room temperature

Extra-virgin olive oil

IN THE bowl of a stand mixer, combine the flours, yeast, and salt and whisk to combine. Place the bowl in the mixer and attached the bread hook. Turn the mixer to low speed, add the water, and mix until the flour is all moistened. Increase the speed to medium and mix until a dough forms and pulls away from the side of the bowl. Continue kneading the dough for 4 to 5 minutes. If your mixer isn't up to the task, transfer the dough to the counter and knead until it springs back quickly when you poke it with a finger.

PLACE THE dough in an oiled bowl and rub with oil. Cover the bowl with plastic and let sit in a cool spot (60°F to 70°F) for at least 12 hours.

IF YOU'RE not using the dough right away, divide it into four pieces (if making Grandma Pies, page 246), five pieces (if making this or other pizzas), or seven pieces (if making Calzones, page 235). Wrap each in plastic, and refrigerate for up to 24 hours, or freeze for up to 2 months. Thaw in the refrigerator.

—— QUICK TOMATO SAUCE ——

MAKES ABOUT 4 CUPS

One 28-ounce can whole tomatoes

2 tablespoons red wine vinegar

1 tablespoon extra-virgin olive oil

1 teaspoon kosher salt

POUR THE tomatoes into a large bowl and add the vinegar, oil, and salt. Crush the tomatoes with your hands until you've made a chunky sauce. Transfer to a storage container and refrigerate for up to 4 days.

—— FOR SERVING ——

3 strips thick-cut bacon, cut into ½-inch lardons

One 250-gram portion Whole-Wheat Pizza Dough

⅓ cup Quick Tomato Sauce

4 ounces fresh mozzarella cheese, torn or cut into 1-inch pieces

⅓ cup freshly grated Parmesan cheese

3 large eggs

1 cup baby arugula

2 teaspoons Pickled Jalapeño Peppers (page 227)

Lemon wedge

Freshly ground black pepper

Extra-virgin olive oil

PREHEAT THE oven to 500°F. Place a pizza stone, pizza steel, or baking sheet in the oven to preheat. In a skillet, cook the bacon over medium-low heat, occasionally pouring off (and reserving) the fat, until the bacon is browned but still has some chew to it, about 10 minutes. Transfer to paper towels to drain.

STRETCH THE dough into a 14-inch round and place on a floured pizza peel. Spread the sauce around the dough, leaving a ½-inch border around the edge. Scatter the mozzarella evenly over the pie and sprinkle with the Parmesan. Transfer to the preheated pizza stone, steel, or baking sheet and bake for 5 minutes. Remove the pie from the oven and use a spoon to make 3 small wells in the cheese, then crack the eggs into the wells. Sprinkle the reserved bacon over the pie. Continue baking the pizza until the egg whites are set but the yolks are still runny, about 10 minutes longer. Remove from the oven and top with the arugula and pickled jalapeños. Squeeze the lemon wedge over the pie, season with black pepper, and drizzle with olive oil. Serve.

Gnocchi
WITH ROASTED TOMATO SAUCE AND BOTTARGA

MAKES 4 SERVINGS

It took me a lot of practice to learn how to properly make gnocchi. My education started at Union Square Cafe, where I would overwork the gnocchi dough and end up with heavy, dense dumplings. Once I learned how to use a lighter hand when making and rolling the dough, I achieved the result I was searching for: soft, pillowy dumplings. Some tips I picked up along the way: Rice the potatoes when they're still warm, then let them cool down to room temperature. Once you've made the dough, let it rest for about 10 minutes, but then roll it out and cut your gnocchi right away—they'll get mushy if you let the dough sit around too long. Cooking the gnocchi is easy: Once they float to the surface of the simmering water, wait 1 minute, then pull them out. You can serve the cooked gnocchi right away, or toss them in olive oil and freeze them.

ROASTED TOMATOES

MAKES ABOUT 3 CUPS

3 tablespoons extra-virgin olive oil

3 garlic cloves, smashed

1 small bunch thyme (about 20 sprigs)

4 rosemary sprigs

1 teaspoon kosher salt

½ teaspoon freshly ground black pepper

4 medium beefsteak tomatoes, halved through the equator

PREHEAT THE oven to 325°F and line a rimmed baking sheet with parchment paper. Drizzle the olive oil on the baking sheet and scatter the garlic, thyme, rosemary, salt, and pepper over. Place the tomatoes, cut side down, on the baking sheet. Transfer to the oven and roast, pouring off (and saving) any accumulated juices and removing any loose tomato skins every 30 minutes or so, until the tomatoes have shrunken slightly but are still juicy, about 2 hours. Transfer the tomatoes and any accumulated juices to a storage container; discard the garlic and herbs. The roasted tomatoes can be covered and refrigerated for a few days.

CONTINUES ➡

THE TAKEAWAY

Bottarga is cured and dried fish roe, usually from the grey mullet or sometimes from bluefin or yellowfin tuna. This ancient preservation technique has been around for at least 2,000 years and has informed food cultures from the Mediterranean to the Middle East and Asia. I love using it as an alternative for grated cheese; it has the same umami-forward flavor of a well-aged Parmesan. A lobe of bottarga is a worthwhile investment; it'll keep forever, and you can grate or shave it over all sorts of dishes, from roasted vegetables and mashed potatoes to pizza and pasta. You can usually find bottarga at a good fish market, and it's widely available online.

--- GNOCCHI ---

4 medium russet
potatoes (about
2 pounds), scrubbed
and let dry

1 tablespoon kosher
salt

1 large egg yolk

1 cup all-purpose flour,
plus more as needed

Extra-virgin olive oil

PREHEAT THE oven to 450°F and set a wire rack inside a rimmed baking sheet. Wrap the potatoes individually in aluminum foil and place on the rack. Bake until tender when pierced with a knife, 1 hour to 1 hour 15 minutes. Unwrap the potatoes and, when cool enough to handle, peel. Pass the potatoes through a potato ricer into a bowl. (You can also use a food mill with the smallest holes, or a potato masher, to do this, but a ricer will give you best results.) Cover the potatoes with plastic wrap, pressing it onto the surface, and let cool to room temperature.

SPREAD THE potatoes out on a clean work surface and sprinkle with the salt. Beat the egg yolk, then spoon it over the potatoes. Use a bench scraper or metal spatula to "cut" the egg into the potatoes. Sprinkle the flour over the potatoes and use the scraper to blend the flour into the potatoes. Gently work the dough into a ball and knead a few times until it's smooth and slightly sticky (the trick is to not overwork it, which results in gummy gnocchi). The dough should spring back slightly when you poke it. Let the dough rest for 10 minutes.

LINE A baking sheet with parchment and dust with flour. Cut the dough into four pieces. Take one piece and roll it on a floured work surface to a ½-inch-thick rope. Use a bench scraper or knife to cut the rope into ¾-inch pieces, then transfer to the parchment. Repeat until all the dough is used up. Using a fingertip, gently press a small indentation in the center of each gnocchi.

BRING A large saucepan of salted water to a boil. Working in batches, poach the gnocchi in simmering water until 1 full minute after they begin to float. Drain, saving a cup of cooking water. If you're using the gnocchi right away, transfer to a baking sheet, drizzle with olive oil, and toss to coat. If you want to make the gnocchi ahead of time, first shock them in ice water until cool, then transfer to a baking sheet and coat with olive oil. Refrigerate the gnocchi for a few hours, or cover with plastic and freeze, then transfer to a large freezer bag and store in the freezer for up to 1 month. (Reheat in simmering water until warmed throughout.)

--- FOR SERVING ---

2 cups chopped
Roasted Tomatoes

2 tablespoons unsalted
butter

1 red finger chile, finely
chopped (with or
without seeds)

¼ cup thinly sliced
basil

Kosher salt

Cooked Gnocchi

1 lemon wedge

Bottarga or Parmesan
cheese, for grating

½ cup Spicy
Breadcrumbs
(page 224)

IN A large skillet, heat the tomatoes until the juices are simmering (add a splash of the gnocchi cooking water if your tomatoes aren't very juicy). Add the butter and stir until melted. Add the chiles and basil and turn off the heat. Season the sauce to taste with salt. Stir in the cooked gnocchi and squeeze some lemon juice over. Divide among serving bowls and grate some bottarga or Parmesan over each serving. Sprinkle with breadcrumbs and serve.

Cavatappi
WITH DUCK CONFIT, SPRING VEGETABLES, RICOTTA, AND MINT

MAKES 4 SERVINGS

When I make a pasta dish that contains lots of vegetables and other fresh produce, I usually don't want to weigh them down with a heavy sauce. Here, I toss pasta with cheese and plenty of pasta water to create a light, silky emulsification, then serve the noodles atop a spoonful of cool, creamy ricotta, which gives you a little surprise at the bottom of the bowl and makes each bite different as you eat your way through the dish.

—— THE TAKEAWAY ——

Homemade duck confit is one of those things that makes home cooks nervous, but it's really one of the most simple and foolproof things you can make. It's basically just duck that's been briefly cured, then cooked in its own fat until it starts to fall off the bone. You end up with both super-tender meat and loads of beautifully flavored duck fat that can be used for confit-ing or roasting vegetables. If you can't find duck fat, you can use canola or sunflower oil instead.

—— DUCK CONFIT ——

1 tablespoon plus 2 teaspoons fennel seeds	3 garlic cloves, coarsely chopped
2 tablespoons allspice berries	2¼ teaspoons ground cinnamon
5 cloves	2 tablespoons kosher salt
4 sage sprigs, finely chopped	¾ teaspoon sugar
Needles from 1 rosemary sprig	2 duck legs with thighs, about 1 pound total
	3 cups duck fat

USING A spice grinder or mortar and pestle, finely grind the fennel seeds, allspice, and cloves. Transfer to a bowl and stir in the sage, rosemary, garlic, cinnamon, salt, and sugar. Rub this mixture all over the duck legs and wrap tightly in plastic. Refrigerate overnight, or up to 24 hours.

PREHEAT THE oven to 200°F. Rinse the duck legs and pat dry. Place the duck in a small baking dish or saucepan (just large enough to hold them in one layer) and cover with duck fat until completely submerged. Bake until the duck is very tender and starting to fall off the bone, 3 to 4 hours. Let cool to room temperature. Cover the dish and refrigerate the duck in the fat until ready to use, up to 1 month. (If using the duck confit right away, drain off the fat and reserve for another use.)

—— MIXED SPRING VEGETABLES ——

6 asparagus spears	1 cup sugar snap peas
1 cup English peas (very fresh or frozen)	

BRING A large saucepan of salted water to a boil and prepare an ice bath. Blanch the vegetables separately until just tender, 3 to 4 minutes for

206

the asparagus, 1 to 2 minutes for the peas, and 1 to 2 minutes for the snap peas. Transfer to the ice bath to cool. Cut the asparagus into ½-inch pieces and the snap peas on the bias into ½-inch pieces. Combine the vegetables in a bowl and set aside.

--- FOR SERVING ---

8 ounces dried cavatappi pasta

1 tablespoon extra-virgin olive oil, plus more for drizzling

Duck Confit, removed from the fat, skin and bones discarded, and meat shredded

¼ cup thinly sliced ramp or scallion whites

Kosher salt

1 cup thinly sliced ramp or scallion greens

Mixed Spring Vegetables

¼ cup coarsely chopped Castelvetrano olives

1 red finger chile, thinly sliced (with seeds)

1 cup finely grated Parmesan cheese

1 lemon wedge

½ cup thinly sliced mint

½ cup ricotta

Flaky sea salt

Freshly ground black pepper

COOK THE pasta in salted boiling water until al dente. Drain, reserving 1 cup of pasta water.

MEANWHILE, IN a skillet, heat the oil over medium heat. Add the shredded duck confit and cook until it starts to crisp, about 2 minutes. Add the ramp whites, season with kosher salt to taste, and cook for a minute or two. Add the ramp greens and cook until wilted, about 1 minute. Add the spring vegetables.

WHEN THE pasta is ready, add the olives, chile, and about ½ cup of the pasta water to the duck mixture. Toss well, then add the pasta. Add the Parmesan and stir until you have an emulsified sauce, adding a little more pasta water if needed. Squeeze lemon over the pasta and add the mint.

DIVIDE THE ricotta among four serving bowls and top with the pasta. Drizzle each serving with olive oil, season with flaky salt and pepper, and serve.

Cavatelli
WITH SPRING VEGETABLES AND CHEESE SAUCE

MAKES 4 SERVINGS

Cavatelli is one of the easiest pastas to make at home—far less work than rolling out long sheets of dough and cutting them into noodles. You can shape the pasta either by hand or by feeding ropes of dough into an inexpensive cavatelli maker (instructions for both methods follow), which will turn out "little caves" of pasta that are perfectly shaped for catching pockets of the cheese sauce. I add some smoky flavor to the dish by revisiting the charred and blanched snap pea combo from the salad on page 85, but you can also adapt this dish throughout the year with other seasonal vegetables.

——— THE TAKEAWAY ———

When you melt cheese into a béchamel (milk thickened with roux), you get Mornay sauce. Classic Mornay is made with Gruyère and/or Emmentaler, and you'll find it on a croque monsieur and similar dishes. Americans are most familiar with cheddar-based Mornay and noodles, aka mac and cheese. My Italianate version is made with Parmesan cheese and scallions (or ramps, if they're in season), and I lighten the sauce with a little bit of water and brighten it with lemon juice, which makes it more vegetable-friendly. Don't be afraid to do the same when you're working with cheesy or other rich sauces, a splash of water and a bit of acid can help make them more versatile.

——— RICOTTA CAVATELLI ———

MAKES 2 POUNDS DOUGH

13 ounces (1½ cups) ricotta

2 large eggs

4⅓ cups all-purpose flour

2¼ teaspoons kosher salt

Semolina flour, for dusting

IN A stand mixer fitted with a dough hook, combine the ricotta, eggs, all-purpose flour, and salt. Mix at medium speed until a dough comes together, about 5 minutes. Transfer to a work surface, wrap in plastic, and let rest for 30 minutes.

DIVIDE THE dough into a few pieces and roll each piece into a ½-inch-thick rope. If you're using a cavatelli maker, feed a rope into the machine and repeat with the remaining dough.

IF YOU'RE making the cavatelli by hand, cut the rope into 1-inch pieces. Using the tips of your index and middle fingers, press down on each piece of dough and pull it towards you so it flattens and curls around your fingertips. See page 23 for a photographic guide.

TOSS THE cavatelli in semolina. At this point, you can spread the cavatelli on a baking sheet and freeze, then transfer to a container and freeze for up to 6 months.

——— CHEESE SAUCE ———

MAKES 1½ CUPS

2 tablespoons unsalted butter

2 tablespoons all-purpose flour

2 tablespoons extra-virgin olive oil

¼ cup thinly sliced ramp or scallion (white parts only)

3 tablespoons water

1⅓ cups milk

Kosher salt

½ teaspoon coarsely ground black pepper

1 cup finely grated Parmesan cheese

2 tablespoons fresh lemon juice

CONTINUES ➡

MAKE THE roux. In a small saucepan, melt the butter over medium-high heat. Add the flour and whisk to form a paste. Continue to cook, stirring, until the raw flour aroma is gone, about 1 minute. Turn off the heat and set the roux aside.

IN A large skillet, heat the olive oil over low heat. Add the ramps and cook until softened, 2 to 3 minutes. Add the water and increase the heat to bring to a simmer. Add the milk and bring to a simmer, then whisk in the roux. Continue cooking until the liquid is thick enough to coat the back of a spoon. Turn off the heat and stir in 2 teaspoons of salt, pepper, and Parmesan. Stir in the lemon juice and season to taste with salt.

SPRING VEGETABLES

8 ounces asparagus, cut on the bias into 1-inch pieces

2 cups sugar snap peas

1 tablespoon extra-virgin olive oil

Kosher salt

BRING A medium saucepan of salted water to a boil and prepare an ice bath. Blanch the asparagus until bright green and crisp-tender, 1 to 2 minutes. Transfer to the ice bath. When cool, transfer to paper towels to drain. Blanch the snap peas until bright green and crisp-tender, 30 to 45 seconds, then transfer to the ice bath. Cut the snap peas in half on the bias, then transfer to paper towels to drain.

HEAT A skillet (preferably cast-iron) over high heat. In a mixing bowl, toss half of the snap peas with the oil and salt. When the skillet is very hot, add the snap peas and let them char on one side without moving them around, 30 to 45 seconds. Turn the snap peas over and char the other side, then transfer to a plate. In a bowl, combine the asparagus, blanched snap peas, and charred snap peas.

FOR SERVING

Kosher salt

12 ounces Ricotta Cavatelli or dried cavatelli pasta

1 tablespoon extra-virgin olive oil

4 slices thick-cut bacon, cut into ¼-inch lardons

1 bunch ramps or scallions, white parts thinly sliced and green parts cut into 1-inch ribbons

Spring Vegetables

1 cup Cheese Sauce

1 jalapeño chile, finely chopped (no seeds)

¼ cup chopped oregano

⅓ cup chopped mint

½ cup finely grated Parmesan cheese

½ cup finely grated pecorino cheese

1 tablespoon fresh lemon juice

1 cup Spicy Breadcrumbs (page 224)

1 lemon, for zesting

Coarsely ground black pepper

COOK THE pasta in salted boiling water until al dente, then drain, reserving about 1 cup of the pasta water.

MEANWHILE, IN a large skillet, heat the olive oil over medium-low heat. Add the bacon and cook, until browned and crisp, about 10 minutes. Add the ramp whites and cook until tender, about 2 minutes. Add the ramp greens and cook until wilted, about 1 minute. Add the spring vegetables.

ADD THE drained pasta along with about ½ cup of the water, season with salt, and toss well. Add the cheese sauce and toss well to coat. Add the jalapeño, oregano, mint, Parmesan, and pecorino and stir well, adding more pasta water if needed. Turn off the heat and stir in the lemon juice. Divide the pasta among four serving bowls and top each with breadcrumbs, freshly grated lemon zest, and pepper to taste. Serve.

Ricotta Cavatelli
WITH TOMATOES, CHILES, AND HERBS

MAKES 4 SERVINGS

I love making this super-simple pasta at the beginning of every tomato season. It uses only a few simple ingredients, but lets the flavor of each shine through. And it's incredibly versatile: Pretty much any shape of pasta can be swapped in for the cavatelli.

THE TAKEAWAY

I don't make many *cooked* tomato sauces for pizza or a bowl of pasta—I like retaining as much of the fresh tomato flavor as possible. My crushed tomato sauce does involve some cooking, but the tomatoes are quickly roasted to loosen their skins and intensify their fresh flavor. Grating the roasted tomatoes on a box grater lets the sauce stay chunky, and a splash of vinegar gives it a sweet and sour flavor profile. You can use the tomatoes anywhere you'd use a cooked tomato sauce, from pizza and pasta to vegetables and fish.

CRUSHED TOMATO SAUCE

MAKES ABOUT 1 CUP

2 large beefsteak tomatoes (about 2½ pounds)

1 tablespoon extra-virgin olive oil

1 teaspoon red wine vinegar

1 teaspoon kosher salt

PREHEAT THE oven to 450°F and line a rimmed baking sheet with parchment. Core the tomatoes and cut an X through the skin on the bottom. Place the tomatoes, cored side down, on the baking sheet and roast for 15 minutes. Let cool, then peel the tomatoes and coarsely grate them into a bowl, using the large holes of a box grater. Stir in the olive oil, vinegar, and salt. Transfer to a storage container and refrigerate for up to 4 days.

FOR SERVING

12 ounces Ricotta Cavatelli (page 208) or dried cavatelli pasta

½ cup oil from Garlic Confit (page 112) or extra-virgin olive oil

1 pint cherry tomatoes, halved

Kosher salt

Red pepper flakes

1 cup finely grated Parmesan cheese

Crushed Tomato Sauce

½ cup chopped mint

½ cup chopped basil

COOK THE pasta in a pot of salted boiling water until al dente. Drain, reserving some of the pasta water.

MEANWHILE, HEAT the oil in a large skillet over medium heat. Add the cherry tomatoes, season with salt, and cook until they start to break down, 3 to 4 minutes. Add the pasta and a pinch of red pepper flakes and toss to combine. Add half of the Parmesan and a splash of pasta water and stir until the pasta is coated in a silky sauce, adding more water as needed.

DIVIDE THE tomato sauce among four serving bowls (about ¼ cup per bowl), spreading the sauce to cover the bottom of the bowl. Spoon the pasta into the center of the bowls and top with the mint and basil. Sprinkle the rest of the Parmesan and small pinch of red pepper flakes over the pasta and serve.

Tomato-Water Risotto
WITH BRAISED LEEKS

MAKES 4 SERVINGS

For most home cooks, making tomato water feels like conspicuous consumption: You pay a premium for a pound for gorgeous heirloom tomatoes, only to puree and strain them for a few ounces of their liquid. But you don't need to blow your bankroll on fancy tomatoes: Your favorite farmers market vendor probably has a stash of bruised tomatoes hiding under the table, or you can use some flavorful beefsteaks. And if you grow your own tomatoes, you can make a quick batch of tomato water anytime some overripened fruit starts to burst on the vine. You can even make a bunch of small batches and freeze them until you're ready to make a dish like this summery risotto.

——— THE TAKEAWAY ———

Some cooks are tomato-water purists, and simply combine chopped tomatoes and salt in a colander. This will yield a clean, purely flavored liquid, but I find it *too* simple (and difficult to flavor later), so I add shallots, basil, salt, and sugar and coarsely puree everything together to get as much liquid out of the tomatoes as possible. The uses for this precious nectar are many: as a broth for braised fish dishes, reduced to make a light tomato sauce or vinaigrette, or as a minimalist mix for Bloody Marys.

——— TOMATO WATER ———

4 pounds tomatoes (about 7 medium), chopped

1 medium shallot, thinly sliced

3 basil sprigs

1 teaspoon kosher salt

1 teaspoon sugar

LINE A fine-mesh sieve with cheesecloth and place over a large bowl. Combine all the ingredients in a food processor and pulse a few times until a coarse puree forms. Transfer to the sieve and let hang overnight (do not stir or press on the solids, or the water will get cloudy). You should end up with about 6 cups of tomato water. Refrigerate until ready to use, up to 3 days ahead.

——— BRAISED LEEKS ———

1 tablespoon unsalted butter

8 baby or 2 full-size leeks, halved lengthwise and washed, then cut crosswise on the bias into ½-inch slices

1 Fresno or Anaheim chile, cut on the bias into ¼-inch slices

Kosher salt

½ cup vegetable stock or water

¼ cup verjus or 2 tablespoons fresh lemon juice

IN A medium skillet, melt the butter over medium-low heat. Add the leeks, chile, a pinch of salt, and the stock and bring to a simmer. Cover the pan and simmer until the leeks are soft, 5 to 7 minutes. Uncover and cook until most of the liquid has evaporated, about 5 minutes. Stir in the verjus, season to taste with salt, and turn off the heat.

--------------- FOR SERVING ---------------

3 tablespoons extra-virgin olive oil

½ cup diced red onion

1 cup Arborio rice

Kosher salt

6 cups Tomato Water, warmed in a saucepan

Braised Leeks

¼ cup thinly sliced basil (preferably Thai basil)

2 cups cherry tomatoes, halved

2 tablespoons unsalted butter

½ cup finely grated Grana Padano cheese

¼ cup finely chopped parsley

IN A large saucepan, heat the oil over medium heat. Add the onion and cook, stirring, until softened, 5 to 7 minutes. Stir in the rice, season with salt, and reduce the heat to medium-low. Cook, stirring, until some of the grains are translucent, about 3 minutes. Ladle in 2 cups of the tomato water, bring to a simmer, and cook, stirring frequently, until absorbed. Add another 1 cup tomato water and continue cooking, stirring frequently and adding more tomato water as the liquid is absorbed, until the rice is tender (with a little bit of bite), about 15 minutes.

STIR IN the leeks and cook for a minute or two to meld the flavors. Add the basil, tomatoes, butter, and cheese and gently stir. Divide the risotto among serving bowls and sprinkle with the parsley. Serve.

Corn Pizza
WITH CORN BÉCHAMEL AND PICKLED PEPPERS

MAKES ONE 14-INCH PIZZA

This pie is an exercise in building big flavors from a single ingredient: corn. The béchamel doubles up on corn, with a cob-infused milk and kernels pureed into the creamy sauce. (Make a double batch and stir cheddar cheese into the extra béchamel to make a corny mac and cheese or queso sauce for nachos.) More charred corn tops the pie, adding little bursts of summery flavor to every bite.

—— THE TAKEAWAY ——

Pickled peppers are a classic pizza topping, but I wanted to make a version that would taste especially good with corn, so I added lime zest and juice to the mix. These peppers are great on sandwiches or chopped up into a tomato salad.

—— CORN BÉCHAMEL ——

MAKES ABOUT 1 CUP

3 ears corn, shucked
2 cups whole milk
2 tablespoons unsalted butter
2 tablespoons all-purpose flour
1 teaspoon kosher salt

CUT THE kernels from the corn cobs and cut the cobs into 1-inch chunks. Measure 2 cups of kernels and set the rest aside for toasting. In a small saucepan, combine the cobs and milk. Bring to a boil, then lower the heat, cover, and simmer for 30 to 40 minutes. Strain through a fine-mesh strainer; discard the cobs.

MAKE THE roux: In a small skillet, melt the butter over medium-low heat. Add the flour and cook, whisking, until the mixture is a light tan color and the texture of wet sand, 2 to 3 minutes. Turn off the heat.

RETURN THE infused milk to the saucepan and add the reserved 2 cups corn kernels and salt. Bring to a simmer, cover, and cook over low heat for 30 minutes. Transfer to a blender and blend until smooth, then strain through a fine-mesh sieve. Return the puree to the saucepan and bring to a simmer. Whisk in the roux and cook until the sauce has thickened, 2 to 3 minutes. Transfer to a bowl and cover with plastic wrap, pressing the plastic onto the surface of the sauce. Let cool. The béchamel can be made up to 1 day ahead and refrigerated until ready to use.

214

PICKLED PEPPERS

MAKES ABOUT 2 CUPS

3 red bell peppers

Strips of zest from 3 limes

1 Thai chile, split lengthwise

1 cup loosely packed mint leaves

1¾ cups red wine vinegar

¼ cup fresh lime juice

½ cup sugar

1 tablespoon kosher salt

CHAR THE peppers over a gas burner or under the broiler until blackened all over. Transfer to a bowl, cover with plastic wrap, and let rest for 10 minutes. Peel away the charred skin and cut away the seeds and white pith. Cut the peppers into ¼-inch strips and place in a pint-size jar.

COMBINE THE lime zest, chile, and mint in a square of cheesecloth and tie into a sachet. Add the sachet to the jar with the peppers. In a small saucepan, bring the vinegar, lime juice, sugar, and salt to a boil. Pour over the peppers and let cool to room temperature. Cover and refrigerate until ready to use. The peppers can be made up to 4 days ahead.

FOR SERVING

¾ cup corn kernels (from the béchamel, opposite)

One 250-gram portion Whole-Wheat Pizza Dough (page 200)

¼ cup to ⅓ cup Corn Béchamel

4 ounces fresh mozzarella, torn

½ cup finely grated Parmesan cheese

¾ cup coarsely grated fontina cheese

2 scallions, thinly sliced

1 tablespoon finely chopped jalapeño chile (no seeds)

½ cup Pickled Peppers

1 tablespoon thinly sliced mint

1 tablespoon chopped tarragon

IN A medium skillet (preferably cast-iron or nonstick), toast the corn kernels over high heat until well browned all over, about 5 minutes. Set aside.

PREHEAT THE oven to 500°F. Place a pizza stone, pizza steel, or baking sheet in the oven to preheat. Stretch the dough into a 14-inch round and place on a floured pizza peel. Spread the béchamel evenly over the dough with a spoon or rubber spatula. Top with the cheeses. Sprinkle the corn, scallions, and jalapeño evenly over the top. Bake the pizza on the preheated pizza stone, steel, or baking sheet until crispy on the bottom, 10 to 12 minutes. Arrange the pickled peppers over the pizza immediately after it comes out of the oven. Top with the mint and tarragon and serve.

Zucchini Pizza
WITH SOPPRESSATA-TOMATO JAM

MAKES ONE 14-INCH PIZZA

Some days you want a classic red-sauced pizza, while others you want an extra-cheesy white pie. This pizza combines the best of both. Although it's technically a white pie, it's studded with the flavors of a tomato and sausage pizza, thanks to the spicy tomato and soppressata jam.

Thinly sliced vegetables are great pizza toppers: They don't need advance cooking, and their edges curl up and caramelize while the pizza bakes in the oven. Just be sure to first squeeze as much water as possible out of the zucchini, or you'll end up with a soggy pie.

THE TAKEAWAY

The soppressata-tomato jam reminds me of *nduja,* the spicy, spreadable Italian salami. And it might become your new favorite pantry staple, as it has so many potential uses: as a topping for roasted vegetables, as a ready-made pasta sauce, or as a sandwich spread.

SOPPRESSATA-TOMATO JAM

MAKES ABOUT 2 CUPS

2 tablespoons extra-virgin olive oil

¼ cup finely chopped soppressata

¼ cup finely chopped prosciutto

1 teaspoon coarsely ground fennel seeds

½ teaspoon sweet smoked paprika

4 teaspoons honey

2 tablespoons red wine vinegar

1½ cups chopped Roasted Tomatoes (page 203), with their juices

IN A medium saucepan, heat the olive oil over medium heat. Add the soppressata and prosciutto and cook, stirring occasionally, until slightly crispy, 3 to 5 minutes. Add the fennel and paprika and cook, stirring, for 1 minute. Add the honey and vinegar, bring to a simmer, and cook until most of the liquid has evaporated. Add the tomatoes and their juices, bring to a simmer, and cook until the mixture is a jam-like consistency, about 30 minutes. Remove from the heat and let cool, then transfer to a storage container and refrigerate until ready to use. The jam can be made a few days ahead.

FOR SERVING

1 small or ½ medium zucchini, thinly sliced (use a mandoline if you have one)

Kosher salt

One 250-gram portion Whole-Wheat Pizza Dough (page 200)

4 ounces fresh mozzarella, torn or cut into 1-inch pieces

½ cup coarsely grated fontina cheese

¼ cup finely grated Parmesan cheese

¼ cup thinly sliced basil

1 teaspoon dried oregano

1 tablespoon oil from Garlic Confit (page 112) or extra-virgin olive oil

Freshly ground black pepper

Red pepper flakes

⅓ cup Soppressata-Tomato Jam

CONTINUES ➡

IN A colander or strainer, toss the zucchini with a couple pinches of salt and let sit for 1 hour. Transfer to a clean towel and squeeze out as much liquid as possible.

PREHEAT THE oven to 500°F. Place a pizza stone, pizza steel, or baking sheet in the oven to preheat. Stretch the dough into a 14-inch round and place on a floured pizza peel. Scatter the cheeses over the dough and top with the basil and oregano.

Arrange the zucchini slices over the pie. Drizzle with the garlic oil and season with salt and black pepper. Bake on the preheated pizza stone, steel, or baking sheet until crispy on the bottom, 10 to 15 minutes. Remove from the oven, sprinkle with a pinch of red pepper flakes, and spoon small dollops of the soppressata-tomato jam over the pie. Serve.

Cavatappi
WITH CORN, CHANTERELLES, AND PICKLED GREEN TOMATOES

MAKES 4 SERVINGS

I tried to pack as much corn flavor as possible into this velvety pasta sauce that provides a sweet counterpoint to the earthy mushrooms. (It is also a great sauce for fish and gnocchi.) Make sure you toss the drained pasta in the sauce for a bit, so it coats the noodles and infuses them with corn flavor. If you want a creamy pasta dish without cheese, you can leave out the Manchego.

THE TAKEAWAY

Every late summer I find myself staring at a bunch of green tomatoes, trying to come up with something new to do with the underripe orbs. So far, these pickles, which add crunch and acidity to this pasta dish, have been my favorite solution. What green tomatoes lack in flavor they make up for in texture, so infusing them with a spicy brine makes a lot of sense. A bit of turmeric in the brine helps prevent their bright green color from turning brown. I've used these pickles in sandwiches, burgers, salads, and as a garnish for Bloody Marys, with many more uses to come.

——— CORN SAUCE ———
MAKES ABOUT 2 CUPS

1 tablespoon extra-virgin olive oil

½ cup diced onion

1½ cups corn kernels (from about 2 ears)

1 teaspoon kosher salt

5 large cloves Garlic Confit (page 112)

⅓ cup dry white wine

1½ cups Corn Stock (page 48)

¼ cup packed summer savory or thyme

Kosher salt

IN A medium saucepan, heat the olive oil over medium-low heat. Add the onion and cook until tender, about 5 minutes. Add the corn and salt and cook, stirring, for 5 minutes. Add the garlic confit and white wine. Increase the heat and simmer until the wine has evaporated. Add the corn stock and savory, bring to a simmer, and cook for 20 minutes. Transfer to a blender and puree until smooth, then strain through a fine-mesh strainer. Season to taste with salt.

——— PICKLED GREEN TOMATOES ———
MAKES ABOUT 4 CUPS

1 pound medium green tomatoes, cut into ⅛-inch wedges

1 small onion, halved and thinly sliced

½ serrano chile, chopped (with seeds)

1¼ cups apple cider vinegar

¾ cup water

¼ cup plus 1 tablespoon sugar

2 tablespoons kosher salt

2 tablespoons yellow mustard seeds

¼ teaspoon celery seeds

¼ teaspoon turmeric

PLACE THE tomatoes, onion, and serrano in a sterilized quart-size jar or divide between two pint-size jars. In a medium saucepan, bring the remaining ingredients to a boil, then pour over the tomatoes. Let cool to room temperature, then seal the jar(s) and refrigerate until ready to use, up to 4 weeks.

CONTINUES ➡

FOR SERVING

- 4 tablespoons extra-virgin olive oil
- 2 cups corn kernels (2 to 3 ears, from stock used in Corn Sauce)
- 2 cups chanterelle or maitake mushrooms, large ones torn in half
- 1 jalapeño chile, diced (with seeds)
- ¼ cup thinly sliced scallion greens
- 8 ounces cavatappi pasta
- 1 cup Corn Sauce
- 1 cup finely grated Manchego cheese
- 1 tablespoon chopped thyme
- 3 tablespoons finely chopped parsley
- ½ cup diced Pickled Green Tomatoes
- Lemon wedges

HEAT 2 tablespoons of the olive oil in a large skillet (preferably cast-iron or nonstick). Add the corn and cook, stirring occasionally, until charred in spots, about 5 minutes. Transfer to a bowl and wipe out the skillet. Add the remaining 2 tablespoons olive oil and heat over high heat. Add the mushrooms and cook, stirring a couple of times, until browned and tender, 4 to 5 minutes. Add the reserved corn, the jalapeño, and scallions and cook for 2 to 3 minutes. Turn off the heat.

MEANWHILE, COOK the pasta in salted boiling water until al dente. Drain and add to the mushroom-corn mixture. Add the corn sauce and toss until the pasta is well coated. Add the Manchego, thyme, and parsley. Transfer to serving bowls and top with the pickled tomatoes. Squeeze some lemon juice over and serve.

Brown Rice Bowl
WITH PEPPER CHUTNEY AND CRISPY JAPANESE EGGPLANT

MAKES 4 TO 6 SERVINGS

Because they're so prevalent in New York City, I've eaten my share of very mediocre rice bowls. There's usually too much rice and not enough texture, and never enough green stuff. This is my vision for the perfect rice bowl: It has a lot of components, yes, but I guarantee it'll be the most interesting rice bowl you'll ever have (and it'll still be good if you skip one or two of the components). As for the rice itself, I deliberately use short-grain brown rice to give it a chewier texture, and season it like sushi rice with vinegar and sugar, as well as kombu for an extra-savory note.

SEASONED BROWN RICE

2 cups short-grain brown rice	½ cup champagne vinegar
4 cups water	2 tablespoons sugar
3 teaspoons kosher salt	4 thyme sprigs
One 6-by-8-inch piece kombu	¼ cup fresh lemon juice

RINSE THE rice in three changes of water and drain. In a medium saucepan, bring the water to a boil and add 1 teaspoon of of the salt and the kombu. Add the rice, cover the pot, and simmer over low heat for 45 minutes. Turn off the heat and let steam for 5 minutes, then fluff with a fork and spread out on a rimmed baking sheet.

MEANWHILE, BRING the vinegar, sugar, and remaining 2 teaspoons salt to a boil. Turn off the heat and add the thyme. Let cool to room temperature, then strain through a fine-mesh strainer and discard the thyme. Stir in the lemon juice. Sprinkle the vinegar solution over the rice and gently fold it in with a spatula.

CRISPY KALE

1 bunch Tuscan kale, stems removed	2 tablespoons extra-virgin olive oil
	Kosher salt

PREHEAT THE oven to 425°F. Brush the kale with the olive oil, spread on a large baking sheet, and season with salt. Bake until crispy, 10 to 12 minutes. Let cool, then break into large pieces.

THE TAKEAWAY

The bell pepper chutney, inspired by my Tabla days, adds a smoky note to the traditional sweet-sour flavor profile of India chutneys with ground chipotle powder, which is a handy spice to have around when you're not in the mood for smoked paprika. Although it has big flavors, the chutney works with a full spectrum of proteins, from lighter fish like bass, to chicken, pork, and steak.

BELL PEPPER CHUTNEY

MAKES 1½ CUPS

1 yellow bell pepper

1 red bell pepper

2 cups white wine vinegar

½ cup sugar

2 tablespoons finely chopped ginger

2 teaspoons chipotle powder

2 tablespoons kosher salt

1 red finger chile, thinly sliced (with seeds)

1 shishito or jalapeño chile, thinly sliced (with seeds)

CHAR THE bell peppers over the flame of a burner or under the broiler until charred all over. Transfer to a bowl and cover with a plate. Let steam for 10 minutes, then rub the skin from the peppers and cut into ½-inch dice. Transfer to a small saucepan and add the remaining ingredients. Bring the liquid to a hard simmer and cook until thickened into a jammy consistency, 3 to 5 minutes. Transfer to a container and let cool to room temperature, then refrigerate until ready to use, up to 1 week.

QUICK KOHLRABI KIMCHI

MAKES ABOUT 2 CUPS

1 medium kohlrabi, peeled and cut into ½-inch pieces (about 2 cups)

1 bunch scallions, thinly sliced (about ½ cup)

1 teaspoon gochugaru (Korean chile flakes)

1 tablespoon kosher salt

½ cup champagne vinegar

IN A small bowl, toss the kohlrabi with the scallions, gochugaru, and salt. Let sit for about 10 minutes, then add the vinegar and toss. The kimchi can be made a few days ahead and refrigerated until ready to use.

CRISPY JAPANESE EGGPLANT

2 Japanese eggplants

Kosher salt

Vegetable oil, for frying

¼ cup cornstarch

PEEL THE eggplants and cut them crosswise into 3-inch pieces, then cut the pieces into 4 wedges each. In a colander, toss the eggplant with 1 tablespoon of salt and let sit for at least 2 hours (or up to overnight). Squeeze as much water as possible out of the eggplants and pat dry with paper towels.

IN A medium saucepan, heat 2 inches of vegetable oil to 360°F. In a bowl, toss the eggplant with the cornstarch until coated. Working in batches, fry the eggplant until golden brown and crispy, 2 to 3 minutes. Drain on paper towels and season with salt.

FOR SERVING

3 tablespoons extra-virgin olive oil

½ cup coarsely chopped cashews

Seasoned Brown Rice

Crispy Kale

Bell Pepper Chutney

1 cup Quick Kohlrabi Kimchi

1 cup mixed diced pickles (such as carrots, turnips, onions, etc.)

Crispy Japanese Eggplant

Lemon wedges

½ cup chopped parsley

Flaky sea salt

Freshly ground black pepper

IN A small skillet, heat the olive oil over medium heat. Add the cashews and cook, stirring frequently, until golden brown, 3 to 4 minutes. Transfer the nuts to a bowl with a slotted spoon and let cool. Reserve the oil in the pan.

IN A large bowl, toss the rice with the crispy kale and drizzle with the oil from the cashews. Divide among serving bowls and top with big spoonfuls of chutney, kohlrabi kimchi, and pickles. Place a few pieces of eggplant in each bowl. Squeeze some lemon juice over each bowl and sprinkle with the cashews and parsley. Season with flaky salt and pepper and serve.

Bucatini
WITH BROCCOLI RABE, BACON, AND BREADCRUMBS

MAKES 4 SERVINGS

Thanks to its hollow, straw-like shape, bucatini is the best of the long pastas for silky, emulsified sauces. Because this dish contains a bitter ingredient—broccoli rabe—I want to tame the bitterness with a bacon fat–enriched sauce, along with cooling bites of goat's milk cheese.

THE TAKEAWAY

Spicy breadcrumbs are one of my most-used crunchy toppings. We make ours with stale whole-wheat sourdough bread, which has a lovely nutty flavor, but you can make yours with any kind of rustic bread. Processed white or wheat bread won't work very well, though; it's too moist and doesn't have the airy pockets that you'll find in artisanal loaves. I like breadcrumbs on the coarser side, so if your bread is stale enough, you can easily grate in on the large holes of a box grater. If it's too moist to grate, pulse bread cubes in a food processor until they're the desired size. In a pinch, you can use panko.

SPICY BREADCRUMBS

MAKES 2 CUPS

8 ounces crustless stale bread (preferably whole-wheat sourdough)

¼ cup extra-virgin olive oil

1 teaspoon kosher salt

¼ teaspoon red pepper flakes

½ teaspoon finely grated lemon zest

USING THE large holes of a box grater, grate the bread into coarse crumbs (you can also do this by pulsing the bread in a food processor). You should end up with about 2 cups crumbs.

IN A skillet, heat the oil over medium-high heat. Add the breadcrumbs and cook, stirring, until they're golden brown and crunchy, about 5 minutes. Stir in the salt and red pepper flakes and transfer to an airtight storage container. Stir in the lemon zest. The breadcrumbs can be stored for a day or two.

FOR SERVING

1 pound broccoli rabe, trimmed

12 ounces bucatini

8 ounces thick-cut bacon, cut into ¼-inch lardons

1 tablespoon extra-virgin olive oil

½ jalapeño chile, thinly sliced (with seeds)

¼ cup chopped parsley

2 tablespoons thinly sliced sage

2 tablespoons thinly sliced basil

1 cup finely grated Parmesan cheese

½ cup Spicy Breadcrumbs

½ cup crumbled goat cheese

BRING A large saucepan of salted water to a boil and prepare an ice bath. Blanch the broccoli rabe until just tender, 1 to 2 minutes. Transfer to the ice bath to cool. Cut the broccoli rabe into 1-inch pieces and set aside.

BRING A large pot of salted water to a boil. Cook the bucatini until al dente. Drain, reserving about 1 cup of the cooking water.

IN A skillet, cook the bacon over medium-low heat, pouring off (and reserving) the fat occasionally, until the bacon is browned but still has some chew to it, about 10 minutes. Transfer to paper towels to drain.

HEAT 1 tablespoon of the reserved bacon fat and the olive oil in a large skillet over medium heat. Add the jalapeño and broccoli rabe and cook until warmed through. Add a splash of pasta water and the herbs and toss well. Add the bucatini and reserved bacon and toss again. Turn off the heat and add the Parmesan, stirring until the pasta is well coated in sauce. Divide the pasta among serving bowls and top with the breadcrumbs and crumbled goat cheese. Serve.

Gemelli
WITH CLAMS AND PICKLED JALAPEÑOS

MAKES 4 SERVINGS

I've eaten many bowls of linguine with clams and spaghetti alle vongole, and every time I have the same complaints: I don't like pulling clams out of the pasta to pick their meat out of their shells, and I think the noodles are too long—it's hard to get everything in one bite when you're twirling noodles around your fork. To solve this problem, I shuck clams before they go into the pasta, and use a shorter, chewier noodle like gemelli, which allows you to enjoy all of the dish's flavors with every forkful. Consider this recipe your hall pass for experimenting with different shapes of pasta; just don't tell your Italian grandmother.

THE TAKEAWAY

A traditional Italian *soffritto* is the "holy trinity" of carrots, onions, and celery slowly cooked to make the base for myriad sauces, soups, and stews. My version is anything but traditional, as it omits the carrots and celery and adds a bit of heat from jalapeños. You can make and freeze a big batch of this soffritto and use it anytime you need a quick foundation for pasta sauces, chili, braises, soups, or stews.

PICKLED JALAPEÑOS

MAKES ABOUT ½ CUP

4 jalapeño chiles	White wine vinegar

THINLY SLICE the jalapeños crosswise and discard the stems. Place in a small sterilized jar or storage container and cover with white wine vinegar. Cover and refrigerate for at least 12 hours before using. The pickled jalapeños will keep for about 2 weeks.

SOFFRITTO

¼ cup plus 2 tablespoons extra-virgin olive oil	2 jalapeño chiles, finely chopped (with seeds)
8 large garlic cloves, finely chopped	¼ cup finely chopped oregano
4 teaspoons kosher salt	¼ cup finely chopped parsley
4 medium onions, finely chopped	3 tablespoons chopped rosemary

IN A medium saucepan, heat the oil over low heat. Add the garlic and salt and cook, stirring, until the garlic is translucent, about 4 minutes. Add the onions and jalapeños and cook, stirring, until softened and lightly browned, about 15 minutes. Turn off the heat and stir in the herbs. The soffritto can be made up to 1 day ahead and refrigerated until ready to use.

CONTINUES ➡

CLAMS

¼ cup extra-virgin olive oil

½ medium white onion, thinly sliced

3 large garlic cloves, thinly sliced

½ Thai chile, split lengthwise

1 teaspoon kosher salt

2 medium beefsteak tomatoes, cored and diced

¾ cup dry white wine

2 pounds littleneck clams, scrubbed

1 teaspoon chopped rosemary

2 teaspoons chopped oregano

1 tablespoon plus 2 teaspoons chopped mint

IN A large saucepan or Dutch oven, heat the olive oil over medium-low heat. Add the onion, garlic, chile, and salt and cook, stirring, until very soft, 5 to 7 minutes. Add the tomatoes and white wine and bring to a boil. Add the clams and cover the pot. Cook the clams, transferring them to a bowl as they open. Discard any clams that don't open after 10 minutes. Once all the clams have been removed, stir the herbs into the pot, cover, and let cool for 10 to 15 minutes. Strain the tomato-clam broth through a fine-mesh strainer, pressing on the solids to extract as much liquid as possible. Meanwhile, remove the clams from their shells and discard the shells.

FOR SERVING

8 ounces gemelli pasta

Tomato-clam broth (from Clams)

1 cup Soffritto

Clams

2 tablespoons unsalted butter

2 tablespoons fresh lemon juice

1 tablespoon chopped Pickled Jalapeños

½ red finger chile, thinly sliced

½ cup thinly sliced mint

½ cup Spicy Breadcrumbs (page 224)

COOK THE pasta in salted boiling water until al dente, then drain. Meanwhile, bring the tomato-clam broth and soffritto to a boil in a large saucepan. Add the clams and butter, stirring until the butter has melted. Bring the liquid to a simmer and add the drained pasta. Add the lemon juice, pickled jalapeños, and finger chile. Stir in the mint and divide the pasta among serving bowls. Sprinkle each serving with 2 tablespoons of breadcrumbs and serve.

Mixed Grains
WITH GRILLED SCALLION RÉMOULADE AND ROASTED FALL VEGETABLES

MAKES 4 TO 6 SERVINGS

I wanted this grain salad to showcase different styles and preparations of grains. You certainly don't need to use three different grains when you make this, as long as you use a combination of crunchy fried grains and creamy grains, which is something you'll keep craving after you've tried it. If you don't want to make the fried grains, you can also swap in puffed-grain cereal.

THE TAKEAWAY

Cooked grains can soak up a ton of flavor, so go heavy when dressing them. Here, I use both a sweet-sour vinaigrette and a smoky, chunky rémoulade to add a double dose of flavor. If you find yourself in the late spring with some ramps or spring onions, use them instead of the scallions.

——— MIXED GRAINS ———

1 cup emmer farro	9 thyme sprigs
1 cup wheatberries	Vegetable or sunflower oil, for frying
1 cup whole freekeh	
3 rosemary sprigs	Kosher salt

BRING THREE saucepans of salted water (at least 4 cups each) to a boil. Divide the grains among the pots, lower the heat, and simmer until al dente, 20 to 30 minutes for the farro, 30 to 35 minutes for the wheatberries, and about 45 minutes for the freekeh. Turn off the heat and divide the rosemary and thyme between the three pots. Let steep for 30 minutes, then drain the grains, discarding the herbs. In a large bowl, combine the grains and stir to mix. Set 1 cup aside for drying and frying and refrigerate the remaining 2 cups until ready to use.

PREHEAT THE oven to 175°F (if your oven doesn't go that low, prop the door open with a wooden spoon). Spread the 1 cup grains on a rimmed baking sheet and roast until completely dry, at least 4 hours.

FILL A medium saucepan with 2 inches of oil and heat to 375°F. Working in batches (about ½ cup at a time), fry the dried grains until they pop like popcorn, 4 to 5 minutes. Transfer to paper towels to drain and season with salt. The grains can be made ahead and stored at room temperature for up to 2 days.

CONTINUES ➡

229

———— ROASTED FALL VEGETABLES ————

4 cups mixed diced
vegetables (I use
a mix of turnips,
carrots, sunchokes,
sweet potato, celery
root, butternut, and
parsnips cut into
½-inch pieces)

¼ cup extra-virgin
olive oil

Kosher salt and freshly
ground black pepper

PREHEAT THE oven to 400°F. In a bowl, toss the vegetables with the olive oil and season with salt and pepper. Arrange on a rimmed baking sheet and roast until just cooked through, 15 to 20 minutes.

———— LEMON-HONEY VINAIGRETTE ————

MAKES ABOUT 1 CUP

3 tablespoons fresh
lemon juice

1 tablespoon sherry
vinegar

1 tablespoon white
balsamic vinegar

1½ teaspoons Dijon
mustard

2 teaspoons Tabasco
hot sauce (or Red Hot
Sauce, page 130)

1 teaspoon honey

1 tablespoon finely
chopped shallot

1 tablespoon chopped
oregano

1 teaspoon kosher salt

¾ cup extra-virgin
olive oil

IN A small bowl, whisk all ingredients together except the olive oil until well mixed. Slowly whisk in the olive oil until emulsified. The vinaigrette can be made a few hours ahead of time and refrigerated until ready to use.

———— GRILLED SCALLION RÉMOULADE ————

MAKES ABOUT 1¼ CUPS

1 bunch scallions
(about 4 ounces),
roots trimmed

1 cup mayonnaise
(preferably House
Mayonnaise,
page 150)

2 tablespoons chopped
Pickled Red Onions
(page 55)

2 chipotle chiles in
adobo, finely chopped

1 teaspoon Dijon
mustard

1 teaspoon Tabasco
hot sauce (or Red Hot
Sauce, page 130)

1 teaspoon
Worcestershire sauce

1 teaspoon fresh lemon
juice

1 teaspoon sugar

1 teaspoon kosher salt

PREPARE A hot grill or preheat a grill pan over high heat. Grill the scallions until charred all over, 3 to 5 minutes. Let cool slightly, then finely chop. In a bowl, combine the scallions with the remaining ingredients and mix well. The rémoulade can be refrigerated for a few days.

———— FOR SERVING ————

Mixed Grains

Roasted Fall
Vegetables

¼ cup diced
watermelon radish
(¼-inch pieces)

¼ cup chopped curly
parsley

¼ cup roughly chopped
dill fronds

½ cup Lemon-Honey
Vinaigrette

Kosher salt

Grilled Scallion
Rémoulade

2 red globe radishes,
thinly sliced

1 lemon, for zesting

IN A large bowl, toss both sets of grains with the roasted vegetables, watermelon radish, parsley, and dill. Add the vinaigrette and toss to coat. Season to taste with salt. Spread about 2 tablespoons of rémoulade on the bottom of each serving bowl and top with the grain salad. Sprinkle the globe radishes on top of the grains and grate some lemon zest over each serving. Serve.

Kale Pizza
WITH FENNEL SAUSAGE

MAKES ONE 14-INCH PIZZA

This is a "kale pizza" with sausage, and not a "sausage pizza" with kale. It's the pizza that convinced me that kale deserves to appear on more pies: I love the way it gets crackly and toasty-flavored in a hot oven, and it can work on pretty much any style of pizza. I prefer Tuscan kale as a pizza topper, because its flat leaves crisp up more evenly, but you can experiment with other kale varieties, as well as spinach. Make sure you really cover the top of the pie with kale before baking, as it will shrink up a bit as it cooks.

—— THE TAKEAWAY ——

If you're feeling ambitious, this pizza is a great reason to make your own sausage. The homemade fennel sausage is a versatile recipe that's easy to make (so long as you have a sausage grinder). Or feel free to use store-bought loose sausage—sweet or hot, depending on your preference. A lot of pizza recipes will have you cook the sausage in a skillet before adding it to the pie, but I like to put dime-size clumps of raw sausage on the pie, which are small enough to cook through as the pizza bakes.

—— FENNEL SAUSAGE ——

MAKES 2 POUNDS

1 pound boneless, skinless chicken thighs

4 ounces pork shoulder

4 ounces fatback (or pork belly)

1 tablespoon ground fennel seeds

1 tablespoon red pepper flakes

1 tablespoon sweet smoked paprika

2 tablespoons kosher salt

¼ cup red wine vinegar

2 teaspoons cold water

CUT THE chicken, pork, and fatback into small cubes and place in a mixing bowl. Add the fennel, red pepper flakes, paprika, and salt and toss well. Line a baking sheet with parchment and scatter the seasoned meat in an even layer. Freeze until the meat is very firm, about 1 hour.

USING A meat grinder fitted with the small die, grind the meat. Transfer to a standing mixer fitted with the paddle attachment. Turn the mixer to low speed and slowly add the vinegar and water. Continue mixing until the meat is tacky to the touch, 2 to 3 minutes. The sausage can be covered and refrigerated for up to 3 days, or frozen for up to 3 months.

One 250-gram portion
  Whole-Wheat Pizza
  Dough (page 200)

⅓ cup Quick Tomato
  Sauce (page 201)

4 ounces (about ½ cup)
  Fennel Sausage or
  loose Italian sausage

1½ cups shredded
  (¼-inch ribbons)
  Tuscan kale

2 tablespoons extra-
  virgin olive oil

Kosher salt

Pinch of red pepper
  flakes

Freshly ground black
  pepper

¼ cup finely grated
  pecorino Toscano
  cheese

PREHEAT THE oven to 500°F. Place a pizza stone, pizza steel, or baking sheet in the oven to pre-heat. Stretch the dough into a 14-inch round and place on a floured pizza peel. Spread the sauce around the dough, leaving a ½-inch border. Top with dime-size pieces of sausage, making sure to cover most of the pie. Top with a layer of kale and lightly press it flat. Drizzle with the olive oil and season with salt. Bake on the preheated pizza stone, steel, or baking sheet until crispy on the bottom, 10 to 15 minutes. Remove from the oven, season with a pinch of red pepper flakes and a good amount of black pepper, and sprinkle the pecorino over the pie. Serve.

Sausage and Soppressata Calzone

MAKES 1 CALZONE (2 SERVINGS)

Most calzones tend to be gut-bombs overstuffed with cheese and other ingredients, like a pizza folded in half. The result is usually wet and mushy, and I end up longing for a slice of pizza instead. My longtime chef de cuisine, Seth Seligman, and I tried to solve these issues by taking a less-is-more approach to the calzone: We put fewer ingredients on the inside, and shape the dough into a long, skinny tube. Bending the tube into a horseshoe shape also helps elongate the calzone and stretch out the filling, so you end up with a thin, crisp crust and just the right amount of gooey filling.

THE TAKEAWAY

By moving some of the calzone's ingredients—tomato sauce, soppressata, and Parmesan cheese—to the outside of the dough, you not only get a better ratio of crust to filling, but the heat of the oven also caramelizes the exterior ingredients, which means more pizza-like flavor. You can apply this technique to focaccia and other homemade breads, or simply brush a store-bought baguette with tomato sauce and cover it with cheese (and pepperoni if you like) to make a quick, calzone-like loaf.

One 200-gram portion Whole-Wheat Pizza Dough (page 200)

½ cup ricotta

4 ounces (about ½ cup) loose hot Italian sausage

2 ounces fresh mozzarella, torn or cut into 1-inch pieces

2 tablespoons roughly chopped basil

¼ teaspoon dried oregano

3 tablespoons Quick Tomato Sauce (page 201), plus 1 cup warm sauce for serving

2 to 3 tablespoons finely grated Parmesan cheese

5 or 6 slices soppressata or pepperoni

PREHEAT THE oven to 450°F. Stretch the dough into a 12-by-5-inch rectangle and place on a floured pizza peel. Spoon a line of ricotta along the bottom fourth of the dough (a long side), leaving a little room at the edges for sealing. Top with small pieces of sausage across the ricotta, and scatter the mozzarella and basil on top of that. Sprinkle with the oregano. Fold the top of the dough over the bottom to form a long tube, and press the edges closed, making sure they're well sealed. Use scissors to cut three 1-inch vents across the top of the calzone to allow steam to escape. Brush the top of the calzone all over with the tomato sauce and sprinkle enough Parmesan on top to give it a light coating. Lay the soppressata across the top of the calzone, making sure not to cover any of the vents.

TRANSFER THE calzone to a baking sheet and carefully push the edges to make a U shape. Bake the calzone until the crust is well browned all over and the cheese is starting to bubble through the air vents, 20 to 25 minutes. Let cool for a few minutes before slicing. Serve with additional tomato sauce for dipping.

Paccheri
WITH ROMANESCO AND SPICY CAULIFLOWER PUREE

MAKES 4 SERVINGS

This is another pasta dish we developed before opening Loring Place. We'd wanted to treat one vegetable different ways in the same pasta, and cauliflower is perfect for this. We always have a ton of cauliflower scraps around the kitchen, which form the basis for the creamy (but dairy-free) sauce that gets blended with fresh chiles and garlic. I love the way chartreuse-colored, fractalized Romanesco broccoli looks—it's almost too pretty to eat—especially when the tips of its little spikes caramelize in the oven. I also love the way tubular paccheri pasta collapses after it's been cooked, which traps little pockets of the sauce inside.

CHILE SAUCE

MAKES ABOUT 1 CUP

4 cups white wine vinegar

1 cup honey

2 tablespoons kosher salt

½ cup extra-virgin olive oil

24 garlic cloves, thinly sliced

2 cups thinly sliced Anaheim and red jalapeño chiles, with seeds (from about 12 ounces peppers)

IN A small saucepan, bring the vinegar, honey, and 4 teaspoons of the salt to a boil. Reduce until syrupy and turn off the heat. In a medium saucepan, heat the olive oil over medium heat. Add the garlic and remaining 2 teaspoons salt and cook, stirring, until golden brown, 2 to 3 minutes. Add the chiles and cook until slightly tender, about 2 minutes. Add the syrup and bring to a boil, then turn off the heat and let cool to room temperature. The chile sauce can be made up to 1 week ahead; refrigerate until ready to use.

SPICY CAULIFLOWER PUREE

13 ounces cauliflower florets

½ cup Chile Sauce

BRING A medium saucepan of salted water to a boil. Add the cauliflower, lower the heat, and simmer until tender, 5 to 10 minutes. Drain the cauliflower and transfer to a blender. Add the chile sauce and puree until smooth.

ROASTED ROMANESCO

½ medium Romanesco broccoli, cut into bite-size florets (about 2 cups)

¼ cup extra-virgin olive oil

2 teaspoons kosher salt

PREHEAT THE oven to 425°F. In a bowl, toss the Romanesco with the olive oil and salt. Spread on a rimmed baking sheet and roast, stirring once or twice, until crisp-tender, 15 to 20 minutes.

FOR SERVING

12 ounces paccheri pasta

Roasted Romanesco

½ cup Chile Sauce

1 cup finely grated Parmesan cheese

¼ cup thinly sliced mint

¼ cup thinly sliced basil

Spicy Cauliflower Puree

½ cup finely grated Asiago or goat's milk Gouda

½ cup Spicy Breadcrumbs (page 224)

COOK THE pasta in a pot of boiling salted water until al dente. Drain, reserving about 2 cups of pasta water. In a large skillet, combine the cooked pasta, Romanesco, chile sauce, Parmesan, and about 1 cup of the pasta water, stirring until the cheese melts into the water and forms a creamy sauce. Stir in the mint and basil. Divide the cauliflower puree among four serving bowls (about ¼ cup per serving), spreading it to cover the bottom of the bowl. Spoon the pasta on top. Sprinkle the Asiago and breadcrumbs over and serve.

Polenta
WITH MUSHROOM JAM

MAKES 4 SERVINGS

This dish looks and sounds similar to the Grits with Mushroom Ragu on page 241, but I'm including both recipes in this book to show how the same set of ingredients can yield very different dishes. Here, I cook the mushrooms further down to make a sweet and sour jam that can stand in anywhere you'd use a chutney. I then stir bite-size chunks of cheese into the polenta, which adds little pockets of intense, earthy flavor, making every bite different. I use Ardith Mae Farmstead's Mammuth, a Camembert-style cheese that's made with goat's milk. You can use anything similar—Camembert's extra-creamy cousin, Brie, is a good substitute as well—but please leave on the rind: It's full of flavor and adds a pleasant chew to the polenta.

——— THE TAKEAWAY ———

Most polenta recipes call for a 4:1 ratio of liquid to polenta. I find this is rarely enough liquid and use a full 6 cups of milk to cook 1 cup of polenta to get the porridge-like texture we want. Coarse, stone-ground cornmeal requires the most liquid; if you're using a finer grain, you might want to start with 4 or 5 cups of milk and add more as needed. You'll know the polenta is finished cooking when it slowly falls off a spoon, like a cake batter, or when you can run a finger through the polenta (be careful, it's hot) and the trench will hold its shape for a couple of seconds before filling back in.

——— POLENTA ———

6 cups whole milk
2 teaspoons kosher salt

1 cup medium or coarse polenta, preferably stone-ground

IN A medium saucepan, bring the milk to a boil and add the salt. Stir in the polenta, lower the heat to medium, and cook, stirring occasionally, until the polenta is creamy and slowly falls off a spoon but still has a little bite, about 45 minutes. It's best to use the polenta right away, but if you want to make it a few hours ahead, press a piece of plastic on top of the polenta and let cool to room temperature. Rewarm gently over medium-low heat with a splash of milk.

——— MUSHROOM JAM ———

MAKES 2 CUPS

¼ cup extra-virgin olive oil

¼ cup finely chopped shallot

2 large garlic cloves, finely chopped

8 ounces button or cremini mushrooms, quartered (large mushrooms cut into sixths)

Kosher salt

½ cup dry sherry

1 cup champagne vinegar

½ cup sherry vinegar

½ cup maple syrup

2 tablespoons finely chopped red finger chiles (with seeds)

1 tablespoon chopped rosemary

IN A medium saucepan, heat the olive oil over low heat. Add the shallot and garlic and cook, stirring, until soft, 5 minutes. Add the mushrooms and a big pinch of salt and cook, stirring occasionally, until golden brown, about 5 minutes. Add the sherry and vinegars, bring to a simmer, and cook until the liquid is syrupy, about 15 minutes. Add the maple syrup, bring to a simmer, and cook until the mushrooms are jammy in texture, 10 to 15 minutes. Stir in the finger chiles and rosemary and let cool. The mushroom jam can be made up to a few days ahead and refrigerated until ready to use.

FOR SERVING

Polenta

1 cup Mushroom Jam

**3 tablespoons unsalted
 butter**

Kosher salt

**3 ounces (about
 ¼ wheel) Camembert
 or Camembert-style
 cheese, cut into
 ½-inch pieces**

**¼ cup mixed chopped
 parsley, chives, and
 tarragon**

Extra-virgin olive oil

REWARM THE polenta and mushroom jam if necessary. Stir the butter into the polenta and season to taste with salt. Gently stir in the cheese. Spoon the polenta into serving bowls and spoon some of the mushroom jam on top. Top with the herbs and a drizzle of olive oil and serve.

Grits
WITH MUSHROOM RAGU

MAKES 4 SERVINGS

This rich dish is an all-around utility player. It's a satisfying meal in itself, a starchy side for braised meat dishes, or, with a fried or poached egg on top, the star of a brunch spread. Buy the highest-quality grits you can find; the difference in flavor between cheap supermarket cornmeal and artisanal grits from Anson Mills or Bob's Red Mill is vast.

The mushroom ragu itself is also versatile: It has a meaty flavor but is completely vegetarian (if you don't use chicken stock). You can serve it on its own as a side dish, and it's wonderful on toast. We make this ragu whenever we have a bunch of mushroom scraps to use up, but if you're starting from scratch, try to combine as many types of mushrooms as you can find, which will make the flavor that much more complex.

—— THE TAKEAWAY ——

You can use grated potatoes as a thickener for sauces, braises, and soups. It's a great trick to keep in your back pocket anytime you want to thicken something on the fly, as the potatoes break down quickly and add more flavor than cornstarch and other thickeners.

—————— GRITS ——————

3½ cups water
½ cup whole milk
1 cup grits or medium cornmeal (preferably freshly ground)

1 tablespoon kosher salt
½ teaspoon freshly ground black pepper

IN A medium saucepan, bring the water and milk to a boil. Add the cornmeal, salt, and pepper. Lower the heat and simmer, stirring frequently, until the grits are tender, 30 to 40 minutes. Cover and keep warm.

—————— KOMBU TEA ——————

MAKES 4 CUPS

1 quart water
One 6-by-8-inch piece kombu
3 strips orange zest (no pith)
4 strips lemon zest (no pith)

2 thyme sprigs
½ green Thai chile (split lengthwise)
1 tablespoon kosher salt

IN A medium saucepan, combine the water and kombu and bring to a simmer. Combine the rest of the ingredients in a bowl and pour the water and kombu over. Cover and let sit for 30 minutes. Strain through a fine-mesh strainer and let cool to room temperature. Transfer to a storage container and refrigerate for up to 4 days or freeze for several months.

MUSHROOM RAGU

MAKES 2 CUPS

¼ cup plus
  2 tablespoons extra-
  virgin olive oil

2 large garlic cloves,
  finely chopped

Kosher salt

½ small onion, diced

¼ cup diced parsnips
  (⅛-inch dice)

¼ cup diced carrot
  (⅛-inch dice)

2 tablespoons white
  wine

½ cup coarsely grated
  russet potato
  (use the large holes
  on a box grater)

¾ cup Kombu Tea,
  chicken stock, or
  vegetable stock

12 ounces mixed
  mushrooms (I use
  trumpet, cremini, hon
  shimeji, and button),
  cut or torn into
  ½-inch pieces (about
  4 cups)

½ Thai chile, finely
  chopped (with seeds)

1 teaspoon thyme
  leaves

FOR SERVING

Grits

2 tablespoons unsalted
  butter

½ cup finely grated
  aged cheddar cheese

½ cup finely grated
  pecorino cheese

Mushroom Ragu

¼ cup mixed chopped
  parsley, chives, and
  tarragon

4 over-easy fried eggs

Extra-virgin olive oil

REWARM THE grits and stir in the butter and cheeses. Rewarm the mushroom ragu and stir in half of the herbs. Divide the grits among four serving bowls and top with the mushroom ragu. Sprinkle the remaining herbs over the mushrooms and top each bowl with a fried egg. Drizzle with olive oil and serve.

IN A medium saucepan, heat the 2 tablespoons olive oil over medium heat. Add the garlic and salt and cook, stirring, until softened, about 2 minutes. Add the onion and cook until translucent, about 5 minutes. Add the parsnips and carrot and cook for 5 minutes. Add the white wine and cook until most of the liquid has evaporated, about 3 minutes. Add the potato and stir well. Add the kombu tea or stock and bring to a boil. Lower the heat and simmer until reduced by half, about 30 minutes. Turn off the heat.

IN A large skillet, heat the remaining ¼ cup olive oil over high heat. Add the mushrooms and 1 teaspoon salt and cook, stirring occasionally, until the mushrooms are nicely browned, 15 to 20 minutes. Add the mushrooms to the vegetable mixture along with the chile and thyme. Let cool. The ragu can be made a day or two ahead of time; rewarm before serving.

Bacon, Date, and Radicchio Pizza

MAKES ONE 14-INCH PIZZA

This pizza started as a late-night snack I'd make at home after a shift at Tabla, using leftover naan dough and some amazing dates I had picked up on a trip to California. I turned it into a well-rounded—even healthy-ish—meal by topping the pie with a chicory salad, and using sweet, chewy dates and a drizzle of balsamic vinegar to cut through the bitterness. You can use other kinds of cured pork, such as chopped prosciutto or pancetta, in place of the bacon.

- 2 ounces bacon, finely chopped
- One 250-gram portion Whole-Wheat Pizza Dough (page 200)
- 2 ounces fresh ricotta
- ¼ cup finely grated Parmesan cheese
- 2 ounces fontina cheese, diced
- 4 Medjool, Halawi, or Khadrawy dates, pitted and quartered lengthwise
- ½ cup thinly sliced radicchio and/or Belgian endive
- 1 tablespoon thinly sliced basil
- 1 tablespoon balsamic vinegar
- 1 tablespoon extra-virgin olive oil
- Flaky sea salt
- Red pepper flakes

IN A skillet, cook the bacon over medium heat, stirring, until crispy, about 5 minutes. Transfer to paper towels to drain.

PREHEAT THE oven to 500°F. Place a pizza stone, pizza steel, or baking sheet in the oven to preheat. Stretch the dough into a 14-inch round and place on a floured pizza peel. Spread the cheeses over the dough, and sprinkle the bacon and dates over. Bake the pizza on the preheated pizza stone, steel, or baking sheet until crispy on the bottom, 10 to 15 minutes.

MEANWHILE, IN a medium bowl, toss the radicchio with the basil, vinegar, and oil. Season with flaky salt and scatter the salad on top of the cooked pizza. Sprinkle with red pepper flakes and serve.

THE TAKEAWAY

Mozzarella is the king of pizza cheeses, and I use it often, but fontina is also a worthy contender for the crown. Fontina melts very easily (it's my favorite grilled cheese filling), gives you a great cheese pull, and is more flavorful than mozzarella, with a sweet, slightly funky profile. As with mozzarella, I usually dice fontina so you get larger melted pieces on the baked pie.

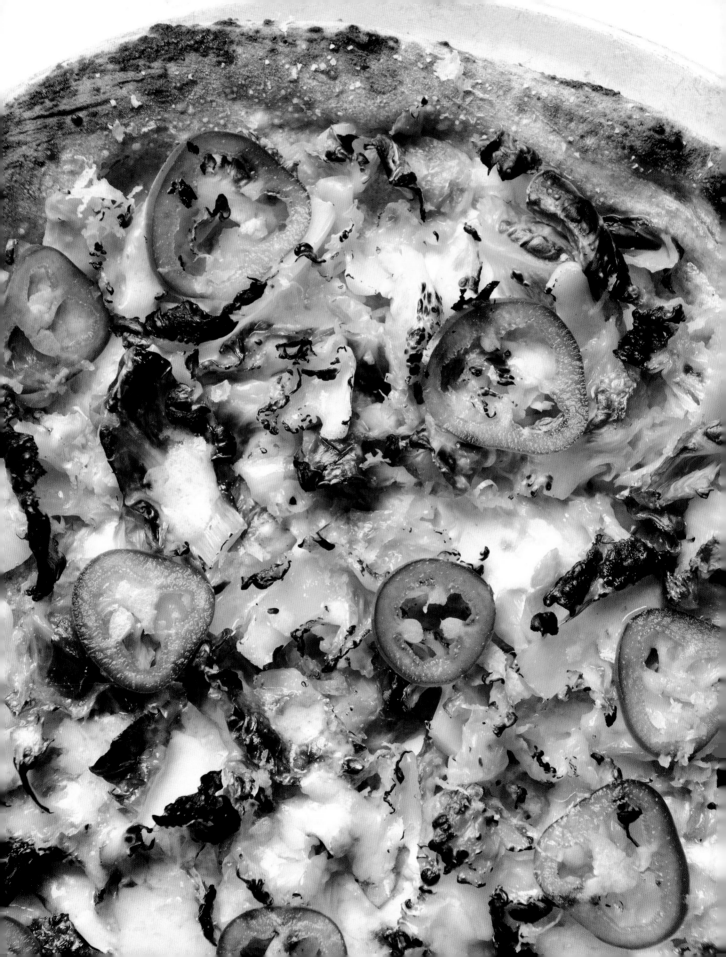

Brussels Sprout Pizza
WITH PICKLED CHILES AND CHEDDAR

MAKES ONE 14-INCH PIZZA

Although Italian cheeses usually get all the love, don't forget about cheddar when making pizzas. It melts easily, has a sweet, nutty flavor that loves Brussels sprouts and other green vegetables, and works on both red and white pies. On this pizza, the pickled jalapeños are vital, as their bright heat and acidity help lift the other flavors.

- 2 cups loosely packed Brussels sprout leaves (dark outer leaves only, from about 1 pound Brussels sprouts)
- One 250-gram portion Whole-Wheat Pizza Dough (page 200)
- ¼ cup ricotta
- ¼ cup finely grated Parmesan cheese
- 2 teaspoons oil from Garlic Confit (page 112) or extra-virgin olive oil
- 1 tablespoon finely chopped parsley
- Kosher salt
- 3 tablespoons finely grated aged cheddar cheese (I use Cabot Clothbound Cheddar)
- 12 Pickled Jalapeño slices (page 227)
- 1 lemon, for zesting

BRING A saucepan of salted water to a boil. Blanch the Brussels sprout leaves until they're bright green and just tender, 1 to 2 minutes. Transfer to paper towels to drain, patting them very dry.

PREHEAT THE oven to 500°F. Place a pizza stone, pizza steel, or baking sheet in the oven to preheat. Stretch the dough into a 14-inch round and place on a floured pizza peel. Using a spoon, place dollops of the ricotta around the dough, leaving a ½-inch border around the edge. Top with the Parmesan. In a bowl, toss the Brussels sprout leaves with the garlic oil, parsley, and a pinch of salt. Spread the leaves evenly over the pizza. Bake on the preheated pizza stone, steel, or baking sheet until crispy on the bottom, 10 to 15 minutes. Remove from the oven and immediately sprinkle the cheddar over the pie. (If you wish, return the pie to the oven for a minute or two to melt.) Sprinkle the pickled jalapeños over the pie and grate some lemon zest over. Serve.

THE TAKEAWAY

When I think about toppings for pizza, I always consider moisture content. The pizza bakes for 10 to 15 minutes, so anything you put on top should cook through in that same window, or you need to slice it more thinly or precook it. But some thin ingredients, like Brussels sprout leaves, will dry out too quickly, so a quick blanch will add the moisture they need to properly crisp up while the pizza bakes.

245

Grandma Pie

MAKES TWO 9-BY-13-INCH PIES (6 SERVINGS)

When we were getting ready to open Loring Place, I knew I wanted to serve a simple, snackable pizza to contrast the more cheffy round pies we offer. Everybody serves a Margherita, so we opted instead for a Sicilian-style "grandma" pizza, so named for the simple treats Italian grandmothers would make for family as they cooked Sunday dinner: some pizza dough in a pan, covered with sauce and cheese.

THE TAKEAWAY

Like the crispy shallots that give crunch to my Little Gem Salad (page 88), crispy fried garlic is a topping that's always good to have on hand, and you'll find new uses for it every time you cook. I like the extra-crunchy bite that you get from frying roughly chopped garlic, but you can make the same recipe with thinly sliced cloves for a lighter texture.

CRISPY GARLIC

MAKES ABOUT ¼ CUP

Cloves from 1 head garlic, peeled and coarsely chopped (about ¼ cup)

1 cup vegetable or canola oil

PLACE THE garlic in a medium saucepan and cover with the oil. Place over medium heat and cook, stirring constantly, until the garlic is light golden brown, about 3 minutes. Pour the garlic and oil through a fine-mesh strainer and press with a spoon or ladle to squeeze out all of the oil. The garlic will continue to cook, so work quickly. Spread the garlic out on paper towels (it will crisp up as it cools). The garlic can be made up to 1 day ahead; store in an airtight container at room temperature.

FOR SERVING

Two 350-gram portions Whole-Wheat Pizza Dough (page 200)

Extra-virgin olive oil, for oiling

All-purpose flour, for dusting

8 ounces fresh mozzarella, torn or cut into 1-inch pieces (about 1½ cups)

1½ cups Quick Tomato Sauce (page 201)

1 teaspoon dried oregano

½ cup freshly grated Parmesan cheese

20 large basil leaves, cut into ribbons

1 teaspoon Crispy Garlic

1 teaspoon flaky sea salt

Red pepper flakes

FORM EACH piece of dough into a ball. Oil two quarter sheet pans (9 by 13 inches) with oil. Dust a work surface with flour and roll one piece of dough with a rolling pin until it's about the size of the sheet pan. Transfer the dough to the sheet pan and press it until it fills the pan. Repeat with the remaining dough. Cover with plastic and let proof at room temperature for 1 hour.

CONTINUES ➡

PREHEAT THE oven to 475°F. Scatter half of the mozzarella over each pie. Divide the tomato sauce between the two pizzas, drizzling it with a spoon to cover each pie. Sprinkle half of the oregano over each pie. Bake the pies in the center of the oven until the edges are crispy and browned and the tomato sauce has thickened, about 15 minutes. Sprinkle each pie with half the Parmesan, basil, crispy garlic, and flaky salt and add a pinch of red pepper flakes. Using a large spatula, transfer the pies to a cutting board, cut each into six pieces, and serve.

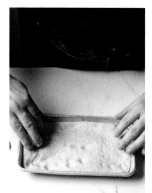

Herbed Grains
WITH STEWED MUSHROOMS AND PRESERVED LEMONS

MAKES 4 TO 6 SERVINGS

Cooking grains can frustrate some cooks, as different varieties of grains—or different styles of the same grain—can have vastly different cooking times and absorb different amounts of water. For this reason, I cook each type of grain separately, and treat them like pasta, cooking them in a good amount of salted water before draining the excess liquid. Here, I combine emmer farro (sometimes labeled "farro medio") and its chewy cousin freekeh (which is made from roasted durum wheat) with intensely flavored glazed mushrooms to make a soul-satisfying porridge that's perfect for the coldest nights of winter.

—— THE TAKEAWAY ——

Most preserved lemons are made with whole fruit, but I learned how to make a different, quicker version from Tom Colicchio. By slicing the lemons first, you can achieve that same salty-sour flavor in a couple of days, rather than weeks. I also love how this method preserves some of the fresh lemon flavor, and you can use the whole slice, rather than throwing away the too-salty flesh. The downside is that quick-preserved lemons don't last as long, so you'll want to use them up within a couple of weeks. Give them a quick rinse and pat dry before using.

—— QUICK PRESERVED LEMONS ——

MAKES ABOUT 1 CUP

2 lemons (preferably organic), washed and dried

1 tablespoon sugar
1 tablespoon kosher salt

THINLY SLICE the lemon into rounds (about $\frac{1}{16}$ inch thick). Arrange the lemon slices in a single layer on a baking sheet and season with the sugar and salt (like you'd season a steak). Stack the lemons and transfer to a jar or container. Seal and refrigerate for at least 2 days before using. The preserved lemons can be refrigerated for up to 1 week. Rinse and pat dry before using.

CONTINUES ➡

249

HERBED GRAINS

1 cup emmer farro

1 cup freekeh

2 rosemary sprigs

6 thyme sprigs

BRING TWO saucepans of salted water to a boil. Add the farro to one and the freekeh to the other and simmer until al dente, 20 to 30 minutes for the farro and about 45 minutes for the freekeh. Turn off the heat and divide the rosemary and thyme between the two pots. Let steep for 30 minutes, then drain and discard the herbs.

SHALLOT CONFIT

MAKES 1½ CUPS

4 medium shallots, peeled and cut crosswise into ¼-inch rings

1½ cups extra-virgin olive oil

IN A small saucepan, combine the shallots and oil. Cook over very low heat (it shouldn't bubble), until the shallots are golden brown and very soft, about 1 hour. Let cool to room temperature, then transfer to a storage container and refrigerate for up to 1 month.

STEWED MUSHROOMS

¼ cup plus 1 tablespoon oil from Shallot Confit or Garlic Confit (page 112) or extra-virgin olive oil

1 medium shallot, finely chopped

2 large garlic cloves, thinly sliced

1 pound mixed mushrooms (I use a combination of silver dollar, shiitake, oyster, and chanterelle), cut or torn into roughly 1-inch pieces

1 teaspoon kosher salt

3 tablespoons white miso paste

1 cup Kombu Tea (page 240) or chicken stock

IN A large saucepan, heat the oil over low heat. Add the shallot and garlic and cook, stirring occasionally, until translucent, about 5 minutes. Add the mushrooms and salt, stir well, and cover the pot. Increase the heat to medium and cook until the mushrooms release some liquid, about 5 minutes. Meanwhile, in a small bowl, whisk the miso into the kombu tea. Add this to the mushrooms, raise the heat to high and cook, uncovered, until the liquid has reduced to a glaze.

FOR SERVING

4 cups Herbed Grains

Stewed Mushrooms

1 jalapeño chile, finely diced (with seeds)

¼ cup chopped mint

¼ cup chopped parsley

¼ cup chopped chives

8 slices Quick-Preserved Lemons, rinsed, patted dry, and chopped

Kosher salt

1 lemon, for zesting

IN A medium saucepan, combine the grains and mushrooms and cook over medium heat until glazy. Turn off the heat and stir in the jalapeño, mint, parsley, chives, and preserved lemon. Season to taste with salt. Divide among serving bowls and finish each with some freshly grated lemon zest.

Whole-Wheat Spaghetti
WITH SPINACH, GARLIC, AND FERMENTED CHILE SAUCE

MAKES 4 SERVINGS

If there's a single dish that represents how I cook, this might be it. One of the first pasta dishes I learned at Union Square Cafe was linguine aglio e olio, *a classic preparation in which you emulsify pasta water and olive oil together to make a light, silky sauce. The dish was so simple, yet elegant, and a demonstration of real technique. It inspired me to make the recipe you see here. I start with whole-wheat spaghetti, which has a nutty flavor that adds so much to the dish. We make our spaghetti from house-milled flour, but unless you own a pasta extruder, a high-quality dried whole-wheat spaghetti will work just as well. The rest of the recipe follows the* aglio e olio *(water and oil) template, but we add handfuls of spinach and herbs that gently wilt into the spaghetti and top the dish with a large spoonful of fermented chile sauce, which adds the acidity you'd get from a squeeze of lemon.*

THE TAKEAWAY

The fermented chile sauce is one of our most-used pantry staples, both by itself and as the base for other sauces, including the Sweet and Spicy Sauce on page 257, and the Chile Aioli on page 34. It's based on *sambal oelek*, the Indonesian chile paste, but is a touch less spicy. If you haven't played around with making fermented sauces at home, this is an easy place to start. As with any fermentation, make sure everything you're using is clean, and use the freshest chiles you can find. It's rare to have a ferment go bad, but if you see any mold forming on your chile puree, throw it out and start over. I like using widely available red finger chiles as the base for the sauce, but you can experiment with other chiles, or a mix of several varieties.

FERMENTED CHILE SAUCE

MAKES 3½ CUPS

4 garlic cloves

1 pound red finger chiles, washed, stems discarded, and coarsely chopped

3 tablespoons sugar

2 tablespoons kosher salt

1 cup extra-virgin olive oil

2 teaspoons hot smoked paprika

½ cup white wine vinegar

IN A food processor, combine the garlic, chiles, sugar, and salt. Pulse until a coarse mash forms. Transfer to a very clean container and cover with cheesecloth. Let ferment at room temperature for 24 hours.

MEANWHILE, COMBINE the olive oil and paprika in a small saucepan. Heat the mixture over low heat until it reaches 180°F, then turn off the heat and let infuse for 2 hours. Strain through a coffee filter and let the oil cool to room temperature.

STIR THE paprika oil and vinegar into the fermented chile mixture. Transfer to a storage container and refrigerate for up to 1 month.

--------------- FOR SERVING ---------------

12 ounces whole-wheat spaghetti

¼ cup extra-virgin olive oil

1 tablespoon finely chopped garlic

¼ cup roughly chopped mint

¼ cup torn basil

5 ounces baby spinach (about 4 loosely packed cups)

Kosher salt

¼ cup Fermented Chile Sauce

½ cup finely grated Parmesan cheese

IN A pot of boiling salted water, cook the spaghetti until al dente. Drain, saving about 1 cup of the pasta water.

MEANWHILE, IN a medium skillet, heat the olive oil over medium-low heat. Add the garlic and cook, stirring, until lightly golden brown, 2 to 3 minutes. Add the mint and basil and cook until they start to wilt, about 30 seconds. Add the spinach, season with salt, and cook, tossing with tongs, until just wilted, about 2 minutes. Add the drained spaghetti to the pan along with a splash of pasta water and toss to emulsify the oil and water, adding more water if needed.

DIVIDE THE spaghetti and spinach among serving bowls. Top each bowl of pasta with a big spoonful of chile sauce, sprinkle with Parmesan, and serve.

Meat
&
Poultry

Chicken Salad
WITH ROASTED BABY VEGETABLES AND SWEET AND SPICY VINAIGRETTE

MAKES 4 SERVINGS

Make this chicken salad whenever you have some leftover roast chicken (perhaps after making the recipe on page 290), or when you see a bounty of baby vegetables at the farmers market, which usually happens in the early summer, then again in the early fall. (In between baby vegetable harvests, you can just cut larger produce into small pieces.) I love roasting turnips and radishes, which mellows out the vegetables' spiciness and makes them sweet and creamy. When carving chicken for a salad, I like to dice the breast meat and shred the leg meat, which gives you two different textures.

─── THE TAKEAWAY ───

Here's a great example of how to turn a condiment into a vinaigrette. I begin with a sweet and spicy sauce (which I also use in the grilled shrimp recipe on page 305), then whisk in some more acid and oil. You can take this same approach to other thicker sauces, including aioli and barbecue sauce.

─── SWEET AND SPICY SAUCE ───

MAKES 2 CUPS

- 2 tablespoons extra-virgin olive oil
- 3 large garlic cloves, finely chopped
- 1½ tablespoons finely chopped ginger
- 2 teaspoons kosher salt
- ½ cup plus 2 tablespoons honey
- 1½ cups white wine vinegar
- 2 red finger chiles, finely chopped (with seeds)
- 1 teaspoon red pepper flakes
- ½ cup Fermented Chile Sauce (page 252)

IN A small saucepan, heat the olive oil over low heat. Add the garlic, ginger, and salt and cook, stirring, until softened, 2 to 3 minutes. Add the honey and vinegar, bring to a boil, and cook until the liquid has reduced by half. Turn off the heat and add the chiles, red pepper flakes, and chile sauce. Transfer to a storage container and refrigerate for up to 1 month.

─── SWEET AND SPICY VINAIGRETTE ───

MAKES ¾ CUP

- ⅓ cup plus 1 tablespoon Sweet and Spicy Sauce
- ¼ cup extra-virgin olive oil
- ¼ cup fresh lemon juice
- 1½ teaspoons kosher salt

COMBINE ALL ingredients in a bowl and whisk until combined. The vinaigrette can be made up to 1 day ahead and refrigerated until ready to use.

CONTINUES ➡

─────── ROASTED BABY VEGETABLES ───────

8 baby turnips, peeled and cut into 4 wedges each; or 1 cup diced turnips

6 baby ball or globe radishes, cut into 4 wedges each

4 baby carrots, peeled and halved lengthwise; or 1 cup diced carrot

6 breakfast radishes, halved lengthwise

3 tablespoons extra-virgin olive oil

Kosher salt

Freshly ground black pepper

PREHEAT THE oven to 375°F and place a wire rack inside a rimmed baking sheet. In a large bowl, toss the vegetables with the olive oil and season with salt and pepper. Scatter on the wire rack and roast, tossing once or twice, until crisp-tender, 15 to 25 minutes (cooking time will vary depending on the size of the vegetables).

─────── FOR SERVING ───────

1 rotisserie or roast chicken

Roasted Baby Vegetables

8 breakfast radishes, thinly sliced

¾ cup Sweet and Spicy Vinaigrette

5 ounces mesclun salad mix

REMOVE THE legs and thighs from the chicken and shred the meat. Cut the breasts off the chicken and dice the meat.

IN A large bowl, toss the chicken with the roasted vegetables, radishes, and vinaigrette. Divide the mesclun among four serving bowls and top with the chicken and vegetables. Serve.

Grilled and Glazed Butterflied Chicken

WITH CORN, TOMATOES, AND JALAPEÑOS

MAKES 4 SERVINGS

Because I grew up a city kid on Manhattan's Upper West Side, it was a treat whenever my family would get invited to someone's country house in the summer. My father would always grill a chicken on those weekends, and because he didn't have a lot of live-fire cooking experience, he'd inevitably end up burning parts of the bird—which I loved. Even today, I'm not afraid to deeply char chicken parts and other grilled meats. I love the bitterness it adds, especially when paired with a sweet barbecue sauce.

This recipe is about as summery as it gets: a juicy, glazy grilled chicken, brushed with a classically flavored barbecue sauce alongside a grill-kissed corn and tomato salad. And it's simple enough to cook at any beach house or weekend rental.

THE TAKEAWAY

When grilling and glazing a whole chicken, the key is to start the bird over lower heat to render some of the fat between the skin and the meat; otherwise, the fat can wash away the glaze and you won't get the crispy coating you want. Once the chicken is about two-thirds of the way to being cooked to my desired temperature, I'll move it to the hot side of the grill and turn it frequently, brushing it with glaze every time I flip it, until it's deeply glazed and crispy all over.

DRY-BRINED BUTTERFLIED CHICKEN

One 4- to 5-pound whole chicken

Kosher salt

USING KITCHEN shears, remove the backbone from the chicken by cutting down each side of the spine (discard the spine or save it for making stock). Flatten the chicken by placing it skin side up on a cutting board and pressing firmly on the breastbone. Cut a 2-inch slash in the thickest part of each leg. Transfer to a wire rack set in a baking sheet. Generously season the chicken all over with salt and refrigerate, uncovered, for up to 24 hours.

BARBECUE SAUCE

MAKES 2 CUPS

1 tablespoon sunflower oil

1 small onion, thinly sliced

2 garlic cloves

1 tablespoon kosher salt

1½ tablespoons ground cumin

1 tablespoon sweet smoked paprika

1 tablespoon chipotle powder

¾ teaspoon yellow mustard seeds

1 tablespoon water

4 cups apple cider vinegar

1 cup canned tomato puree

¾ cup maple syrup

½ cup packed dark brown sugar

IN A medium saucepan, heat the oil over medium-low heat. Add the onion, garlic, and salt and cook, stirring occasionally, until softened, about 7 minutes. Add the cumin, paprika, chipotle, mustard seeds, and water and cook for 2 to 3 minutes. Add the vinegar, tomato puree, maple syrup, and brown sugar, bring to a boil, and reduce until thick like a sauce. Season to taste with salt and more vinegar, if needed, and let cool. The barbecue sauce can be made ahead and refrigerated for up to 2 weeks.

CONTINUES ➡

— GRILL-ROASTED TOMATOES AND CORN —

2 beefsteak tomatoes, halved crosswise

4 ears corn, in their husks

PREPARE A two-stage grill with low and high heat sides: On a charcoal grill, spread 1 chimney of coals over half of the grate and scatter a few coals over the other side. On a gas grill, heat half of the burners to high heat and half to low. Clean and oil the grill.

PLACE THE tomatoes, cut side down, in a small skillet or baking sheet. Place the tomatoes over the cool side of the grill, close the grill, and roast until the tomatoes are softened and the skin begins to loosen, about 1 hour. When cool enough to handle, peel the tomatoes and coarsely chop.

GRILL THE corn over the high heat side of the grill, turning frequently, until the husk is charred all over and the corn kernels are beginning to brown, about 15 minutes. When cool enough to handle, shuck the corn and cut the kernels off the cob into a bowl.

—————— FOR SERVING ——————

Dry-Brined Butterflied Chicken

Barbecue Sauce

1 tablespoon extra-virgin olive oil

1 tablespoon unsalted butter

1 jalapeño chile, finely chopped (with seeds)

Grill-Roasted Tomatoes and Corn

2 tablespoons chopped savory

2 tablespoons chopped parsley

Kosher salt

PLACE THE chicken, skin side down, on the cooler side of the grill with its legs facing toward the hotter side. Cover the grill (if using a charcoal grill, leave the vents on the top and bottom open). Cook until an instant-read thermometer inserted into the thickest part of the breast reads 130°F, 20 to 30 minutes. Turn the chicken over and brush the top side with some barbecue sauce. Using two sets of tongs, rotate the chicken over onto the hot side of the grill, skin side down. Press the chicken down firmly and brush the underside with barbecue sauce. Grill the chicken, flipping it every 2 minutes and brushing it with sauce a couple of times, until it is charred all over, well glazed in sauce, and an instant-read thermometer inserted into the thickest part of the leg reads 160°F, 10 to 15 minutes. Transfer to a cutting board and let rest 10 minutes before carving.

MEANWHILE, IN a large skillet, heat the olive oil and butter over medium-high heat. When the butter has melted, add the jalapeño and cook, stirring, until soft, about 1 minute. Add the corn and sauté for 1 minute. Stir in the tomatoes, turn off the heat, and stir in the savory and parsley. Season to taste with salt and transfer to a serving bowl.

CARVE THE chicken and serve, family-style, alongside the corn and tomatoes.

Grilled Chicken Thighs

WITH CAROLINA RICE, PEAS, AND CARROT BARBECUE SAUCE

MAKES 4 SERVINGS

This dish started with the creamy, risotto-like rice, which is an excellent side or vegetarian main course (if you use vegetable stock) on its own. I use Carolina Gold rice, a long-grain variety that has been grown in the American Southeast since the colonial days. I cook it like pasta in plenty of simmering liquid, but use a seaweed-infused chicken stock instead of water to pack it with as much flavor as possible. The carrot barbecue sauce that glazes the chicken thighs is a riff on the Carrot-Hazelnut Romesco (which you'll find on page 54), but made without nuts and with the addition of coffee beans, which add a deep, toasty flavor.

THE TAKEAWAY ───

Any time I'm cooking something in liquid, whether it's water or stock, I treat it as an opportunity to impart more flavor to a dish. I often use kombu as an infusion because the dried kelp adds lots of umami without making the liquid taste seaweed-y. You can play around with the ingredients you use for your infusion, but typically you want some herbs, citrus peels, and a touch of heat from aromatic chiles.

─── PICKLED CARROTS ───

MAKES ABOUT 2 CUPS

1 pound carrots, peeled and cut into sticks (long enough to fit your jar)

1 teaspoon coriander seeds

1 teaspoon fennel seeds

½ teaspoon cumin seeds

½ teaspoon yellow mustard seeds

1 small dried red chile

1 bay leaf

2 cups apple cider vinegar

1 cup sugar

1 tablespoon kosher salt

PLACE THE carrots in a sterilized pint-size jar and add the spices, chile, and bay leaf. In a small saucepan, bring the vinegar, sugar, and salt to a boil. Pour over the carrots and let cool to room temperature. Seal the jar and refrigerate for at least 2 days before using.

─── CARROT BARBECUE SAUCE ───

MAKES ABOUT 2½ CUPS

3 cups carrot juice

3 cups white wine vinegar

1¾ cups sugar

3 tablespoons ground coriander

2 tablespoons ground cumin

1½ tablespoons sweet smoked paprika

1 tablespoon red pepper flakes

1½ teaspoons mustard powder

¼ cup crushed coffee beans

2 tablespoons sunflower or vegetable oil

½ medium white onion, thinly sliced

5 garlic cloves, thinly sliced

2 medium carrots, peeled and thinly sliced

1½ tablespoons kosher salt

Strips of zest from 1 medium lemon

IN A medium saucepan, combine the carrot juice, vinegar, sugar, spices, and coffee beans. Bring to a boil, then turn off the heat, cover the pot, and let steep for 30 minutes. Strain through a fine-mesh strainer.

CONTINUES ➡

CLEAN OUT the saucepan, add the sunflower oil, and heat over medium-low heat. Add the onions, garlic, carrots, and salt and cook, stirring frequently, until the onions are translucent, about 5 minutes. Add the strained carrot juice mixture, bring to a simmer, and cook until reduced by half. Transfer to a blender along with the lemon zest and blend until very smooth. The sauce can be made a few days ahead and refrigerated until ready to use.

INFUSED CHICKEN STOCK

MAKES ABOUT 6 CUPS

6¼ cups chicken stock

Two 6-by-8-inch sheets kombu

Strips of zest from 1 large orange

Strips of zest from 1 medium lemon

2 Thai green chiles, split lengthwise

1½ tablespoons thyme leaves

1 tablespoon kosher salt

IN A medium saucepan, combine the stock and kombu and bring to a boil. Combine the remaining ingredients in a heatproof bowl and add the hot stock and kombu. Cover and let steep for 30 minutes. Strain through a fine-mesh strainer, pressing on the solids to extract as much liquid as possible.

CAROLINA RICE

6 cups Infused Chicken Stock

1 cup Carolina Gold long-grain rice (we use Anson Mills brand)

IN A medium saucepan, bring the stock to a boil. Lower the heat to a simmer, add the rice, and cook until the rice is tender with a little bit of bite, about 8 minutes. Drain the rice, reserving about 2 cups stock.

FOR SERVING

8 bone-in, skin-on chicken thighs

Kosher salt and freshly ground black pepper

Carrot Barbecue Sauce

2 cups cooked Carolina Rice, plus reserved chicken stock

½ cup English peas (blanched if fresh)

¼ cup thinly sliced ramp bulbs or scallion whites

1 cup sliced ramp leaves or scallion greens

1 tablespoon finely grated lemon zest

½ lemon, for juicing

¼ cup chopped Pickled Carrots

2 tablespoons chopped parsley

2 tablespoons thinly sliced mint

Extra-virgin olive oil

PREPARE A medium-hot grill or preheat a grill pan over medium-high heat. Clean and oil the grate. Season the chicken with salt and pepper and grill, skin side down, until golden brown, about 5 minutes. Turn the chicken over and brush the top with the barbecue sauce. Continue grilling and brushing with sauce, turning the chicken over every few minutes, until nicely charred and glazed and an instant-read thermometer inserted into the thickest part of the thigh reads 165°F, 15 to 20 minutes longer. Transfer to a platter and let rest.

WHILE THE chicken rests, combine the rice and 1 cup reserved stock in a large saucepan. Bring the stock to a simmer and add the peas, ramp whites and leaves, lemon zest, and a squeeze of lemon juice. Add the pickled carrots, parsley, and mint and season to taste with salt. Transfer the rice to a platter, top with the chicken, drizzle with olive oil, and serve.

Grilled Hanger Steak
WITH SPICE-ROASTED ZUCCHINI AND LIME YOGURT

MAKES 4 SERVINGS

In order to stand up to the big flavors of spice-rubbed steaks, I coat zucchini in a thick, spicy paste made with pureed dried chiles, and cool the whole dish off with a tangy lime yogurt sauce. Not in the mood for steak? The zucchini alone will make an excellent side dish, and the technique can be used with other varieties of summer squash.

THE TAKEAWAY
Because there's only one per cow, hanger steak (aka butcher's steak) is a prized cut that you usually only find at a butcher shop or a well-stocked meat counter. It's worth seeking out, though, because it has a pronounced beefy flavor and is usually priced well below rib-eyes, strips, and other grilling steaks. Whether you're cooking the steak over a grill or in a pan, think of it like a sausage: You need to turn the long, round cut frequently—about every minute or so—to ensure even browning on all sides.

SPICE-ROASTED ZUCCHINI

- 1 ancho chile, stem and seeds removed
- 2 guajillo chiles, stems and seeds removed
- 1 teaspoon coriander seeds
- ½ teaspoon caraway seeds
- ½ teaspoon cumin seeds
- ¼ cup Shallot Confit (page 250), drained
- 1 tablespoon Aleppo pepper
- 4 teaspoons maple syrup
- 4 teaspoons fresh lemon juice
- 1 teaspoon kosher salt
- ¼ cup sunflower or vegetable oil
- 2 medium zucchini or other summer squash, cut crosswise into 1-inch-thick rounds

PREHEAT THE oven to 400°F and set a wire rack inside a rimmed baking sheet. Place the dried chiles in a heatproof bowl and cover with boiling water. Cover the bowl with plastic and let sit for 30 minutes, then drain.

IN A small skillet, toast the coriander, caraway, and cumin seeds until fragrant and a shade darker, about 3 minutes. Finely grind the spices in a grinder or with a mortar and pestle.

IN A blender, combine the rehydrated chiles, ground spices, shallot confit, Aleppo pepper, maple syrup, lemon juice, and salt. Puree until smooth. With the machine running, slowly drizzle in the sunflower oil until emulsified.

IN A large bowl, toss the zucchini with the chile marinade until well coated. Scrape the zucchini onto the rack and roast until tender, 15 to 20 minutes.

CONTINUES ➡

LIME YOGURT

1 cup Greek yogurt

2 tablespoons extra-virgin olive oil

2 garlic cloves, finely grated on a Microplane

2 teaspoons finely grated lime zest

2 teaspoons fresh lime juice

1 teaspoon kosher salt

COMBINE ALL ingredients in a bowl and blend with a fork until well mixed. Refrigerate until ready to use. The yogurt can be made up to 1 day ahead.

FOR SERVING

One 1½- to 2-pound hanger steak, trimmed

Oil from Garlic Confit (page 112) or extra-virgin olive oil

Kosher salt and freshly ground black pepper

Lime Yogurt

Spice-Roasted Zucchini

Extra-virgin olive oil

2 tablespoons chopped parsley

2 tablespoons chopped mint

Flaky sea salt

PREPARE A hot grill or preheat a grill pan over high heat. Rub the steak with the garlic oil and generously season with kosher salt and pepper. Grill the steak, turning frequently, until well charred all over and an instant-read thermometer inserted into the center reads 130°F for medium-rare, about 10 minutes. Transfer to a cutting board and let rest for 5 minutes before carving across the grain into thick slices.

SPREAD ¼ cup lime yogurt on the bottom of four plates. Top with the steak and scatter the zucchini around. Drizzle with olive oil, sprinkle with the parsley, mint, and flaky salt, and serve.

Roasted Chicken Thighs

WITH BEANS, POTATOES, AND HONEY-BUTTER HOT SAUCE

MAKES 4 SERVINGS

This is the perfect recipe for a weeknight dinner as you can make it start to finish in under an hour (especially if your oven has enough space to roast everything at once). I finish the dish with a drizzle of honey-butter hot sauce and a sprinkle of blue cheese, my nod to Buffalo chicken wings, one of my favorite comfort foods from college.

———— THE TAKEAWAY ————

The honey-butter hot sauce is very similar to the orangey glaze that covers Buffalo wings, but I add some sweetness to the hot-and-sour flavor with honey. The sauce is also great on roasted potatoes, cauliflower, and (trust me) swordfish. Or brush it on some chicken wings and roast them to make your own Buffalo-style snack.

———— HONEY-BUTTER HOT SAUCE ————

¼ cup Tabasco hot sauce (or Red Hot Sauce, page 130)

2 tablespoons honey

1 teaspoon kosher salt

6 tablespoons cold unsalted butter, cut into cubes

IN A small saucepan, heat the hot sauce, honey, and salt over medium heat. When the liquid is about to simmer, turn off the heat and whisk in the butter, a few pieces at a time, until emulsified. Keep warm until ready to use.

—— ROASTED CHICKEN AND VEGETABLES ——

8 bone-in, skin-on chicken thighs

Extra-virgin olive oil

Kosher salt and freshly ground black pepper

1 pound baby potatoes

2 cups mixed summer beans (such as green and yellow wax beans and Romano beans), trimmed and cut into 2-inch pieces

IF YOUR oven is large enough, you can roast the chicken and both vegetables at the same time. If it isn't, roast the chicken and potatoes first, then put the green beans in the oven when the potatoes are finished.

PREHEAT THE oven to 400°F and place a wire rack inside a rimmed baking sheet. Brush the skin side of the chicken with olive oil and season with salt and pepper. Place the chicken on the rack and roast until an instant-read thermometer inserted into the center reads 165°F, 35 to 45 minutes.

MEANWHILE, IN a bowl, toss the potatoes with 1 tablespoon olive oil and season with salt and pepper. Transfer to a rimmed baking sheet and roast until golden brown and tender, 20 to 30 minutes (depending on the size of the potatoes). In the same bowl, toss the beans with 1 tablespoon olive oil and season with salt and pepper. Transfer to a rimmed baking sheet and roast until just tender, about 10 minutes.

─────── FOR SERVING ───────

Roast Chicken and Vegetables

Honey-Butter Hot Sauce

2 tablespoons chopped parsley

1 tablespoon chopped tarragon

Kosher salt and freshly ground black pepper

2 tablespoons fresh lemon juice

1 tablespoon extra-virgin olive oil

½ cup crumbled blue cheese (optional)

PREHEAT THE broiler. Brush the chicken liberally with hot sauce and broil until the skin is crisp and the sauce caramelizes, about 2 minutes.

IN A bowl, toss the roasted vegetables with the parsley and tarragon. Season with salt and pepper and add the lemon juice and olive oil. Divide the vegetables among four plates and top with the chicken. Drizzle some of the hot sauce over and top with the blue cheese, if using. Serve.

Grilled Pork Chops

WITH SWEET AND SOUR GLAZE

MAKES 4 SERVINGS

When I grill pork chops, chicken, and other glaze-friendly meats, I like to build up a thick layer of the glaze, which becomes sticky with little crunchy bits of caramelized sugar. To do this, I build a pretty hot fire and turn and brush the meat frequently. It's OK to let the occasional flame kiss the meat as it grills, but if your grill is flaring up a bunch (which is common with fattier cuts of pork, especially when they're dripping with glaze), keep moving the meat around the grill away from the flame. Leave the spray bottle alone; water will just create smoke that makes the meat taste sooty.

These sweet-and-sour chops will pair nicely with lots of vegetable sides from this book, including Roasted Sunchokes with Paprika Oil and Lemon-Oregano Vinaigrette (page 186), Fresh-Corn Polenta with Butter and Herbs (page 156), Grilled Broccoli with Orange Aioli and Pistachio Vinaigrette (page 158), and Pan-Roasted Asparagus with Spring Onions and Lemon-Mayo Dressing (page 150).

THE TAKEAWAY

I think it's a waste to throw away a marinade after it's done flavoring meat, so I'll turn it into a sauce or glaze—or in this case, both. (In addition to this recipe, I use the technique in the pot roast on page 289). One thing to remember when creating a double-duty marinade is to hold back on the salt; otherwise the reduced glaze will be too salty.

---

1 tablespoon Dijon mustard

Finely grated zest of 1 medium orange

6 tablespoons fresh orange juice

½ cup fresh lemon juice

2 tablespoons maple syrup

2 teaspoons ground coriander

½ teaspoon hot smoked paprika

1 teaspoon ground cumin

2 teaspoons kosher salt, plus more for seasoning

1 tablespoon chopped oregano

1 teaspoon chopped thyme

4 bone-in pork chops (about 1 inch thick)

2 tablespoons extra-virgin olive oil

1 large white onion, halved and cut into ¼-inch slices

Flaky sea salt

IN A bowl, whisk together the mustard, orange zest, orange juice, lemon juice, maple syrup, coriander, paprika, cumin, kosher salt, oregano, and thyme. Transfer to a large resealable plastic bag, add the pork chops, and marinate in the refrigerator for 6 hours.

CONTINUES ➡

REMOVE THE pork chops from the marinade and pat dry. Strain the marinade and discard the solids. In a medium skillet, heat the olive oil over medium-high heat. Add the onions and sauté until they begin to soften and caramelize, 3 to 4 minutes. Add the marinade, bring the liquid to a boil, and reduce until glazy. Set aside about ½ cup of the glaze for brushing on the pork, and pour the rest into a bowl.

PREPARE A medium-hot grill or preheat a grill pan over medium-high heat. Season the pork chops with kosher salt and grill, turning once, until browned on both sides, about 3 minutes per side. Brush the pork chops with the reserved glaze and continue grilling, flipping, and glazing them every minute or two, until nicely charred and coated with glaze, about 4 minutes. The pork chops are done when an instant-read thermometer inserted near the bone registers 130°F. Transfer to a platter and spoon the onions and the glaze from the bowl over the pork. Sprinkle with flaky salt and serve.

Grilled Porterhouse Steak

WITH GRILLED MAITAKE MUSHROOMS AND SHALLOT BUTTER

MAKES 4 SERVINGS

I like making this recipe with different cuts of steak (especially a bone-in rib eye), but a double thick T-bone is the perfect size for four people. Both the T-bone and the porterhouse include a T-shaped rib bone that separates two steaks: a large strip and a smaller tenderloin. The only difference between the two is how much tenderloin meat you get (the por- terhouse offers a larger piece of tenderloin). You can make this recipe with either, of course. The perfect accompaniment for a beefy steak is earthy mush- rooms, which can be grilled at the same time, so this recipe can be made start to finish at the grill.

THE TAKEAWAY

When grilling thick cuts of meat (1½ inches or thicker), I like to grill the steak over low heat (or cook in a low oven) until it reaches a temperature about 20°F below my desired final temperature, then I blast the thing over a hot fire to give it a deeply charred crust. This is called a "reverse sear," and at a restaurant it allows cooks to "parcook" meat, then finish it to order. Because you're cooking the steak to a specific temperature, make sure you have a trusty instant-read thermometer—the reverse sear won't work on intuition alone.

One 24-ounce porterhouse or T-bone steak, about 2 inches thick

Kosher salt and freshly ground black pepper

Extra-virgin olive oil

8 garlic cloves, smashed and peeled

5 thyme sprigs, lightly bruised

½ cup (1 stick) unsalted butter

¼ cup finely chopped shallots

Two 8-ounce maitake mushrooms, halved through the stem

3 tablespoons fines herbes (equal parts finely chopped chervil, chives, parsley, and tarragon)

1 serrano chile, seeded and finely chopped

Flaky sea salt

Lemon wedge

LINE A baking dish with parchment paper. Season the steak generously with salt and pepper, drizzle with olive oil, and rub it all in. Drizzle some more olive oil on the parchment and scatter on half of the garlic and thyme. Place the steak on top, then add the remaining garlic and thyme on top of the steak. Let sit at room temperature for about 1 hour.

MEANWHILE, IN a small saucepan, melt the but- ter over low heat. Add the shallots and gently cook until they're translucent, 5 to 7 minutes. Turn off the heat.

PREPARE A two-stage grill with low and high heat sides: On a charcoal grill, spread 1 chimney of coals over half of the grate and scatter a few coals over the other side. On a gas grill, heat half of the burners to high heat and half to low. In a bowl, gently toss the mushrooms with about ¼ cup of the shallot butter (leave the shallots in the sauce- pan) and season with salt and pepper.

CONTINUES ➡

273

PLACE THE steak on the cooler side of the grill and cook, uncovered and turning occasionally, until an instant-read thermometer registers 105°F for rare, 115°F for medium-rare, or 125°F for medium. Transfer the steak to the hot side of the grill and cook, turning frequently, until charred all over, about 2 minutes total. Transfer the steak to a wire rack set over a plate, loosely cover with foil, and let rest for 10 minutes.

MEANWHILE, GRILL the mushrooms over the hot part of the grill, turning a few times, until lightly charred and beginning to soften, 3 to 4 minutes. Transfer to a serving plate and spoon the shallots and some of the remaining butter over. Sprinkle with the herbs, serrano, and flaky salt and squeeze a lemon wedge over.

TO SLICE the steak, cut the meat off both sides of the bone, leaving you with two large pieces of steak. Trim off any large pieces of excess fat, slice each steak across the grain, then rearrange the slices around the bone on a platter and serve with the mushrooms.

Lamb Rib Chops
WITH SWEET AND SPICY TOMATO COMPOTE AND HERBED BREADCRUMBS

MAKES 4 SERVINGS

This recipe was on one of our first Loring Place menus. I wanted to offer a great piece of grilled meat with an exceptional sauce, and the sweet, sour, and slightly smoky tomato compote was just the thing. A handful of breadcrumbs adds both texture and the herby flavors you need to tie everything together.

——— HERBED BREADCRUMBS ———

MAKES 1 CUP

1 cup panko

¼ cup extra-virgin olive oil

2 tablespoons finely chopped mint

1 tablespoon finely chopped thyme

Kosher salt and freshly ground black pepper

IN A skillet, combine the panko and olive oil and cook over medium-low heat, stirring frequently, until the panko is golden brown. Transfer to a bowl and let cool, then stir in the mint and thyme and season to taste with salt and pepper. The breadcrumbs can be stored in an airtight container for up to 3 days.

——— FOR SERVING ———

1 bunch (16 to 20 stems) broccoli rabe

Four 6- to 8-ounce double lamb rib chops

Kosher salt and freshly ground black pepper

1 cup Tomato Compote (page 170)

Herbed Breadcrumbs

BRING A large saucepan of salted water to a boil and prepare an ice bath. Trim the bottom inch or so off the end of the broccoli rabe stems. Working in batches, blanch the broccoli rabe until bright green and crisp-tender, 2 to 3 minutes. Transfer to the ice bath to cool, then drain and lightly squeeze dry.

PREPARE A medium-hot grill or preheat a grill pan over medium-high heat. Season the lamb chops with salt and pepper and grill, turning every minute or so, until cooked to the desired temperature, 8 to 10 minutes total for medium-rare. About halfway through cooking the lamb, grill the broccoli rabe until lightly charred, 2 to 4 minutes. Transfer the lamb to a platter and let rest for 5 minutes before serving.

SPOON SOME of the tomato compote on four plates. Place a lamb chop on top and sprinkle with some of the breadcrumbs. Serve with the broccoli rabe on the side.

——— THE TAKEAWAY ———

I frequently use crispy breadcrumbs to add crunch to a variety of dishes, especially salads, pastas, and vegetables. They're also a great way to add texture to meaty dishes, like these lamb chops. Instead of sprinkling the finished dish with herbs, I add them to the fried breadcrumbs—here I use lamb-loving mint and thyme, but you can tweak this recipe with any kind of herbs to complement the meat they're accompanying.

277

Grilled Pork Chops
WITH BRAISED CABBAGE

MAKES 4 SERVINGS

I use not one but two glazes for these deeply savory grilled chops. While this may sound like overkill, each glaze adds something unique: The simple red wine vinegar glaze helps you build a deeply caramelized coating while you grill the pork, and a finishing drizzle of the pomegranate glaze adds the fruit's sweet-tart brightness that bridges the pork with the buttery braised cabbage.

——— THE TAKEAWAY ———

Braised cabbage is often a one- or two-note dish, and not that exciting to me. So to add a lot more complexity (while avoiding extra knife work), I like to finely chop a bunch of aromatics in a food processor, then cook them down with some kombu-infused water to create a very flavorful base for braising the cabbage. You can use this technique for any kind of hearty green, and it works equally well with braised vegetables, including leeks, onions, and fennel.

——— BRINED PORK CHOPS ———

4 cups water
½ cup kosher salt
¼ cup packed light brown sugar
Two 4-by-6-inch sheets kombu

1 rosemary sprig
2 garlic cloves, smashed and peeled
4 bone-in pork chops (about 1 inch thick)

IN A medium saucepan, bring all ingredients except the pork chops to a simmer. Turn off the heat and let cool to room temperature. Place the pork in a large resealable bag, add the brine, and seal the bag. Refrigerate at least 4 hours or up to 8 hours.

——— POMEGRANATE GLAZE ———

1 cup pure pomegranate juice
¼ cup sugar
1 teaspoon kosher salt

3 tablespoons fresh lemon juice
¼ teaspoon coarsely ground black pepper

IN A medium saucepan, combine the pomegranate juice, sugar, and salt. Bring to a boil and reduce until thick and glazy. Turn off the heat and stir in the lemon juice and pepper. The glaze can be made ahead and refrigerated for a day or two.

——— RED WINE VINEGAR GLAZE ———

1¼ cups red wine vinegar

¼ cup sugar

IN A medium saucepan, combine the vinegar and sugar. Bring to a boil and reduce until thick and glazy. Turn off the heat. The glaze can be made ahead and refrigerated for a day or two.

CONTINUES ➡

278

—————— BRAISED CABBAGE ——————

1 Granny Smith apple, quartered, cored, and sliced crosswise into ⅛-inch slices

¼ cup white wine vinegar

1½ cups water

Three 4-by-6-inch sheets kombu

½ cup extra-virgin olive oil

1 medium or 2 small fennel bulbs, cored and thinly sliced

6 scallions, roughly chopped

One 2-inch piece ginger, peeled and thinly sliced

1 jalapeño chile, seeded and roughly chopped

1 tablespoon sugar

Kosher salt

½ head savoy cabbage, cored and chopped into 1-inch squares

4 tablespoons unsalted butter

2 teaspoons finely chopped rosemary

2 tablespoons finely chopped parsley

IN A small bowl, cover the apple slices with the vinegar and let sit while you make the rest of the cabbage.

IN A medium saucepan, bring 1 cup water to a boil. Turn off the heat, add the kombu, and cover the pot. Let sit for 30 minutes. Remove the kombu, squeezing out as much liquid as possible.

IN A food processor, combine the kombu-infused water, olive oil, fennel, scallions, ginger, jalapeño, sugar, and 4 teaspoons salt. Pulse until finely chopped. Transfer to a large saucepan and cook over medium heat until all of the liquid has evaporated, 10 to 15 minutes. Add the cabbage, butter, and remaining ½ cup water. Cover the pan and cook over medium heat for 15 minutes, then uncover and continue cooking, stirring occasionally, until the cabbage is very tender and glazy, about 15 minutes longer. Turn off the heat. Drain the apples and add to the pan. Stir in the rosemary and parsley and season to taste with salt.

—————— FOR SERVING ——————

Brined Pork Chops

Pomegranate Glaze

Red Wine Vinegar Glaze

¼ cup pomegranate seeds (optional)

Flaky sea salt

Braised Cabbage

PREPARE A medium-hot grill or preheat a grill pan over medium-high heat. Remove the pork from the brine and pat dry with paper towels. Grill the pork chops, turning a few times, until browned on both sides, about 5 minutes. Brush the chops all over with the vinegar glaze and continue grilling, flipping and brushing with glaze every couple of minutes, until well coated with glaze and charred in spots, 5 to 7 minutes longer (the pork is cooked through when an instant-read thermometer inserted into the center reads 140°F).

TRANSFER THE pork to a serving platter and drizzle some of the pomegranate glaze over. Sprinkle with pomegranate seeds (if using) and flaky salt. Serve with the braised cabbage.

Herb-Marinated Roasted Lamb Shoulder

MAKES 6 TO 8 SERVINGS

Here's a super-easy lamb you can slowly roast on a Sunday afternoon. The herby marinade is thick and almost pesto-like and becomes a light crust as the lamb slowly cooks. You can serve this lamb with many of the side dishes in the vegetable chapter, but my favorite accompaniments are the Crispy Salt and Pepper Potatoes (page 191), Citrus-Glazed Carrots with Pickled Chiles and Lime (page 194), Glazed Sweet Potatoes with Yogurt and Dill (page 185), and Roasted Brussels Sprouts with Avocado and Apple (page 175).

THE TAKEAWAY

The slow-roasting technique I use for fish (see page 309) also works great for large cuts of meat. The long cooking time helps render the fat and break down the meat to become more tender, while the low temperature prevents it from drying out, yielding results that are similar to braised meat, but a little lighter in texture. This roasting method works especially well with pork shoulder and short ribs.

4 cups loosely packed parsley leaves

1 cup loosely packed sage leaves

½ cup rosemary needles

2 dried chiles de arbol or 1 teaspoon red pepper flakes

2 tablespoons finely grated lemon zest

3 cloves Garlic Confit (page 112) or 1 tablespoon chopped fresh garlic

1 tablespoon kosher salt

½ cup white wine

½ cup extra-virgin olive oil

One 3- to 4-pound boneless lamb shoulder, tied in 2-inch intervals

IN A food processor, combine the parsley, sage, rosemary, chiles, lemon zest, garlic confit, and salt. Pulse until finely chopped, then, with the machine running, slowly pour in the wine and olive oil; puree until smooth. Place the lamb in a large resealable bag and add the marinade. Seal and make sure the marinade is covering all of the lamb. Refrigerate for at least 8 hours.

PREHEAT THE oven to 250°F and place a wire rack or roasting rack inside a roasting pan. Add enough water to cover the bottom of the pan. Remove the lamb from the marinade and place on the rack, leaving the meat covered in as much marinade as possible. Roast the lamb until an instant-read thermometer inserted into the center reads 130°F for medium, 2½ to 3 hours. Transfer to a cutting board and let rest for at least 15 minutes before slicing and serving.

Pan-Roasted Chicken Breasts
WITH PAN JUS AND WARM POTATO SALAD

MAKES 4 SERVINGS

This juicy pan chicken with a creamy potato salad works pretty much any time of the year, and it's a pretty quick dinner. The warm potato salad is equally good served cold, and gifts you some leftover whole-grain mustard mayo, a versatile marriage of two condiments that you'll find yourself spreading on sandwiches, spooning over vegetables, or using as the base for a creamy salad dressing (just add a squeeze of lemon juice and you're all set).

——— WHOLE-GRAIN MUSTARD MAYO ———

MAKES ABOUT ¾ CUP

½ cup mayonnaise (preferably House Mayonnaise, page 150)

¼ cup whole-grain mustard, store-bought or homemade (page 62)

2 tablespoons Dijon mustard

3 tablespoons apple cider vinegar

1½ teaspoons kosher salt

IN A medium bowl, combine all of the ingredients and stir until well mixed. The mayonnaise can be made ahead and refrigerated for up to 2 weeks.

——— POTATO SALAD ———

1½ pounds fingerling or other small potatoes

2 tablespoons kosher salt

⅓ cup Whole-Grain Mustard Mayo

4 radishes, thinly sliced

2 tablespoons chopped tarragon

2 tablespoons parsley leaves

1 jalapeño chile, thinly sliced (with seeds)

PLACE THE potatoes in a medium saucepan, cover with 3 inches of water, and add the salt.

CONTINUES ➡

THE TAKEAWAY

This recipe teaches you how to make a basic pan jus, which is one of the quickest ways to create a sauce for any manner of pan-seared meat. The process is simple: Cook a piece of meat in the pan, then pour off most of the fat. Add some aromatics (shallots, garlic, onions, etc.) to the pan and deglaze with liquid (wine, dry vermouth, and stock are great), making sure to scrape up any fond (the browned bits stuck to the bottom of the pan). About that fond: It's hard to build up a fond in a nonstick or cast-iron skillet, so this is the time to use your stickiest stainless steel. For extra flavor, I like to add some herbs while the sauce is reducing. While many folks will finish a pan sauce with a knob of butter, I add lemon juice and honey to lighten and brighten it up.

Bring the water to a boil, reduce the heat to medium-low, and simmer until the potatoes are tender, 15 to 20 minutes (cooking time will vary depending on the size of the potatoes). Drain the potatoes and let cool for a couple of minutes. In a large bowl, toss the potatoes with the mustard mayo until coated. Add the radishes, tarragon, parsley, and jalapeño and gently toss.

————————— FOR SERVING —————————

4 boneless, skin-on chicken breast halves

Kosher salt and freshly ground black pepper

1 tablespoon vegetable oil

2 tablespoons finely chopped shallot

1 garlic clove, finely grated on a Microplane (or similar grater)

1 cup dry white wine

1 teaspoon chopped rosemary

2 thyme sprigs

4 teaspoons honey

1 tablespoon fresh lemon juice

Potato Salad

PREHEAT THE oven to 450°F. Pat the chicken dry and season with salt and pepper. In a large ovenproof skillet, heat the oil over medium-high heat until it shimmers. Add the chicken, skin side down, and cook, occasionally rocking it with a spatula to make sure all of the skin comes in contact with the pan, until the skin is deeply golden brown and crisp, about 6 minutes. Flip the chicken over and transfer the pan to the oven. Roast until an instant-read thermometer inserted into the center of the breasts reads 155°F, 9 to 12 minutes. Transfer the chicken to a cutting board.

POUR OFF all but 1 tablespoon of the fat from the pan and place over medium-low heat. Add the shallot, garlic, and 1 teaspoon salt and cook until softened, 2 to 3 minutes. Add the wine, rosemary, and thyme and bring the liquid to a boil, scraping up any browned bits from the bottom of the skillet with a wooden spoon. Continue cooking until the liquid is reduced by half, then turn off the heat and stir in the honey and lemon juice.

SLICE EACH chicken breast into three or four pieces, then transfer to serving plates. Divide the potato salad among the plates, drizzle the pan sauce over the chicken, and serve.

Raisin-Stuffed Pork Loin

MAKES 8 SERVINGS

The herby stuffing for this pork is based on one my father and I developed over the years—first for leg of lamb and later pork loin—that is also great in chicken and game birds. I first made this dish for a dinner to benefit Cookies for Kids' Cancer, a charity I care very much about. The roast goes great with a host of other vegetable sides, including Glazed Sweet Potatoes with Yogurt and Dill (page 185), Grilled Asparagus with Broken Chile Sauce and Potato Ribbons (page 145), Grilled Chard Stems with Lemon-Balsamic Vinaigrette (page 169), and Roasted Acorn Squash with Spicy Granola and Apple Gastrique (page 188).

—————— RAISIN STUFFING ——————

¾ cup yellow raisins

¾ cup dry white wine

2 tablespoons white wine vinegar

2 tablespoons extra-virgin olive oil

2 garlic cloves, finely chopped

2 tablespoons finely chopped parsley

1 tablespoon finely chopped sage

1 tablespoon finely chopped rosemary

1 tablespoon finely grated lemon zest

1 serrano chile, seeded and finely chopped

½ cup coarse fresh breadcrumbs

1 teaspoon kosher salt

IN A small saucepan, combine the raisins, wine, and vinegar. Bring to a boil, cover, and remove from the heat. Let the raisins sit for 1 hour, then drain, reserving the liquid.

IN A small skillet, heat the olive oil and garlic over medium-low heat until the garlic is soft, 3 to 4 minutes. Transfer the garlic and oil to a bowl and add the raisins and remaining ingredients; stir to combine. The stuffing should be moist (but not soggy); add some of the reserved raisin liquid if needed.

—————— FOR SERVING ——————

One 3-pound boneless center-cut pork loin

Raisin Stuffing

Kosher salt and freshly ground black pepper

3 tablespoons extra-virgin olive oil

Flaky sea salt

PREHEAT THE oven to 300°F. Using a long, thin-bladed knife (such as a butcher's knife), start cutting a 1½-inch-wide tunnel into the center of the loin from one end. Repeat with the other side so there's a single tunnel through the center of the pork. Stand the pork on end, holding it in one hand, and begin pushing the stuffing into the pork with your fingers. Turn the pork over and continue filling it with stuffing until it won't take any more. Set the pork on its side and gently roll it under your hands to even out the stuffing while smoothing out any large lumps. Tie the pork in 1-inch intervals and season all over with kosher salt and pepper.

IN A large ovenproof skillet, heat the oil over medium heat. Sear the pork on all sides until golden brown. Transfer the pan to the oven and bake, rotating the pork every 15 minutes, until an instant-read thermometer inserted into the middle of the stuffing reads 130°F, about 45 minutes total. Transfer the pork to a platter and loosely cover with foil. Let rest for 20 minutes, then remove the string. Sprinkle with flaky salt and pepper, carve into 1-inch medallions, and serve.

CONTINUES ➡

THE TAKEAWAY

It's not hard to fill the pork loin with stuffing, but it takes a bit of care to get an even stuffing. Use a long meat carver (if you have one) or a butcher's knife to make a tunnel through the center of the roast, then stretch it into a bigger cavity using your fingers or a (very clean!) sharpening steel. Stand the roast on its end and jam in as much stuffing as it will hold, turn the roast over, and repeat; you'll know when it can't take any more stuffing. Then, in order to get an even tube of stuffing down the center of the roast, turn it on its side and feel for any lumps, smoothing them out by rolling the roast against the counter with your hands.

THE TAKEAWAY

In addition to giving the beef the "roast, slice, and sear" treatment, I also reduce its braising liquid down into a glaze, which I brush on the medallions as they're seared in a hot skillet. While some glazes are meant to layer a big, bold flavor on top of, say, a grilled piece of chicken or pork, the glaze in this recipe tastes much like meat it was used to braise, which enhances its flavor.

Crispy Pot Roast
WITH BROCCOLI RABE

MAKES 4 TO 6 SERVINGS

Most roasted meats don't have the texture or super-savory caramelized flavor of a well-seared steak, and most steaks don't have the super-tender texture of a slow-cooked hunk of meat. This recipe has both, thanks to a technique I call "roast, slice, and sear." It's as straightforward as it sounds: Roast a large-format piece of meat, then cut it into slices and sear them until they're well browned, like a steak.

———————— POT ROAST ————————

One 4-pound boneless beef chuck roast

Kosher salt and freshly ground pepper

2 tablespoons extra-virgin olive oil

2 large white onions, halved and thinly sliced

3 cups chicken stock, preferably homemade (page 75)

2 cups red wine

⅔ cup red wine vinegar

¼ cup sugar

10 thyme sprigs

PREHEAT THE oven to 275°F. Season the chuck roast with salt and pepper and let sit for 30 minutes.

IN A Dutch oven or large saucepan, heat the olive oil over medium heat. Add the onions and 2 teaspoons salt and cook, stirring occasionally, until lightly caramelized, about 15 minutes. Add the stock, wine, vinegar, and sugar and bring to a boil. Add the roast and cover the pot. Braise, turning the pot roast over and adding the thyme after 1 hour, until the pot roast is tender throughout, about 2½ hours total. Remove the pot roast from the pot and place on a cutting board.

REMOVE THE thyme from the braising liquid and discard. Bring the braising liquid and onions to a boil, then reduce until thickened and glazy. The pot roast can be made a day ahead and refrigerated until ready to use.

———————— FOR SERVING ————————

1 bunch (16 to 20 stems) broccoli rabe

Extra-virgin olive oil

Kosher salt

1 tablespoon thinly sliced sage

Pinch of red pepper flakes

Pot Roast

All-purpose flour

Reduced braising liquid and onions (from the Pot Roast)

2 tablespoons chopped chives

BRING A large saucepan of salted water to a boil and prepare an ice bath. Trim the bottom inch or so off the ends of the broccoli rabe stems. Working in batches, blanch the broccoli rabe until bright green and crisp tender, 2 to 3 minutes. Transfer to the ice bath to cool, then drain and lightly squeeze dry.

IN A large skillet, heat 3 tablespoons olive oil over medium-high heat. Add the broccoli rabe, season with salt, and cook, flipping a few times, until warmed through and tender, about 2 minutes. Add the sage and red pepper flakes and season with salt.

SLICE THE pot roast into 1-inch-thick medallions and season with salt. In a large skillet, heat 3 tablespoons olive oil over medium-high heat. Dust the cut sides of the medallions with flour and pat off the excess. Sear the medallions in the hot oil until browned on both sides, 2 to 3 minutes per side. Add the reduced braising liquid and onions and spoon them over the beef until it's well coated. Arrange the pot roast slices on a platter (or individual plates) and drizzle with olive oil. Top with the chives and serve with the broccoli rabe.

Roast Chicken on a Bed of Vegetables

MAKES 4 SERVINGS

You've likely seen dozens of roast chicken recipes that promise perfectly browned, crispy skin. I honestly don't see what all the fuss over crispy skin is about: When your goal is crispy chicken skin, you usually sacrifice the moisture of the meat inside. Plus, once the bird is rested and carved, most of that crispy skin will get soggy with the steam and juices that are released. Instead, I use my favorite method for roasting a chicken, adapted from Jean-Georges Vongerichten's, in which he bakes the bird in a roasting pan filled with chunks of potatoes (a recipe he calls Potatoes That Taste Better than the Chicken). Instead of a roasting pan, I use a Dutch oven, which helps keep the bird extra moist. As the chicken cooks, its juices and fat get absorbed by the vegetables, making some of the best roasted carrots and potatoes you've ever tasted.

——— THE TAKEAWAY ———

The Dutch oven method itself is this recipe's main takeaway, but I use a couple of other tricks that you can borrow no matter how you approach roasting a chicken. First, I make a 2-inch slash in the thickest part of each leg, which will help it cook at the same speed as the breast. And I cook the bird breast side down for the first 10 minutes of roasting, which steams the meat and helps it stay extra moist.

---

1 pound baby potatoes, fingerling potatoes, or halved small potatoes

4 medium carrots, cut into 1-inch pieces

1 large onion, cut into ½-inch wedges

2 garlic cloves, finely chopped

4 tablespoons extra-virgin olive oil

Kosher salt and freshly ground black pepper

One 3- to 4-pound whole chicken

1 bunch herbs (such as thyme, rosemary, sage, marjoram, and parsley)

½ lemon

1 red finger chile, thinly sliced (with seeds)

2 tablespoons chopped parsley

2 tablespoons chopped chives

Flaky sea salt

PREHEAT THE oven to 450°F. In a large bowl, toss the potatoes, carrots, onion, and garlic with 3 tablespoons of the olive oil and season with kosher salt. Pour the vegetables into the bottom of a Dutch oven or large saucepan.

RUB THE chicken with the remaining 1 tablespoon olive oil and season all over with kosher salt and pepper. Stuff the bunch of herbs into the cavity. Cut a 2-inch slash in the thickest part of each leg. Place the chicken on top of the vegetables, breast side down, and roast, uncovered, for 10 minutes. Flip the chicken and continue roasting until an instant-read thermometer inserted into the thickest part of the thigh reads 165°F, about 45 minutes longer. Transfer the chicken to a cutting board and let rest for 10 minutes before carving. Meanwhile, check the vegetables; if they aren't completely tender, return the pot to the oven and continue roasting until they're finished.

CARVE THE chicken. (I like to carve the bird into eight pieces: four breast pieces, two thighs, and two drumsticks.) Scatter the vegetables on a serving platter and arrange the chicken pieces on top. Squeeze the lemon over the chicken. Sprinkle with the chile, parsley, chives, and flaky salt and serve.

Braised Short Ribs

WITH HORSERADISH GREMOLATA AND POTATO PUREE

MAKES 8 SERVINGS

Short ribs are always a crowd-pleaser and difficult to mess up, so keep this decadent dish in mind for your next dinner party. I prefer to braise a whole rack of short ribs—this makes slicing easier—but individual ribs are fine as well. The creamy potatoes that accompany the short ribs are downright gluttonous, with just enough garlic confit to give them a sweet, roasted flavor without making them into garlic mashed potatoes.

——— THE TAKEAWAY ———

Even with super-tender braised meats like these short ribs (and the brisket on page 295), I like to slice and broil the meat with a sweet glaze. This "braise and glaze" technique builds a wonderfully caramelized crust that crackles like the top of a crème brûlée.

——— BRAISED SHORT RIBS ———

- 2 tablespoon extra-virgin olive oil
- 2 medium onions, thinly sliced
- 4 pounds beef short ribs on the bone (preferably one 8-rib or two 4-rib racks, but individual ribs are fine)
- 2 heads garlic, cloves separated and peeled
- 1 tablespoon kosher salt
- 1 tablespoon freshly ground black pepper
- 4 rosemary sprigs
- 12 thyme sprigs
- 2 cups water
- 3½ cups red wine vinegar
- 3 tablespoon sugar

PREHEAT THE oven to 250°F. In a large Dutch oven, heat the oil over medium-high heat and add the onions. (If you don't have a large Dutch oven, cook the onions in a skillet and transfer to a roasting pan before adding the ribs.) Cook, stirring occasionally, until the onions are well browned, about 10 minutes. Add the short ribs, garlic, salt, pepper, rosemary, thyme, water, and 2½ cups of the vinegar. Bring the liquid to a simmer, then place a piece of parchment on top of the ribs. Cover the pot with aluminum foil and bake until the meat is very tender, 4 to 5 hours. Remove the pot from the oven and let cool to room temperature. Remove and discard the rosemary and thyme. The ribs can be cooked a day ahead and refrigerated overnight (which will also make it easier to remove the fat).

WHILE THE ribs braise, combine the remaining 1 cup vinegar and the sugar in a small saucepan. Bring to a boil and reduce until you have a glaze thick enough to coat the back of a spoon. Turn off the heat.

CONTINUES ➡

293

REMOVE THE ribs from the pot and use a ladle to discard the fat. Pass the braising liquid through a fine-mesh strainer into a medium saucepan and reserve the liquid and the garlic and onions. Bring the braising liquid to a boil and reduce until it's thick enough to coat the back of a spoon. Transfer to a blender and add the reserved garlic and onions. Blend until smooth (the mixture should be the thickness of ketchup).

PREHEAT THE broiler. Cut the meat off the bones and trim any connective tissue. If you braised a whole rack of ribs, divide the meat into eight portions. Place the ribs in a skillet and spread the puree over the ribs. Add just enough water to cover the bottom of the skillet. Broil until a crust forms on the ribs, 4 to 6 minutes (if the ribs start to char or burn, remove them from the oven). Brush the top of the ribs with the vinegar glaze and return to the broiler for about 1 minute, or until the top of the meat is caramelized (remove the meat if the glaze begins to burn).

creamy. Season to taste with salt. Cover the top of the potatoes with plastic wrap and keep warm.

--- HORSERADISH GREMOLATA ---

½ cup finely chopped parsley

½ cup finely chopped chives

1 red finger chile, seeded and finely chopped

1½ tablespoons finely grated fresh horseradish

1 tablespoon finely grated lemon zest

IN A bowl, combine the parsley, chives, chile, horseradish, and lemon zest.

--- FOR SERVING ---

Potato Puree

Braised Short Ribs

Horseradish Gremolata

½ cup Pickled Red Onions (page 55)

SPOON SOME potato puree into the center of eight serving plates and top with the short ribs. Pour any leftover liquid from broiling the ribs over the meat. Sprinkle the gremolata and pickled onions over the meat and serve.

--- POTATO PUREE ---

2 pounds Yukon Gold potatoes, peeled and cut into 2-inch chunks

1 cup heavy cream

¾ cup milk

4 tablespoons unsalted butter

5 cloves Garlic Confit (page 112)

Kosher salt

IN A medium saucepan, cover the potatoes with cold water. Bring the water to a boil over medium-high heat and cook the potatoes until soft, 15 to 20 minutes. While the potatoes cook, combine the cream, milk, butter, and garlic confit in a small saucepan and warm over low heat (do not boil). Drain the potatoes and, when cool enough to handle, pass them through a ricer or food mill into a saucepan, adding the garlic as well. Heat the puree over low heat, stirring in enough of the hot cream until the puree is very smooth and

Braised Brisket
WITH BARBECUE SAUCE

MAKES 8 TO 10 SERVINGS

This saucy brisket takes a bit of advanced planning, but it doesn't require much active work. I prepare it over the course of a week to serve on the weekend. It's another example of a dish that uses the marinade throughout the recipe: The smoky, tomato-based marinade becomes the brisket's braising liquid, then is reduced into a sweet and sticky glaze that caramelizes under the broiler. I like to let the cooked braised brisket rest in its braising liquid overnight, which makes slicing easier, but you can also serve it right away—and even skip the glazing and broiling step, if you're in a hurry. Serve it with Fresh-Corn Polenta with Butter and Herbs (page 156), Crispy Salt and Pepper Potatoes (page 191), Grilled Carrots with Sweet and Sour Carrot Sauce (page 147), or Brussels Sprouts with Mustard Vinaigrette (page 182).

THE TAKEAWAY

It's common to salt large cuts of meat a day or two ahead of time, but I like to add sugar to my cure, which also penetrates the meat. It doesn't make the meat taste sweet, just more flavorful, as when sugar is used to cure bacon. I also use the 2:1 salt-to-sugar cure on other braised or roasted meats, such as pork shoulder, larger cuts of lamb, and chicken thighs.

¼ cup kosher salt, plus more for the sauce

2 tablespoons granulated sugar

One 6- to 8-pound beef brisket (first/flat cut), trimmed

2 tablespoons ancho chile powder

2 tablespoons ground cinnamon

1 tablespoon coarsely ground black pepper

1 teaspoon chipotle powder

3 tablespoons Dijon mustard

¼ cup roughly chopped ginger

6 garlic cloves, peeled

1½ cups red wine vinegar, plus more for the sauce

2 white onions, cut into ⅛-inch slices

One 28-ounce can crushed tomatoes (or whole tomatoes, crushed with your hands)

12 ounces pilsner beer

¼ cup packed light brown sugar, plus more for the sauce

¼ teaspoon liquid smoke (optional)

IN A small bowl, mix the salt and granulated sugar. Rub the cure all over the brisket, wrap in plastic, and refrigerate overnight, or for up to 2 days.

CONTINUES ➡

IN A blender, combine the spices, mustard, ginger, garlic, and vinegar. Puree until smooth. Pour into a bowl and add the onions, tomatoes, beer, brown sugar, and liquid smoke (if using). Stir to combine. Place the brisket in a roasting pan and pour the marinade over. Cover with plastic and refrigerate for 2 days, flipping the meat over after the first day.

PREHEAT THE oven to 275°F. Cover the roasting pan with foil (after discarding the plastic) and bake, flipping the brisket every 30 minutes or so, until the meat is fork-tender, 3 to 4 hours. (If time allows, let the brisket cool in its liquid after it's done cooking, then cover the pan and refrigerate overnight. Follow the instructions for slicing the brisket and reducing the sauce in the next step, but rewarm the brisket for about 10 minutes in a 350°F oven before broiling.)

TO SERVE the brisket right away, remove it from the pan and transfer to a cutting board. Preheat the broiler. Strain the braising liquid into a medium saucepan and discard the solids. Bring the liquid to a boil and reduce until thick enough to coat the back of a spoon. Season the sauce to taste with salt, vinegar, and brown sugar. Slice the brisket against the grain into ¼-inch slices. Transfer to a baking dish and pour the sauce over. Broil until the brisket is browned and glazed, watching carefully to prevent burning, 4 to 5 minutes. Serve.

Seafood

—

Grilled Salmon

WITH ORANGE MARMALADE, HARICOTS VERTS, AND CHARRED SNAP PEAS

MAKES 4 SERVINGS

I love making this dish in the early spring, when citrus season is winding down and green beans and snap peas are starting to ring in the season. It's also a great excuse to uncover the grill, perhaps for the first time in months, for cooking the salmon. While I usually like to cook protein over a hot fire to get as much char as possible, with salmon I usually back off the heat a bit and grill it over a medium or medium-hot grill. There's so much fat in salmon that too much char can bring out a bitter, burnt flavor.

——— THE TAKEAWAY ———

Oranges and salmon are an unexpectedly great combination: The oranges have a sweet acidity that makes the salmon taste amazing. In this recipe, I top the salmon with an orange marmalade that's probably too spicy for a piece of toast but is great with a wide variety of vegetables and proteins, from carrots and broccoli to shrimp and pork.

——— ORANGE MARMALADE ———

1 large orange
2 tablespoons sugar
¾ cup fresh lemon juice

3 tablespoons Fermented Chile Sauce (page 252)

USING A sharp knife, cut the peel and pith off the orange. Working over a bowl, cut the orange between the membranes to release the segments. Dice the segments, then return them to the bowl. Cut the peel (with the pith) into ¼-inch dice.

IN A small saucepan, cover the orange peel with cold water and bring to a boil. Turn off the heat, drain, and repeat, blanching the peel two more times.

IN A saucepan, combine the orange peel and segments, sugar, and lemon juice. Bring to a boil and cook until the liquid is reduced by half. Turn off the heat and let cool to room temperature, then stir in the chile sauce. The marmalade can be made up to 2 weeks ahead and refrigerated until ready to use.

——— HARICOTS VERTS ———

4 ounces haricots verts, trimmed

BRING A medium saucepan of salted water to a boil and prepare an ice bath. Blanch the haricots verts until bright green but still crunchy, 30 to 60 seconds, then transfer to the ice bath. When cool, transfer to paper towels to drain. Cut enough beans into ¼-inch pieces to make ¼ cup. Cut the rest of the haricots verts in half.

CONTINUES ➡

CHARRED SNAP PEAS

2 cups sugar snap peas (about 8 ounces)

1 tablespoon extra-virgin olive oil

1 teaspoon kosher salt

HEAT A skillet (preferably cast-iron) over high heat. In a mixing bowl, toss the sugar snap peas with the oil and salt. When the skillet is very hot, and working in batches to not crowd the pan, add the snap peas and let them char on one side without moving them around, 30 to 45 seconds. Turn the snap peas over and char the other side, then transfer to a plate and let cool.

FOR SERVING

Orange Marmalade

Haricots Verts

4 teaspoons chopped mint

Charred Snap Peas

1 cup thinly sliced scallion greens (or roughly chopped ramp greens)

2 teaspoons thinly sliced Pickled Ramps (page 154), plus 2 tablespoons pickling liquid

2 teaspoons finely chopped jalapeño chile (with seeds)

4 teaspoons chopped basil

Four 5-ounce salmon fillets with skin

2 tablespoons extra-virgin olive oil

Kosher salt

IN A bowl, combine the marmalade, haricots verts, and mint.

IN A large skillet, combine the snap peas with the scallions, pickled ramps, and jalapeños and cook over medium-low heat until warm. Add the pickling liquid and basil, stir well, and turn off the heat.

PREPARE A medium-hot grill or preheat a grill pan over medium-high heat. Pat the salmon dry, then rub the skin side with the olive oil and season both sides with salt. Clean and oil the grill grate, then grill the salmon, skin side down, until the skin is crisp and well browned, about 4 minutes. Using a thin spatula, flip the salmon over and grill for 2 minutes longer, or until the fish is just cooked through. Remove from the grill.

DIVIDE THE vegetables among four serving plates. Top with the salmon and then spoon some of the marmalade over each piece of fish. Serve.

Grilled Shrimp
WITH SWEET AND SPICY SAUCE

MAKES 4 SERVINGS

You can serve smaller portions of this dish by itself as an appetizer or first course, or pair it with Grilled Broccoli with Orange Aioli and Pistachio Vinaigrette (page 158), Citrus-Glazed Carrots (page 195), Grilled Asparagus with Broken Chile Sauce (page 145), or the Corn and Herb Salad with Lime Vinaigrette (page 93). Even if you're not planning to eat them, leave the heads on the shrimp, which add a lot of flavor. You'll know the shrimp are cooked through when they start to turn pink around the area where the vein used to be.

─────── SWEET AND SPICY SAUCE ───────

MAKES 2 CUPS

2 tablespoons extra-virgin olive oil

3 large garlic cloves, finely chopped

1½ tablespoons finely chopped ginger

2 teaspoons kosher salt

½ cup plus 2 tablespoons honey

1½ cups white wine vinegar

2 red finger chiles, finely chopped (with seeds)

1 teaspoon red pepper flakes

½ cup Fermented Chile Sauce (page 252)

IN A small saucepan, heat the olive oil over low heat. Add the garlic, ginger, and salt and cook, stirring, until softened, 2 to 3 minutes. Add the honey and vinegar, bring to a boil, and cook until the liquid has reduced by half. Turn off the heat and add the chiles, red pepper flakes, and chile sauce. Refrigerate for up to 1 month.

─────── FOR SERVING ───────

2 pounds whole shrimp (16–20 per pound size), with shells

½ cup extra-virgin olive oil (or oil from Garlic Confit, page 112)

1 tablespoon finely grated lemon zest

2 tablespoons chopped parsley

2 tablespoons chopped mint

½ teaspoon red pepper flakes

Kosher salt and freshly ground black pepper

1 cup Sweet and Spicy Sauce

PEEL THE shrimp shells and devein the bodies, leaving the heads and tails intact. (You can also remove the heads, but you're throwing away flavor!) In a bowl, combine the olive oil, lemon zest, parsley, mint, and red pepper flakes. Stir to combine, then add the shrimp and toss well. Cover and refrigerate for 2 to 3 hours.

PREPARE A hot grill or preheat a grill pan over high heat. Remove the shrimp from the marinade and season with salt and pepper. Grill the shrimp until well browned on one side, about 2 minutes. Turn the shrimp over and continue grilling until opaque, about 2 minutes longer. Transfer to a serving platter and serve the sweet and spicy sauce on the side.

─────── THE TAKEAWAY ───────

The sweet and spicy sauce is my fresher take on an Asian sweet chile sauce, and another reason to keep some Fermented Chile Sauce (page 252) on hand. It makes a great dipping sauce for fried foods, and becomes the base for the sweet and spicy vinaigrette in the chicken salad on page 257.

Grilled Tuna Steaks

WITH ORANGE-CHILE TOPPING

MAKES 4 SERVINGS

At Loring Place, we make this dish with extra-fatty tuna bellies, which we cook to medium. If your fishmonger has some tuna bellies to spare, I highly encourage doing the same, but I've adapted the recipe for easier-to-find tuna steaks. With this thicker, less-fatty cut of tuna, I like to grill it just until it picks up some char, leaving the fish as rare as possible, but feel free to cook it to your preferred doneness.

THE TAKEAWAY

I like contrasting soft, fatty tuna with a crispy topping, and the combination of fried garlic, chile, and herbs that tops the grilled tuna here is just what the dish needs to make it complete. Technique-wise, this is the inverse of the Ginger-Scallion Topping (page 172), in which hot oil is poured over the other ingredients. Here, I heat a larger amount of olive oil, to which I add the herbs and other ingredients. This both makes the herbs extra crispy and infuses the oil with their flavor, creating a sauce that is brightened with a squeeze of citrus. The topping works really well on any crudo, sashimi, or other raw fish preparation, or you can add it to soba to make a lovely noodle salad.

MARINATED TUNA

2 teaspoons kosher salt

2 teaspoons sugar

Four 6-ounce tuna steaks

⅓ cup red wine vinegar

½ cup extra-virgin olive oil

2 teaspoons red pepper flakes

COMBINE THE salt and sugar and season the tuna steaks all over with the mixture. In a bowl, whisk together the vinegar, olive oil, and red pepper flakes. Transfer to a large resealable plastic bag, add the tuna, and marinate for 30 to 60 minutes.

ORANGE-CHILE TOPPING

1½ cups extra-virgin olive oil

3 large garlic cloves, thinly sliced

1 red finger chile, thinly sliced (with seeds)

Strips of zest from 1 medium orange, finely chopped

1 cup lightly packed mint, large leaves torn

1 cup lightly packed basil, large leaves torn

IN A medium saucepan, heat the olive oil over medium-high heat to 325°F. Add the garlic and fry for 1 minute, then add the chile and fry for 1 minute longer. Add the orange zest, mint, and basil and fry until the herbs are crisp, 30 to 60 seconds longer. Strain the oil into a heatproof bowl and let cool to room temperature. Return the fried garlic, chiles, orange zest, and herbs to the oil.

CONTINUES ➡

PICKLED SHALLOTS

MAKES ABOUT 2 CUPS

8 medium shallots,
thinly sliced

1½ teaspoons yellow
mustard seeds

1 tablespoon coriander
seeds

2 teaspoons fennel
seeds

1 tablespoon cumin
seeds

1 dried red chile

1 dried bay leaf

1¾ cups apple cider
vinegar

2 tablespoons sugar

PLACE THE shallots in a sterilized pint-size jar.

IN A small skillet, toast the mustard, coriander, fennel, and cumin seeds over low heat until fragrant, about 30 seconds. Let cool. Add to the jar along with the chile and bay leaf.

IN A small saucepan, combine the vinegar and sugar. Bring to a boil, stirring until the sugar dissolves. Pour over the shallots and let cool to room temperature. Seal the jar and refrigerate for up to 2 weeks.

FOR SERVING

Marinated Tuna

Kosher salt and freshly
ground black pepper

Extra-virgin olive oil

1 clementine half or
2 orange wedges

2 lemon wedges

Orange-Chile Topping

¼ cup Pickled Shallots

1 clementine or orange,
for zesting

Flaky sea salt

PREPARE A hot grill or preheat a grill pan over high heat. Remove the tuna from the marinade and pat dry. Season with kosher salt and pepper and rub all over with olive oil. Clean and oil the grill grate, then grill the tuna until well browned on one side, 3 to 4 minutes. Using a thin metal spatula, flip the tuna over and continue grilling until browned on the other side, about 3 minutes longer for rare. Transfer to a platter or individual plates and squeeze some clementine and lemon juice over the fish. Spoon some of the topping over the fish, then scatter the pickled shallots over. Grate some clementine zest over, season with flaky salt and pepper, and serve.

Slow-Roasted Halibut
WITH SUMMER BEANS AND PEACH-TOMATO SAUCE

MAKES 4 SERVINGS

When conceiving a fish-based entrée, texture is always at the top of my mind, and this dish is four-part harmony of textures: buttery halibut, velvety peach-tomato sauce, snappy summer beans, and crunchy almond and fried herb topping. I'd serve it at the height of peach season, when summer beans and tomatoes are also showing up at the market.

THE TAKEAWAY

As a kid, I loved peach-tomato salsa, so that pairing of summer fruit has always made a lot of sense to me. As a chef, I use the combination often, and this bright, slightly spicy sauce can work with any kind of fish. You can also double up on the amount of tomatoes and turn it into a quick, chilled soup.

PEACH-TOMATO SAUCE

MAKES 3 CUPS

2 medium yellow tomatoes

2 ripe peaches

¼ cup fresh lemon juice

2 tablespoons honey

2 tablespoons plus 2 teaspoons champagne vinegar

1 red Thai chile, thinly sliced (with seeds)

1½ teaspoons kosher salt

BRING A large saucepan of water to a boil and prepare an ice bath. Lightly score the bottom of the tomatoes and peaches with an X. Blanch the fruit until the skin begins to loosen, about 1 minute. Transfer to the ice bath to cool, then remove the skins with a paring knife. Core and cut the tomatoes into chunks. Pit and cut the peaches into chunks. In a blender, combine the tomatoes and peaches with all of the remaining ingredients and puree until very smooth. Strain through a fine-mesh strainer. Refrigerate until ready to use. (The sauce can be made up to a day ahead of time, but it's best the same day it's made.)

ALMOND-HERB TOPPING

½ cup extra-virgin olive oil

½ cup roughly chopped raw almonds

¼ cup torn basil

¼ cup torn mint

IN A small skillet, combine the olive oil and almonds and place over high heat. Cook until the almonds start to turn brown, 2 to 3 minutes. Add the basil and mint and cook until the herbs are crispy, 1 to 2 minutes. Pour the contents of the skillet into a heatproof bowl and let cool.

CONTINUES ➡

309

─────── FOR SERVING ───────

Four 5-ounce portions skinless halibut

Kosher salt and freshly ground black pepper

¼ cup extra-virgin olive oil

8 ounces yellow wax beans

8 ounces green wax beans

2 tablespoons oil from Garlic Confit (page 112) or extra-virgin olive oil

¼ cup thinly sliced mint

1⅓ cups Peach-Tomato Sauce

Almond-Herb Topping

Flaky sea salt

PREHEAT THE oven to 250°F. Season the halibut with kosher salt and pepper and place in a baking dish just large enough to fit the fish in a single layer. Drizzle the fish with the olive oil and add just enough water to cover the bottom of the dish. Cover with foil and roast until the halibut is opaque in the center, 20 to 30 minutes (depending on the thickness of the fish).

WHILE THE halibut is roasting, bring a saucepan of salted water to a boil. Add the yellow and green beans and blanch until just tender, 2 to 3 minutes. Transfer to paper towels to drain, then cut into ½-inch pieces.

IN A skillet, heat the garlic oil over medium-high heat. Add the beans and sauté until warmed through, then add the mint, season with kosher salt, and toss.

LADLE ABOUT ⅓ cup of peach-tomato sauce in the bottom of four serving bowls. Top with the beans. Place the fish on top of the vegetables and spoon some of the almond topping over each piece of fish. Sprinkle with flaky salt and serve.

Slow-Roasted Halibut

WITH TOMATOES AND ALMONDS

MAKES 4 SERVINGS

This summery seafood dish is a celebration of tomatoes. Two different tomato preparations—crushed tomato sauce on the bottom and a pile of sweet, roasted cherry tomatoes on top—sandwich tender halibut and showcase the tomato's versatility. Toasted almonds add crunch, and I'm always surprised at how great everything tastes together.

——— THE TAKEAWAY ———

My method for low-and-slow roasting is a great way to use your late-summer surplus of cherry or Sungold tomatoes. My goal is to intensify their flavor and sweetness without drying them out all the way, so you still get little bursts of fresh, juicy tomato flavor when you bite into them. The key is to keep an eye on the skins: When they start to shrivel around the tomato edges, the tomatoes are done. You can make a big batch of these and use them in a bunch of ways: in my baked ricotta starter (page 43), on pizzas, in pasta, or as a garnish for salads. If you want to preserve them for a week or two, cover them completely with olive oil and store in the refrigerator.

——— ROASTED CHERRY TOMATOES ———

1½ cups cherry and/or Sungold tomatoes, halved through the equator

1 tablespoon extra-virgin olive oil

½ teaspoon kosher salt

¼ teaspoon freshly ground black pepper

PREHEAT THE oven to 200°F and line a rimmed baking sheet with parchment paper. In a bowl, toss the tomatoes with the olive oil and season with salt and pepper. Arrange the tomatoes, cut side up, on the parchment and roast until they begin to shrivel around the edges, about 1 hour.

——— ALMOND-HERB TOPPING ———

½ cup roughly chopped almonds

¼ cup roughly chopped parsley

¼ cup extra-virgin olive oil

2 tablespoons roughly chopped oregano

IN A medium saucepan, combine the almonds and olive oil. Turn the heat to medium and cook, stirring occasionally, until the almonds are lightly browned, 3 to 4 minutes. Add the parsley and oregano and turn off the heat. Pour the contents of the skillet into a heatproof bowl and let cool. The topping can be made a day ahead and refrigerated until ready to use.

——— SPICY RED WINE VINAIGRETTE ———

MAKES ⅔ CUP

2 garlic cloves, roughly chopped

½ habanero chile, seeded and roughly chopped

⅓ cup red wine vinegar

2 teaspoons kosher salt

½ teaspoon sugar

¼ cup plus 1 tablespoon extra-virgin olive oil

IN A blender, combine all of the ingredients except the olive oil. Puree until smooth, then slowly add the olive oil until emulsified. The vinaigrette can be made a day or two ahead and refrigerated until ready to use.

Four 5-ounce portions skinless halibut

Kosher salt and freshly ground black pepper

Extra-virgin olive oil

5 ounces baby spinach (about 5 cups)

Roasted Cherry Tomatoes

¼ cup thinly sliced shallots

½ red finger chile, thinly sliced (with seeds)

¼ cup Spicy Red Wine Vinaigrette

1½ cups Crushed Tomato Sauce (page 211)

Almond-Herb Topping

¼ cup thinly sliced basil

PREHEAT THE oven to 250°F. Season the halibut with salt and pepper and place in a baking dish just large enough to fit the fish in a single layer. Drizzle the fish with ¼ cup olive oil and add just enough water to cover the bottom of the dish. Cover with foil and roast until the halibut is opaque in the center, 20 to 30 minutes (depending on the thickness of the fish).

MEANWHILE, IN a medium skillet, heat 1 tablespoon olive oil over medium heat. Add the spinach and cook, tossing frequently, until wilted, 1 to 2 minutes. If there's any liquid in the skillet, pour it out, then season the spinach with salt.

IN A small bowl, toss the roasted tomatoes, shallots, and chile with the vinaigrette.

DIVIDE THE crushed tomato sauce among four shallow serving bowls. Divide the spinach among the bowls, placing it over the sauce. Spoon about 2 tablespoons of the almond-herb topping over and around each portion of spinach. Top with a piece of fish. Spoon the roasted tomato mixture over the fish, sprinkle with basil, and serve.

Braised Black Bass
WITH CHERRY TOMATOES, WHITE WINE, AND ZUCCHINI

MAKES 4 SERVINGS

Once you've prepped all of the ingredients, this summery one-pot dish comes together rather quickly. You'll notice a couple of unusual additions to the braising liquid: elderflower syrup and fish sauce. These ingredients are imperceptible in the final dish, but they add a lot of complexity.

Four 6-ounce black sea bass fillets with skin

Kosher salt and freshly ground black pepper

2 tablespoons vegetable oil

2 tablespoons extra-virgin olive oil, plus more for drizzling

1 large garlic clove, thinly sliced

2 teaspoons chopped marjoram or oregano

1 tablespoon finely chopped jalapeño chile (with seeds)

1 large green zucchini, cut into ½-inch dice (about 2 cups)

1 large yellow zucchini, cut into ½-inch dice (about 2 cups)

2 cups Sungold tomatoes, halved

½ cup white wine

1 tablespoon fresh lime juice

1 tablespoon elderflower syrup or 1½ teaspoons light honey

1 tablespoon fish sauce

2 tablespoons thinly sliced basil

2 tablespoons finely chopped parsley

1 lemon, for zesting

Flaky sea salt

USING A sharp knife, score the skin side of each piece of fish a couple of times in the thickest part of the fillet. Pat the fish dry and season with kosher salt and pepper. In a large skillet, heat the vegetable oil over high heat until it shimmers. Add the fish, skin side down, and cook for 1 minute, then press down on the fish with a spatula to flatten. Continue cooking the fish until the skin is golden brown, 2 to 3 minutes. Transfer the fish to a plate and wipe out the skillet.

ADD THE olive oil to the same skillet and heat over low heat. Add the garlic and 2 teaspoons kosher salt and cook, stirring frequently, until the garlic is lightly browned, 2 to 3 minutes. Add the marjoram and jalapeño and cook for 1 minute. Increase the heat to high and add the zucchini. Cook, stirring frequently, until the zucchini starts to brown, about 3 minutes. Add the tomatoes and wine and bring the liquid to a simmer. Add the fish, skin side up, and braise until opaque throughout, 2 to 3 minutes. Turn off the heat and add the lime juice, elderflower syrup, fish sauce, basil, and parsley.

DIVIDE THE fish and vegetables among four shallow bowls. Grate over lemon zest, sprinkle with flaky salt, and drizzle with olive oil. Serve.

THE TAKEAWAY

If you've braised chicken thighs, you're probably familiar with the process of searing the skin side of the meat first, then removing it to build the braising liquid before returning the meat to the pan to finish cooking. This technique gives you the best of both worlds: crisp, caramelized skin and juicy, braised meat. I like taking the same approach with fish, and black bass has a skin that will stay crispy even after simmering in the liquid (so long as you leave the skin exposed). You can do the same with other kinds of skin-on fish: Red snapper works well, as does salmon.

Black Bass

WITH MARINATED PEPPERS AND KALE

MAKES 4 SERVINGS

Make this speedy supper whenever you can find a nice piece of black bass. I love this fish for its skin, which gets extra crispy and turns a beautiful brown color when cooked properly. There are a few keys to doing it right: Get the skin as dry as possible and the pan very hot before you add the oil and fish. When the fish hits the pan, it will seize up for 30 to 45 seconds, then relax a bit. That's when you should begin pressing down on it with a spatula, to prevent curling and to crisp up the skin as much as possible.

—— THE TAKEAWAY ——

The marinated bell peppers that add acidity and texture to this fish dish are based on the peppers you'd find on an antipasto platter. They're super versatile and will keep for about a week, so use the leftovers in sandwiches, mix into salads, or place over toast spread with goat cheese.

—— MARINATED PEPPERS ——

1 each red, yellow, and orange bell peppers

½ cup plus 2 tablespoons extra-virgin olive oil

12 garlic cloves, thinly sliced (use a mandoline if you have one)

½ serrano chile, halved lengthwise and thinly sliced (with seeds)

½ cup coarsely chopped oregano

1 tablespoon kosher salt

⅓ cup fresh lemon juice

¼ cup balsamic vinegar

CHAR THE peppers over the flame of a gas burner (or under a broiler), turning with tongs until blackened and blistered all over, about 10 minutes. Transfer the peppers to a bowl, cover with a plate, and let stand for 15 minutes. Scrape off the skins with a paring knife and wipe the flesh clean with a paper towel. Discard the stem and seeds. Cut the peppers lengthwise into ¼-inch-thick strips.

IN A medium skillet, heat the olive oil over medium heat. Add the garlic and cook, stirring frequently, until very lightly browned, about 7 minutes. Turn off the heat and add the serrano and oregano. Transfer to a bowl and add the salt, lemon juice, and vinegar. Stir in the roasted peppers. Stir well and let cool to room temperature. Let sit for at least an hour before serving. The marinated peppers can be made ahead and refrigerated for up to 1 week.

CONTINUES ➡

SAUTÉED KALE

3 tablespoons extra-virgin olive oil

1 bunch Tuscan kale, stems removed and leaves roughly chopped

Kosher salt

IN A medium skillet, heat the olive oil over medium heat. Add the kale, season with salt, and toss to coat with the oil. Cover the pan and cook for 5 minutes. Remove the lid and continue cooking, stirring frequently, until the kale is soft and the liquid has mostly evaporated, about 3 minutes. Keep warm.

FOR SERVING

Four 6-ounce black sea bass fillets with skin (use red snapper if you can't find bass)

Kosher salt and freshly ground black pepper

2 tablespoons extra-virgin olive oil

Sautéed Kale

¼ cup coarsely chopped toasted almonds

¼ cup roughly chopped basil

2 lemon wedges

Marinated Peppers

Flaky sea salt

PAT THE fish very dry with paper towels and season with kosher salt and pepper. In a large skillet, heat the olive oil over medium-high heat until it shimmers. Add the fish, skin side down, and let it cook, undisturbed, for 30 to 45 seconds. Press down on the fish with a spatula for about 30 seconds to prevent the skin from curling, then continue cooking, pressing frequently with the spatula, until the skin is browned and crisp and the fish is nearly opaque, 6 to 7 minutes. Flip the fish over and cook until opaque throughout, about 1 minute longer.

DIVIDE THE warm kale among four shallow bowls. Sprinkle the almonds and basil over the kale and squeeze some lemon juice over. Top with the fish and scatter the marinated peppers around the bowl. Sprinkle with flaky salt and serve.

Roasted Snapper
WITH PUREED CORN AND PICKLED PEPPERS

MAKES 4 SERVINGS

Although they basically contain the same ingredients, the corn puree in this summery fish dish is the opposite of the Fresh-Corn Polenta on page 156, where the raw corn is pureed, then cooked into a thick, polenta-like porridge. Here, I first cook the corn kernels, then puree them until the mixture is completely smooth and velvety, becoming both starch and sauce for the lean, moist fish.

THE TAKEAWAY

When I want to add a touch of heat and acidity to a dish, I'll often use pickled jalapeños or finger chiles. But when I want the flavor of chiles to come through, I'll use a mix of hot and sweet peppers, which I quickly pickle in the simplest of brines. This medley of pickled peppers is a great topping for burgers and sandwiches, or you can chop them up and add them to mayonnaise to make a deliciously chunky, spicy dressing.

PICKLED MIXED PEPPERS

MAKES 1 CUP

2 jalapeño chiles, halved, seeded, and sliced crosswise into ⅛-inch pieces

2 Anaheim chiles, halved, seeded, and sliced crosswise into ⅛-inch pieces

2 cherry peppers, halved, seeded, and sliced crosswise into ⅛-inch pieces

1 red bell pepper, seeded, cut into 8 wedges, and sliced crosswise into ⅛-inch pieces

2 cups white wine vinegar

¼ cup sugar

2 tablespoons kosher salt

PLACE ALL the chiles and peppers in a sterile pint-size jar. In a small saucepan, bring the vinegar, sugar, and salt to a boil. Pour over the peppers and let cool to room temperature. The pickled peppers can be made ahead and refrigerated for up to 2 weeks.

CORN PUREE

4 ears corn, shucked

2 tablespoons extra-virgin olive oil

Kosher salt

1 tablespoon water

CUT THE kernels from the corn. (You can save the cobs for making Corn Stock, page 48.) In a large skillet, heat the olive oil over medium heat. Add the corn and 1 teaspoon salt and cook, stirring frequently, until the corn is cooked through but has a little bit of crunch, 3 to 4 minutes. Turn off the heat and transfer half of the corn to a blender along with the water. (Save the rest of the corn kernels for serving.) Puree the corn in the blender until smooth and season to taste with salt. Gently rewarm before serving.

--------- FOR SERVING ---------

Four 5-ounce pieces red snapper with skin

Kosher salt

2 tablespoons extra-virgin olive oil, plus more for drizzling

Sautéed corn kernels (from the Corn Puree)

½ cup thinly sliced basil

2 tablespoons chopped tarragon

Corn Puree

½ cup Pickled Mixed Peppers

Flaky sea salt

PAT THE snapper dry and season with kosher salt. In a large skillet, heat the olive oil over medium heat. Add the fish, skin side down, and cook, occasionally pressing it down with a spatula to prevent curling, until the skin is brown, 4 to 5 minutes. Turn the fish over and cook until just opaque in the center, 1 to 2 minutes longer. Transfer the fish to a plate to rest. Add the corn kernels to the skillet and cook over medium heat until warmed through, about 1 minute, then add the basil and tarragon and toss. Turn off the heat.

DIVIDE THE corn puree among four plates. Spoon the corn and herb mixture over the puree, then top with a piece of fish. Place a small pile of pickled peppers on top of each piece, drizzle with olive oil, season with flaky salt, and serve.

Grilled Arctic Char

WITH CHICKPEA SAUCE, QUINOA, AND GRILLED AVOCADO

MAKES 4 SERVINGS

There's a lot of texture going on in this dish, which you could consider a grain salad topped with fish (leave out the fish and you have a tasty vegan main course). The chunky, slightly spicy chickpea sauce is an unexpected dressing for grilled fish, but I just love how it bridges all of the ingredients together. You could also serve the sauce by itself, spread it on toast, or use it as a dip for crudités.

THE TAKEAWAY

A hot grill can magically elevate an avocado into something slightly crispy on the outside, but soft and unctuous on the inside. This trick was inspired by a salad I ate (and loved) in Puerto Rico that was made with grilled avocados and tomatoes. I like to peel avocados after halving them, which gives you lots more flesh to char on the grill. I usually start by searing the flat sides, then roll the avocado around until the rounded side picks up some color as well. Grilled avocados are great pretty much anywhere you'd use a raw one, from chunky guacamole and tacos to ceviche and salads.

QUINOA

1 cup quinoa
2 cups water
1 teaspoon kosher salt

RINSE THE quinoa with cold water and drain. In a small saucepan, bring the water to a boil and add the salt. Add the quinoa and cover the pot. Reduce the heat to very low and simmer the quinoa for 15 minutes. Turn off the heat, then let the quinoa steam, covered, for 20 minutes. Uncover the pot and fluff the quinoa with a fork.

BRAISED CARROTS

3 medium carrots, cut into obliques (about 1 cup)
2 cups water
1 teaspoon kosher salt

IN A medium saucepan, combine the carrots, water, and salt. Bring the liquid to a boil, then reduce the heat to medium, cover the pot, and simmer until the carrots are just tender throughout, 8 to 10 minutes. Drain before serving.

RED WINE VINAIGRETTE

MAKES ¾ CUP

½ cup red wine vinegar
½ teaspoon kosher salt
¼ cup extra-virgin olive oil

IN A small bowl, combine the vinegar and salt. Slowly whisk in the olive oil until emulsified. The vinaigrette can be made a day or two ahead, but whisk well before using.

CHICKPEA SAUCE

MAKES 2 CUPS

½ cup dried chickpeas

1 teaspoon baking soda

1 cup Hummus
 (page 30, or another
 hummus)

¼ cup fresh lemon juice

¼ cup Fermented Chile
 Sauce (page 252)

IN A bowl, cover the chickpeas by at least 2 inches of water (they'll soak up more than you'd expect). Add ½ teaspoon of the baking soda and stir until dissolved. Let the chickpeas soak at room temperature for at least 8 hours or overnight. Drain and rinse.

PLACE THE soaked chickpeas in a saucepan and cover with 4 cups water. Add the remaining ½ teaspoon baking soda. Bring the water to a boil, then reduce the heat and simmer until the chickpeas are very tender, 45 to 60 minutes. Drain the chickpeas and transfer to a bowl. Using a whisk, gently mash the chickpeas until some are broken up (the sauce will be chunky). Add the hummus, lemon juice, and chile sauce and stir to combine. The sauce can be made a day ahead and refrigerated until ready to use.

FOR SERVING

Four 6-ounce arctic
 char fillets with skin

Extra-virgin olive oil

Kosher salt

1 ripe (but firm)
 avocado

2 cups Quinoa

1 tablespoon
 chopped dill

1 tablespoon chopped
 basil

1 tablespoon chopped
 parsley

1 tablespoon chopped
 mint

Braised Carrots,
 drained

½ cup Red Wine
 Vinaigrette

1 cup Chickpea Sauce

PREPARE A medium-hot grill or preheat a grill pan over medium-high heat. Pat the char dry, then rub the skin side with olive oil and season both sides with salt. Clean and oil the grill grate, then grill the fish, skin side down, until the skin is crisp and well browned, about 4 minutes. Using a thin spatula, flip the char over and grill for 2 minutes longer, or until the fish is just cooked through. Remove from the grill.

MEANWHILE, CUT the avocado in half lengthwise and remove the pit and skin. Brush the avocado with olive oil and season with salt. Grill the avocado cut side down, then roll it around to get some char all over, 2 to 3 minutes. Transfer to a cutting board and dice.

IN A bowl, toss the quinoa with the herbs, carrots, and vinaigrette. Spread about ¼ cup chickpea sauce on the bottom of four shallow bowls. Divide the quinoa salad among the bowls, spooning it over the sauce. Spoon the diced avocadoes over the quinoa. Place the fish on top, drizzle with olive oil, and serve.

Grilled Swordfish
WITH OLIVE TAPENADE AND FENNEL SALAD

MAKES 4 SERVINGS

I created this recipe to highlight the buttery, meaty flavor of grilled swordfish. Because the fish has so much flavor, I didn't want to overpower it with an intense sauce or heavy vegetables, so I took the classic Italian pairing of swordfish and olives and added a simple fennel salad.

Swordfish is one of the more oily fishes, so it can stand up to the heat of a hot grill and takes on char well, especially when it's sprinkled with a little sugar before cooking. However, it tends to stick to the grill more easily than other fish, so I oil both the fish and the grill grates, and I don't move the fish around much as it cooks.

THE TAKEAWAY

My olive tapenade is everything that jarred tapenade isn't. Whereas the jarred stuff is muddy puree made mostly from black olives, mine is a chunky, brightly flavored topping made with two varieties of green olives that are boosted with flavor from herbs, a touch of jalapeño, and the leftover oil from my Marinated Olives (page 104). The tapenade will keep for about a week, so feel free to use any leftovers in pasta, on toasts, or as part of an antipasto spread.

OLIVE TAPENADE

MAKES ABOUT 2 CUPS

¼ cup roughly chopped Sevillano olives

¼ cup roughly chopped Castelvetrano olives

1 cup thinly sliced scallions

½ cup finely chopped parsley

1 teaspoon finely chopped jalapeño chile (no seeds)

2 tablespoons finely grated lemon zest (preferably Meyer lemons)

1½ teaspoons kosher salt

1 teaspoon sugar

⅓ cup extra-virgin olive oil

¼ cup oil from Marinated Olives (page 104) or extra-virgin olive oil

IN A medium heat-proof bowl, combine the olives, scallions, parsley, jalapeño, lemon zest, salt, and sugar. Combine the olive oils in a small saucepan and heat over medium-high heat until almost smoking. Pour over the olive mixture. Let cool to room temperature. The tapenade can be made ahead and refrigerated for up to 1 week.

FENNEL SALAD

1 medium fennel bulb, halved, cored, and thinly shaved (use a mandoline if you have one)

¼ cup chopped fennel fronds

2 tablespoons chopped tarragon

1 tablespoon fresh lemon juice (preferably Meyer lemon)

3 tablespoons extra-virgin olive oil

Kosher salt and freshly ground black pepper

IN A bowl, toss all the ingredients together, seasoning with the salt and pepper. Refrigerate until ready to serve.

––––––––– FOR SERVING –––––––––

Four 6-ounce center-
cut swordfish steaks
(about 1 inch thick)

Extra-virgin olive oil

Kosher salt and freshly
ground black pepper

Sugar

Fennel Salad

Olive Tapenade

PREPARE A hot grill or preheat a grill pan over high heat. Oil the grates or pan well. Brush the swordfish steaks with olive oil and season with salt, pepper, and a little bit of sugar (this will help with caramelizing). Grill the fish until well browned on one side, about 4 minutes, then flip the fish over and continue grilling until well browned on the other side and just cooked through, about 4 minutes longer.

DIVIDE THE fennel salad among four plates and top with the swordfish. Spoon some of the tapenade over each piece of fish, drizzle with olive oil, and serve.

Grilled Mackerel and Fennel

WITH GRILLED PICKLES AND YOGURT SAUCE

MAKES 4 SERVINGS

My former chef de cuisine, Karen Shu, brought the idea for this dish to me, and we developed it together. Spanish mackerel is the perfect fish for grilling whole, as it has a tough skin that crisps up nicely on the grill, and its rich, oily flesh is difficult to overcook. With any whole grilled fish, I'll make a couple of slashes through the thickest part of the body to help it cook in the same amount of time as the thinner tail end. If you don't want to fire up the grill, you can also roast the fish in a 450°F oven for about 25 minutes, but you'll miss out on the smoky charred flavor. The yogurt sauce is like a Greek tzatziki, but I swap out the grated cucumber for cucumber juice to create a smooth, creamy accompaniment to the unctuous fish.

THE TAKEAWAY

Homemade pickled ginger is much, much different than the pink stuff that comes with your takeout sushi. Jarred pickled ginger is too cloying and lacks the spicy punch that can add a big flavor in small amounts. My version (recipe on page 115) is a little saltier and a lot less sweet, and also gifts you with a delicious, gingery brine that's great in vinaigrettes. When buying fresh ginger to pickle, look for roots with smooth, tight skin—that's an indication of freshness.

YOGURT SAUCE

1 cup Greek yogurt

3 tablespoons fresh cucumber juice

4 teaspoons fresh lemon juice

1 teaspoon finely grated lemon zest

1 small garlic clove, finely grated on a Microplane (or similar grater)

½ teaspoon kosher salt

Pinch of sugar

COMBINE ALL ingredients in a medium bowl and whisk until smooth. The yogurt sauce can be made up to 1 day ahead and refrigerated until ready to use.

FRIED CAPERS

⅓ cup capers (preferably salt-packed)

Vegetable oil

SOAK THE capers in cold water for a few minutes and squeeze gently. Repeat two times. Transfer the capers to paper towels and pat dry. In a medium saucepan, heat about ¼ inch of oil over medium-high heat. When the oil is hot, add the capers (they might splatter at first, so stand back) and fry until just golden brown, 45 to 60 seconds. Transfer to paper towels to drain. The capers can be made a day or two ahead; cover and store at room temperature.

GRILLED FENNEL

1 medium bulb fennel, cut into 6 wedges through the core

3 tablespoons extra-virgin olive oil

1 teaspoon kosher salt

PREHEAT THE oven to 375°F. Place the fennel wedges in a baking dish and toss with the olive oil and salt. Add just enough water to cover the bottom of the dish and cover the dish with foil. Bake for 20 minutes, or until the fennel is crisp-tender.

CONTINUES ➡

PREPARE A hot grill or preheat a grill pan over high heat. Grill the fennel, turning a few times, until nicely browned and tender throughout, about 4 minutes. Transfer to a cutting board, remove the core, and cut the fennel into 1- to 2-inch pieces.

—————— FOR SERVING ——————

One 3-pound whole Spanish mackerel (with head and tail), scaled, gutted, and gills removed

Extra-virgin olive oil

Kosher salt and freshly ground black pepper

Grilled Fennel

2 Persian or ½ English seedless cucumber, quartered lengthwise, seeded, and cut on the bias into ¼-inch pieces

½ cup diced Grilled Cucumber Pickles (page 101), or another pickled cucumber

1 tablespoon julienned Pickled Ginger (page 115)

2 tablespoons chopped black (taggiasca or kalamata) olives

3 tablespoons chopped parsley

3 tablespoons chopped mint

2 tablespoons chopped dill

Yogurt Sauce

Fried Capers

Flaky sea salt

PREPARE A two-stage grill with medium and hot sides. Using a sharp knife, make a few 1-inch-long slits down the middle of the fish on both sides. Brush the fish all over with olive oil and season with kosher salt and pepper.

CLEAN AND oil the grill, then grill the fish over medium heat for 15 minutes. Using two spatulas, carefully turn the fish over and grill for 15 minutes longer. Move the fish to the hotter side of the grill and cook until the skin is nicely browned on both sides, 1 to 2 minutes per side. Transfer to a baking sheet and let rest.

IN A bowl, toss the grilled fennel with the raw and pickled cucumber, pickled ginger, olives, parsley, mint, and dill. Spread the yogurt sauce on the bottom of a serving platter, top with the fennel mixture, and place the fish on top. Drizzle with olive oil, sprinkle with fried capers and flaky salt, and serve.

Pan-Seared Arctic Char

WITH MISO-GLAZED BUTTERNUT SQUASH AND TAMARIND SAUCE

MAKES 4 SERVINGS

I fell in love with tamarind during my tenure at Tabla, and have continued finding new ways to add its sweet-sour flavor and fruity acidity to marinades, broths, glazes, and dressings. Here, I use it to create a sweet-sour sauce that has a big hit of black pepper and coriander flavors. The sauce will be intense when you taste it by itself, but when paired with fish and sweet roasted squash, its flavor mellows out and pulls everything together.

You'll find tamarind paste sold in two different forms at most Asian markets: as dense blocks (usually labeled "tamarind pulp") or in jars of "tamarind paste." I usually work with the less-refined pulp, steeping it in water or another liquid to loosen it up, then straining out the seeds.

—— THE TAKEAWAY ——

When tossed with butternut squash and roasted, the miso glaze becomes a slightly sticky, sweet-and-salty coating that will make you happy eating the squash forever. Luckily, the glaze can be used on all kinds of oven-bound ingredients, including fish, chicken, and beef, but I especially like what it brings to vegetables.

—— TAMARIND SAUCE ——

MAKES 1 CUP

- 1 cup water
- ¼ cup packed tamarind pulp
- 6 Medjool, Halawi, or Khadrawy dates, pitted and chopped
- 1 tablespoon maple syrup
- One 1-inch piece ginger, peeled and coarsely chopped
- ¼ cup fresh lime juice
- 2 tablespoons fresh orange juice
- 1 tablespoon ground coriander
- 1 tablespoon kosher salt
- 1 teaspoon freshly ground black pepper

IN A small saucepan, bring the water and tamarind pulp to a simmer over medium-low heat. Cover the pot and simmer for 20 minutes, then turn off the heat and let sit for 30 minutes. Strain through a fine-mesh strainer, pressing on the tamarind to extract as much juice as possible. Discard the solids.

IN A small saucepan, combine 3 tablespoons of the tamarind water, the dates, maple syrup, and ginger. Bring to a boil, turn off the heat, cover the pot, and let steep for 20 minutes. Transfer to a blender and add the remaining ingredients. Blend until smooth. The tamarind sauce can be made a few hours ahead and refrigerated until ready to use.

—— MISO GLAZE ——

- 1 red finger chile
- 8 cloves Garlic Confit (page 112)
- ¼ cup yellow miso paste
- 3 tablespoons honey
- ¼ cup fresh lemon juice
- Strips of zest (no pith) from 1 lemon
- 1 teaspoon kosher salt

CONTINUES ➡

CHAR THE chile over the flame of a burner or under the broiler until charred all over. Transfer to a bowl and cover with a plate. Let steam for 10 minutes, then peel and trim the stem. Combine the chile and the remaining ingredients in a blender or food processor and blend until smooth. The glaze can be made a day or two ahead of time and refrigerated until ready to use.

─────── ROASTED SQUASH ───────

1 butternut squash   Miso Glaze
   (2½ to 3 pounds)

PREHEAT THE oven to 450°F and place a wire rack inside a rimmed baking sheet. Cut the squash in half crosswise (where the bulbous bottom meets the narrower top) and reserve the top half for another use. Peel the bottom half, cut it in half, and remove the seeds. Cut the squash into blocks about 2 inches wide and 3 inches long. In a bowl, toss the squash with the miso glaze. Arrange the squash on the rack and roast until tender and browned, 20 to 25 minutes.

─────── FRIED PUMPKIN SEEDS ───────

½ cup plus   ½ cup raw pumpkin
  2 tablespoons extra-   seeds
  virgin olive oil   1 rosemary sprig

IN A medium skillet, heat the olive oil over medium heat. Add the pumpkin seeds and cook, stirring constantly, until golden brown (they might start to sizzle and pop), 3 to 4 minutes. Add the rosemary and turn off the heat. Wait 1 minute, then strain the oil and let cool; discard the rosemary. When the oil has cooled to room temperature, return the seeds to the oil. The fried seeds can be made a day or two ahead; cover and store at room temperature.

─────── FOR SERVING ───────

Four 5-ounce arctic   Roasted Squash
  char fillets with skin   Fried Pumpkin Seeds

Kosher salt   2 tablespoons thinly
               sliced mint
2 tablespoons extra-
  virgin olive oil   Flaky sea salt

Tamarind Sauce

PAT THE skin side of the fish dry and season both sides with kosher salt. In a large skillet, heat the olive oil over medium-high heat. Place the fish, skin side down, in the skillet and cook, occasionally pressing it down with a spatula to prevent curling, until the skin is brown, 4 minutes. Turn the fish over and cook until just opaque in the center, about 1 minute longer.

SPOON ABOUT ¼ cup of the tamarind sauce on the bottom of four serving plates and run the back of a spoon through it to make a long stripe of sauce. Place the fish on top of the sauce. Divide the squash among the plates, shingling the slices next to the fish. Spoon some of the pumpkin seeds and their oil over the squash. Sprinkle the fish with the mint and flaky salt and serve.

Cornmeal-Crusted Hake

WITH MASHED BUTTERNUT SQUASH AND SOY-BROWN BUTTER VINAIGRETTE

MAKES 4 SERVINGS

This dish delivers the crunchy texture of a corn-meal-crusted fish but avoids the heaviness that comes with a battered-and-fried fish. It's also gluten-free, thanks to the sticky paste of egg whites and cornstarch that helps the cornmeal adhere to the fillet. I've used this technique with skate, and it works with other flaky fish as well. I love the way the squash, spinach, and herbs all come together at the end of the dish to create a very flavorful mash, one that you could also serve on its own or with any kind of protein. Be sure to cook the spinach and herbs long enough so they completely wilt and the whole thing becomes one mass, rather than sautéed spin-ach with little pieces of squash mixed in.

THE TAKEAWAY

Using brown butter as the fat in a vinaigrette is an old-school French thing, but classic applications tend to be too creamy and heavy for fish. I lighten my vinaigrette up with tamari and lime juice, so it ends up being more like a vibrant pan sauce, one that you could also use to dress green vegetables or a salad.

SOY-BROWN BUTTER VINAIGRETTE

MAKES ¾ CUP

4 tablespoons unsalted butter	2 teaspoons kosher salt
1 medium shallot, finely chopped	3 tablespoons tamari or soy sauce
⅓ cup finely chopped ginger	2 tablespoons fresh lime juice
	¼ cup maple syrup

IN A medium saucepan, melt the butter over medium-low heat. Continue cooking until the butter begins to turn brown and smells nutty, 6 to 8 minutes. Reduce the heat to the lowest setting and add the shallot, ginger, and salt. Continue cooking until the shallots are translucent, 4 to 5 minutes. Add the tamari, lime juice, and maple syrup and cook, whisking occasionally, for 5 minutes. Turn off the heat and store at room temperature until ready to use.

MASHED BUTTERNUT SQUASH

2 cups diced butternut squash (½-inch dice)	⅔ cup water
	Kosher salt

IN A medium saucepan, bring the squash, water, and ½ teaspoon salt to a simmer. Cover the pot and cook over medium heat until the squash is very tender, about 10 minutes. Drain the water and mash the squash with a fork or potato masher. Season to taste with salt. The squash can be made up to 1 day ahead and refrigerated until ready to use.

CONTINUES ➡

2 tablespoons extra-
 virgin olive oil

8 ounces baby spinach

⅓ cup chopped basil

⅓ cup chopped mint

⅓ cup chopped dill

Mashed Butternut
 Squash

Kosher salt

2 large egg whites

1 teaspoon water

½ cup cornstarch

Four 5-ounce hake
 fillets

½ cup finely ground
 cornmeal

¼ cup vegetable oil

Soy–Brown Butter
 Vinaigrette

1 lime, for zesting

Lime wedges

Flaky sea salt

Freshly ground black
 pepper

IN A medium skillet, heat the olive oil over medium-high heat. Add the spinach and cook, stirring frequently, until it begins to wilt, about 2 minutes. Add the herbs, stir to combine, and cook for 1 minute. Add the squash and stir to combine; the spinach should completely wilt and blend into the squash. Turn off the heat, season to taste with kosher salt, and keep warm.

IN A bowl, whisk the egg whites with the water and cornstarch. Season the hake all over with kosher salt and brush one side with the egg white mixture. Dredge that side in the cornmeal, pressing it into the fish until well coated. In a large skillet, heat the vegetable oil over high heat. Add the hake, cornmeal side down, and cook until golden brown, 3 to 4 minutes. Turn the fish over and continue cooking until opaque throughout, 3 to 4 minutes longer.

DIVIDE THE spinach and squash among four plates. Top with the fish and drizzle some of the vinaigrette over. Top with freshly grated lime zest, a squeeze of lime juice, flaky salt, and pepper. Serve.

Slow-Roasted Halibut
WITH BRAISED MUSHROOMS

MAKES 4 SERVINGS

The combination of sweet, flaky halibut with earthy, umami-rich mushrooms is as satisfying as any slow-braised winter dish, and this quick dinner comes together in less than an hour—or half that time if you make the mushrooms the day before.

THE TAKEAWAY

The braised mushrooms are like a looser version of the mushroom ragu that I use as the rich topping for grits on page 240. It's based on a classic white wine mushroom sauce, but flavor-boosted with miso and a touch of heat from chiles. As with any mixed-mushroom recipe, feel free to use whatever (and as many) kinds of mushrooms you can find. Pair the mushrooms with chicken breasts for a lighter take on chicken marsala.

BRAISED MUSHROOMS

3 tablespoons oil from Garlic Confit (page 112) or extra-virgin olive oil

1 pound mixed mushrooms (I like shiitake, hon shimeji, silver dollar, and king trumpet), cut into ⅛-inch slices

Kosher salt

1 small shallot, finely diced

5 tablespoons dry white wine

4 teaspoons yellow miso

¼ cup plus 2 tablespoons water

½ red finger chile, halved and thinly sliced (with seeds)

IN A large skillet, heat the garlic oil over medium heat. Add the mushrooms and 1 teaspoon salt and cook, stirring frequently, until slightly tender and starting to brown, about 5 minutes. Add the shallot and cook for 5 minutes. Add the wine and cook for 5 minutes. In a small bowl, stir the miso into the water. Add this mixture to the mushrooms and bring the liquid to a boil. Turn off the heat and stir in the chile. Season to taste with salt. The mushrooms can be made a day ahead and refrigerated until ready to use.

FOR SERVING

Four 5-ounce portions skinless halibut

Kosher salt and freshly ground black pepper

¼ cup extra-virgin olive oil, plus more for drizzling

Braised Mushrooms

¼ cup fines herbes (equal parts finely chopped chervil, chives, parsley, and tarragon)

1 lemon, for zesting

Flaky sea salt

PREHEAT THE oven to 250°F. Season the halibut with kosher salt and pepper and place in a baking dish just large enough to fit the fish in a single layer. Drizzle the fish with the ¼ cup olive oil and add just enough water to cover the bottom of the dish. Cover with foil and roast until the halibut is opaque in the center, 20 to 30 minutes (depending on the thickness of the fish).

DIVIDE THE braised mushrooms among four shallow serving bowls and sprinkle with the herbs. Top with the halibut and drizzle with olive oil. Grate some lemon zest over the fish, sprinkle with flaky salt, and serve.

Pan-Seared Snapper

WITH APPLE PUREE, BRUSSELS SPROUTS, AND BEET VINAIGRETTE

MAKES 4 SERVINGS

This beautiful, colorful dish plays with the same flavors as the recipe for Roasted Brussels Sprouts with Avocado and Apple (page 175), but in a different configuration. Here, I combine apples and avocado to make a puree that's rich, but doesn't overpower the fish. A sprinkling of blanched Brussels sprout leaves provides texture, while a crimson-colored beet vinaigrette adds the intense flavors of reduced beet, apple, and fennel juices.

───── THE TAKEAWAY ─────

Avocados have a subtle flavor and soft, buttery texture, which makes them the perfect ingredient in purees when you want to avoid using butter or oil. In this recipe, they turn what's essentially apple sauce into a richer accompaniment for fish. They blend very easily into other starchy vegetable purees (broccoli-avocado and edamame-avocado are both excellent pairings), and you can even mash them into potatoes, if you don't mind the resulting light-green hue. They can also thicken creamy dressings, like green goddess.

───── APPLE PUREE ─────

2 medium Mutsu (aka Crispin) apples

2 tablespoons extra-virgin olive oil

2 teaspoons kosher salt

1 medium ripe avocado, diced

¼ cup fresh lime juice

2 tablespoons chopped jalapeño chile (no seeds)

PEEL THE apples and set the peels aside. Core and cut the apples into 1-inch chunks (you should have about 1½ cups). In a medium saucepan, combine the apples, olive oil, and salt. Cover the pot and cook over medium-low heat until the apples are completely tender (lower the heat if they begin to brown), 10 to 15 minutes. Transfer to a blender and let cool to room temperature. Add the apple peels and the remaining ingredients and blend until smooth.

───── BEET VINAIGRETTE ─────

1 cup red beet juice (from about 2 medium beets)

½ cup apple juice (preferably fresh, from 1 large apple)

1 cup fennel juice (from 1 medium bulb)

2 tablespoons plus 1 teaspoon white wine vinegar

1 tablespoon plus 2 teaspoons pickling liquid from Pickled Jalapeños (page 227)

¾ teaspoon kosher salt

IN A medium saucepan, combine the beet juice, apple juice, fennel juice, and vinegar. Bring to a boil and cook, skimming away any foam as needed, until the liquid is reduced by half, then turn off the heat. Stir in the pickling liquid and salt.

— SAUTÉED BRUSSELS SPROUT LEAVES —

4 cups Brussels sprout leaves (from about 1 pound sprouts)

1 tablespoon extra-virgin olive oil

BRING A saucepan of salted water to a boil. Blanch the Brussels sprouts until they're bright green and just tender, 1 to 2 minutes. Transfer to paper towels to drain.

IN A skillet, heat the olive oil over high heat. Add the sprouts and cook, stirring frequently, until golden brown and tender. Transfer to a plate and let cool.

— FOR SERVING —

Four 5-ounce pieces red snapper with skin

Kosher salt

2 tablespoons extra-virgin olive oil

1 cup Apple Puree

Sautéed Brussels Sprout Leaves

Flaky sea salt

1 cup Beet Vinaigrette

PAT THE snapper dry and season with kosher salt. In a large skillet, heat the olive oil over medium heat. Place the fish, skin side down, in the skillet and cook, occasionally pressing it down with a spatula to prevent curling, until the skin is brown, 4 to 5 minutes. Turn the fish over and cook until just opaque in the center, 1 to 2 minutes longer. Transfer the fish to a plate to rest.

DIVIDE THE apple puree among four shallow serving bowls (about ¼ cup puree each). Divide the Brussels sprouts over the puree. Top with the fish and season with flaky salt. Spoon the vinaigrette around the fish and serve.

Pan-Seared Sea Trout

WITH BUTTERNUT SQUASH PUREE, PARSNIPS, AND CRISPY HERBS

MAKES 4 SERVINGS

Make this whenever you find yourself in the dead of winter yet yearning for a lighter fish dish. I brighten up a butternut squash puree with ginger, orange juice, and the slightly tropical flavors of coconut water and coconut oil, and pair it with sweet, flaky trout.

THE TAKEAWAY

When I was developing the recipe for Roasted Acorn Squash with Spicy Granola and Apple Gastrique (page 188), I loved how the coconut and ginger in the granola tasted with the squash, and I wanted to explore that flavor combination in a squash puree. Cooking with coconut is common in Indian and other Asian food cultures, but I didn't want the heavy richness that coconut milk brings to the table, so I use a combination of coconut oil and coconut water instead, which adds subtle nutty and fruity flavors to the puree without making it all about the coconut. Try using this coconut oil and water combination to cook other big-flavored vegetables, such as carrots, parsnips, or bell peppers, or use it as the base of a braising liquid for fish.

BUTTERNUT SQUASH PUREE

½ medium butternut squash, peeled and roughly chopped (about 4 cups)

One 2-inch piece ginger, peeled and roughly chopped

½ red finger chile, roughly chopped (with seeds)

¾ cup coconut water

⅓ cup fresh orange juice

2 tablespoons coconut oil

2 teaspoons kosher salt

IN A medium saucepan, combine all ingredients and bring to a simmer over medium heat. Cover the pot and cook until the squash is very tender, about 15 minutes. Transfer to a blender or food processor and puree until smooth. Keep warm until ready to serve.

PAN-ROASTED PARSNIPS AND SQUASH

2 tablespoons extra-virgin olive oil

1 cup butternut squash, cut into ½-inch batons

1 cup medium parsnips, sliced on the bias into ½-inch pieces

Kosher salt

IN EACH of two medium skillets, heat 1 tablespoon olive oil over medium heat. Add the squash to one pan and the parsnips to the other, season with salt, and cook, stirring frequently, until the vegetables are crisp-tender, about 10 minutes for the squash and 12 minutes for the parsnips. Season to taste with salt and transfer to a plate.

FOR SERVING

Four 5-ounce sea trout
  fillets with skin

Kosher salt

4 tablespoons extra-
  virgin olive oil

½ cup small basil leaves

¼ cup mint leaves

Pan-Roasted Parsnips
  and Squash

Butternut Squash
  Puree

Lemon wedges

Flaky sea salt

PAT THE trout dry and season both sides with kosher salt. In a large skillet, heat 1 tablespoon of the olive oil over medium heat. Place the fish, skin side down, in the pan and cook, pressing with a spatula, until the skin is browned and crisp, about 6 minutes. Turn the trout over and continue cooking until the flesh is opaque, about 2 minutes longer. Transfer to a plate and wipe out the skillet.

ADD THE remaining 3 tablespoons olive oil to the skillet and heat over medium-high heat. Add the basil and mint and fry, stirring frequently, until crisp, 1 to 2 minutes. Add the parsnips and squash and cook until heated through.

DIVIDE THE squash puree among four shallow serving bowls or plates. Divide the vegetables and herbs over the squash. Top with a piece of fish and spoon some of the oil from the crispy herbs over. Squeeze some lemon over each serving, season with flaky salt, and serve.

Pan-Seared Black Bass

WITH CAULIFLOWER AND CHUNKY LEMON VINAIGRETTE

MAKES 4 SERVINGS

Like the seared scallops on page 341, this is another example of pairing a chunky and boldly flavored vinaigrette with a rich, creamy puree. As you eat the fish, the vinaigrette and puree mingle, giving you a full spectrum of flavors and textures. I pack as much flavor as possible into the cauliflower puree by cooking the florets in water that I've infused with lemon zest, lemongrass, ginger, garlic, and jala-peño. The result is the most layered puree you've ever tested.

—— THE TAKEAWAY ——

Recipes for deeply caramelized cauliflower usually take you to the oven. While roasting cauliflower will give you the color and nutty flavor you desire, you usually end up sacrificing texture and are left with florets that are nicely browned on the outside, but mushy on the inside. Pan-roasting cauliflower, on the other hand, will give you lots more control over caramelization, and is quick enough so the florets retain their crunch—and that textural contrast is important when pairing the florets with a silky cauliflower puree. Make sure you cut your cauliflower into small florets, each about the size of a dime, or you'll run into the same problem as roasting.

—— LEMON INFUSION ——

MAKES 2 CUPS

2 cups water
½ cup chopped lemongrass
Strips of zest (no pith) from 1 lemon
⅓ cup thyme leaves
⅓ cup roughly chopped ginger
½ jalapeño chile, split lengthwise (with seeds)
1 garlic clove, peeled
½ teaspoon kosher salt

IN A saucepan, bring the water to a boil. Add the remaining ingredients to a heatproof bowl and cover with the boiling water. Cover the bowl with plastic wrap and let sit for 30 minutes. Strain through a fine-mesh strainer. The lemon infusion can be made a day ahead; cover and refrigerate until ready to use.

—— CAULIFLOWER PUREE ——

1 tablespoon extra-virgin olive oil
1 small yellow onion, thinly sliced
1 garlic clove, thinly sliced
½ teaspoon kosher salt, plus more for seasoning
3½ cups cauliflower florets
¼ cup Lemon Infusion

IN A medium saucepan, heat the olive oil over low heat. Add the onion, garlic, and salt and cook until the onions are soft, about 8 minutes. Add the cauliflower and lemon infusion, bring the liquid to a simmer, and cover the pot. Cook until the cauliflower is very tender, about 10 minutes. Uncover the pot and continue cooking until most of the liquid has evaporated. Transfer to a blender and puree until smooth. Season to taste with salt. The puree can be made a day ahead and refrigerated until ready to use. Rewarm gently in a saucepan.

PAN-ROASTED CAULIFLOWER

3 tablespoons extra-virgin olive oil

1½ cups small cauliflower florets (½- to 1-inch pieces)

Kosher salt and freshly ground black pepper

IN A medium skillet, heat the olive oil over medium-high heat until it shimmers. Add the cauliflower, season with salt, and cook until browned on one side, about 2 minutes. Stir and continue cooking, stirring occasionally, until the cauliflower is just tender and browned all over, about 6 minutes. Season to taste with salt and pepper.

CHUNKY LEMON VINAIGRETTE

¼ cup extra-virgin olive oil

2 tablespoons chopped lemon segments

1 tablespoon Lemon Infusion

1 tablespoon fresh lemon juice

1 tablespoon finely chopped jalapeño chile (no seeds)

1 teaspoon finely grated ginger

1 tablespoon thinly sliced basil

1 tablespoon finely chopped parsley

2 teaspoons finely chopped chives

1 teaspoon finely chopped tarragon

2 teaspoons sugar

½ teaspoon kosher salt

¼ teaspoon Tabasco hot sauce (or Red Hot Sauce, page 130)

COMBINE ALL ingredients in a small bowl and stir to combine. The vinaigrette can be made up to 1 day ahead; cover and refrigerate until ready to use.

FOR SERVING

Four 6-ounce black sea bass fillets with skin

Kosher salt and freshly ground black pepper

2 tablespoons extra-virgin olive oil

Cauliflower Puree

Pan-Roasted Cauliflower

Chunky Lemon Vinaigrette

1 lemon, for zesting

Flaky sea salt

USING A sharp knife, score the skin side of each piece of fish a couple of times in the thickest part of the fillet. Season the fish with kosher salt and pepper and pat the skin dry. In a large skillet, heat the olive oil over high heat until it shimmers. Add the fish, skin side down, and cook for 30 to 45 seconds, then press down on the fish with a spatula to flatten. Continue cooking the fish, pressing frequently with the spatula, until the skin is golden brown and the flesh is turning opaque around the edges, about 4 minutes. Turn the fish over and continue cooking until opaque throughout, 1 to 2 minutes. Transfer to a plate.

DIVIDE THE cauliflower puree among four shallow serving bowls or plates. Scatter the pan-roasted cauliflower over the puree and top each with a piece of fish. Spoon the vinaigrette over and around the fish. Grate some lemon zest over the fish and season with flaky salt. Serve.

Seared Scallops
WITH SUNCHOKE SAUCE AND APPLE VINAIGRETTE

MAKES 4 SERVINGS

Each component of this elegant dish is interesting on its own, but served together the three elements—creamy sunchoke sauce, buttery scallops, and sharp apple vinaigrette—create something entirely amazing. I love the way the vinaigrette mingles with the sunchoke puree on the plate to form a creamy dressing that's perfect with the seared scallops. The plating is a bit cheffy, yes, but sometimes it's fun to play restaurant at home. You can also serve these scallops individually as a sophisticated starter.

SUNCHOKE SAUCE

2 tablespoons extra-virgin olive oil

1 medium shallot, thinly sliced

1 tablespoon kosher salt

1 pound sunchokes (about 12 medium), peeled and roughly chopped

1 Mutsu (aka Crispin) apple, peeled, cored, and roughly chopped (about 1 cup)

1 tablespoon roughly chopped ginger

½ green Thai chile (with seeds)

4 teaspoons white wine vinegar

1 tablespoon water

IN A medium saucepan, heat the olive oil over low heat. Add the shallot and salt and cook, stirring occasionally, until softened, 8 to 10 minutes. Add the remaining ingredients, cover the pot, and simmer over medium heat until the sunchokes and apples are very tender, about 15 minutes. Transfer to a blender or food processor and puree until smooth, then strain in a fine-mesh strainer, pressing on the solids with a rubber spatula. Keep warm.

APPLE VINAIGRETTE

1 tablespoon extra-virgin olive oil

½ cup diced red onions

¼ cup champagne vinegar

4 teaspoons maple syrup

1 large Mutsu apple (aka Crispin), peeled, cored, and cut into ⅛-inch dice (about 1 cup)

¼ cup fresh lime juice

Kosher salt

IN A medium saucepan, heat the olive oil over low heat. Add the onions and cook until softened, 8 to 10 minutes. Add the vinegar and maple syrup and bring the liquid to a boil. Turn off the heat and let cool to room temperature. Stir in the apple and lime juice and season to taste with salt.

FOR SERVING

12 dry-packed U/10 scallops, side muscles removed

Kosher salt

2 tablespoons extra-virgin olive oil, plus more for drizzling

2 tablespoons unsalted butter

Sunchoke Sauce

Flaky sea salt

Apple Vinaigrette

2 tablespoons roughly chopped parsley

1 tablespoon roughly chopped tarragon

SEASON THE scallops on both sides with kosher salt. Let sit for about 15 minutes, then pat dry. In a large skillet, heat the olive oil over medium-high heat until it shimmers. Add the scallops and cook, without moving, until the bottoms are deeply browned, 3 to 4 minutes. Add the butter to the pan and turn the scallops over. Continue cooking, basting the scallops with the melted butter, until the scallops are just opaque, 1 to 2 minutes longer. Transfer to a plate.

CONTINUES ➡

ON A serving plate, spoon 1-tablespoon dollops of the sunchoke sauce for each scallop. Top each dollop with a scallop. Season the scallops with flaky salt, then spoon some of the apple vinaigrette over each. Drizzle some of the liquid from the vinaigrette around the scallops, then drizzle with olive oil. Sprinkle the parsley and tarragon over the dish and serve.

THE TAKEAWAY

There's an art to searing scallops, but the most important thing to remember is that you only need to get a beautifully browned crust on one side of the scallop. If you try to brown both sides, you're going to overcook them. I salt scallops about 15 minutes before I'm ready to cook them, which draws out some of the water (scallops expel a lot of liquid as they cook, and steam is the enemy of caramelization). Then I pat them very, very dry with paper towels right before I season them again and add them to a very hot pan. Now comes the important part: Don't do anything! Just leave the scallops alone for a few minutes, as they build up a deeply browned crust. Once you see a little color building up the side of the scallops, gently poke them with a spatula to see if they easily release from the pan. Once they do, add some butter to the pan, give it a swirl, and flip the scallops over. Then start basting the scallops with butter, which will further brown their tops and infuse them with the nutty flavor of browned butter. The scallops are done when you give their sides a squeeze and they're soft and slightly springy. Or you can look at their color: The flesh at the top and bottom of the scallop should be opaque, with a thin band of translucent flesh in the middle.

Slow-Roasted Halibut

WITH GRILLED FENNEL, BLOOD ORANGE VINAIGRETTE, AND OLIVES

MAKES 4 SERVINGS

I love recipes where the vegetable component is something you'd be happy to eat by itself. The grilled fennel in this light, wintry fish dish is one of those components. I like it so much that I couldn't resist using it three times in this cookbook: You'll also find it in the roasted beet recipe on page 127 and the grilled mackerel on page 325. The citrusy vinaigrette that unites the deeply caramelized fennel with the soft, flaky fish is simple but has an interesting texture thanks to the addition of diced orange peel confit.

——— BLOOD ORANGE VINAIGRETTE ———

Strips of zest (with pith) from 4 blood oranges, cut into ¼-inch pieces (about ½ cup)

½ cup plus ¼ cup blood orange juice (from about 6 oranges)

1 tablespoon sugar

¼ cup plus 2 teaspoons extra-virgin olive oil

¼ cup champagne vinegar

Kosher salt

2 tablespoons finely chopped shallot

IN A small saucepan, cover the orange zest with cold water. Bring the water to a boil, then drain. Repeat two times. Add the ½ cup orange juice and the sugar to the saucepan and bring to a boil. Cook until the liquid is reduced by about half and syrupy. Turn off the heat and let the orange confit cool.

IN A blender, combine the olive oil, vinegar, 1½ teaspoons salt, and the remaining ¼ cup orange juice. Blend until smooth, then transfer to a bowl and whisk in the orange confit and shallots. Season to taste with salt.

CONTINUES ➡

——— THE TAKEAWAY ———

If cooking fish is your white whale, so to speak, then I highly recommend starting with my method for slow-roasted fish. It's virtually foolproof, and my favorite method for cooking thicker, flakier varieties of fish, including halibut and cod, as well as fattier species like salmon, arctic char, and swordfish. The results are similar to those achieved in sous vide cooking: soft, moist, uniformly cooked fish that's very hard to overcook. A couple of things to remember: Cut your fish into individual portions before roasting, as the fish will be too soft to cut after. And add enough water to cover the bottom of the pan, which will keep the fish from drying out. I usually add a drizzle of olive oil as well, for good measure. You can add other aromatics to the pan: Some citrus slices, spices, herbs, ginger, or chiles will all gently perfume the fish as it cooks.

GRILLED FENNEL

1 teaspoon fennel seeds, coarsely ground in a spice grinder or mortar and pestle

1 teaspoon sugar

1 teaspoon kosher salt

1 medium fennel bulb, halved, cored, and cut into ½-inch wedges

¼ cup extra-virgin olive oil

PREHEAT THE oven to 375°F. In a small bowl, combine the fennel seeds, sugar, and salt and stir until combined. In a medium bowl, toss the fennel wedges with the fennel sugar until well coated. Arrange the fennel in a single layer on a rimmed baking sheet (sprinkle with any remaining fennel sugar from the bowl) and drizzle with the olive oil. Cover with aluminum foil and roast for 10 minutes, then uncover and roast until just tender, about 10 minutes longer.

PREHEAT THE broiler, prepare a hot grill, or preheat a grill pan over high heat. Broil or grill the fennel until caramelized all over, a minute or two per side.

FOR SERVING

Four 5-ounce portions skinless halibut

Kosher salt and freshly ground black pepper

¼ cup extra-virgin olive oil

Grilled Fennel

¼ cup roughly chopped Sevillano or other green olives

Blood Orange Vinaigrette

2 tablespoons chopped fennel fronds

Flaky sea salt

PREHEAT THE oven to 250°F. Season the halibut with kosher salt and pepper and place in a baking dish just large enough to fit the fish in a single layer. Drizzle the fish with the olive oil and add just enough water to cover the bottom of the dish. Cover with foil and roast until the halibut is opaque in the center, 20 to 30 minutes (depending on the thickness of the fish).

DIVIDE THE grilled fennel among four serving plates and sprinkle with the olives. Spoon the vinaigrette (about ¼ cup per plate) over and around the fennel. Top the fennel with the fish. Sprinkle some fennel fronds and flaky salt on top of the fish and serve.

Slow-Roasted Arctic Char

WITH PARSNIP PUREE AND ROASTED ROOT VEGETABLES

MAKES 4 SERVINGS

I built this dish from the bottom up, starting with the parsnip puree. I love the fresh, sweet flavor you get when cooking parsnips in their own juice (more on that below), so I started there and topped it with chunks of deeply caramelized root vegetables, which add both texture and a rich vegetable flavor. I could top this combo with pretty much anything, but I landed on the mild, lightly sweet flavor of arctic char, which falls somewhere between trout and salmon. If you're not in the mood for fish, serve the parsnip puree and vegetables with some roast chicken, pork, or braised beef.

THE TAKEAWAY

Braising vegetables in their own juice will give you a dramatically different result than cooking them in water. You'll notice how much richer and sweeter they become, in addition to tasting like the best versions of themselves. You also don't need a fancy juicer: Just puree raw parsnips with enough water to let the blender do its job, then strain. You can apply this technique to carrots, beets, and asparagus, as well as winter squash if it's going to be pureed into a soup.

PARSNIP PUREE

2 pounds parsnips (about 5 medium), peeled and diced

2 tablespoons fresh lemon juice (preferably Meyer lemon)

Kosher salt

PLACE HALF of the parsnips in a blender along with a splash of water and blend until smooth. (If you have a juicer, skip the water and just juice the parsnips.) Strain in a fine-mesh strainer; you should have about 1 cup parsnip juice.

IN A small saucepan, combine the remaining parsnips with the parsnip juice. Bring the liquid to a simmer and cook, skimming any foam that rises to the surface, until the parsnips are very soft, 10 to 15 minutes. Drain the parsnips, reserving the cooking liquid. Transfer the parsnips to a blender and puree, added some cooking liquid as needed, until very smooth. Scrape the puree into the saucepan and stir in the lemon juice. Season to taste with salt and keep warm.

ROASTED CARROTS AND PARSNIPS

2 medium carrots, peeled and cut into obliques

1 large parsnip, peeled and cut into obliques

2 tablespoons extra-virgin olive oil

Kosher salt

PREHEAT THE oven to 425°F. In a bowl, toss the carrots and parsnips with the olive oil and season with salt. Spread on a rimmed baking sheet and roast, stirring once or twice, until tender and deeply caramelized, about 15 minutes.

FOR SERVING

2 serrano chiles

Four 5-ounce skinless arctic char fillets

Kosher salt

Extra-virgin olive oil

Roasted Carrots and Parsnips

¼ cup roughly chopped basil (or whole small leaves)

Parsnip Puree

1 lemon (preferably Meyer), for zesting

Flaky sea salt

CHAR THE chiles over the flame of a gas burner (or under a broiler), turning with tongs until blackened and blistered all over, about 4 minutes. Transfer the chiles to a bowl, cover with a plate, and let stand for 10 minutes. Scrape off the skins with a paring knife and wipe the flesh clean with a paper towel. Discard the stem and seeds. Cut the chiles lengthwise into ¼- by ½-inch pieces.

PREHEAT THE oven to 250°F. Season the char with kosher salt and place in a baking dish just large enough to fit the fish in a single layer. Drizzle the fish with olive oil and add just enough water to cover the bottom of the dish. Cover with foil and roast until the char is opaque in the center, 15 to 20 minutes.

MEANWHILE, IN a skillet, heat 1 tablespoon olive oil over medium heat. Add the carrots and parsnips and sauté until warmed through and caramelized in spots, 2 to 3 minutes. Add the roasted chiles and the basil and cook for 1 minute. Season with salt and turn off the heat.

DIVIDE THE parsnip puree among four plates. Top the puree with the roasted vegetable mixture. Place the char on top of the vegetables, grate some lemon zest over each piece of fish, and sprinkle with flaky salt. Serve.

Slow-Roasted Salmon
WITH SUNCHOKE PUREE AND SWEET-SOUR ONIONS

MAKES 4 SERVINGS

Here's a super-simple dish that hits all of the flavors you want. When slow-roasting salmon, you won't see as much of a color change as when you use high heat—your salmon is cooked through when its color changes from bright rosy pink to a slightly dull pink.

——— SWEET-SOUR ONIONS ———

1 tablespoon vegetable oil	Kosher salt and freshly ground black pepper
2 large Vidalia onions, cut crosswise into ½-inch rings	1 cup red wine
¼ cup sugar	¼ cup red wine vinegar
	1 teaspoon thyme leaves

IN A large skillet, heat the oil over medium heat. Add the onions and cook, stirring occasionally, until lightly caramelized, 10 to 15 minutes. Add the sugar and cook, stirring, until it melts into the onions, about 2 minutes. Season with salt and pepper and add the wine and vinegar. Bring the liquid to a boil, reduce the heat to a steady simmer, and cook, stirring occasionally, until the liquid is syrupy, about 30 minutes. Turn off the heat and let cool, then stir in the thyme. The onions can be made up to a day ahead and refrigerated until ready to use.

——— SUNCHOKE PUREE ———

1 pound sunchokes, cut into 1-inch pieces	1 cup water
	Kosher salt

IN A medium saucepan, combine the sunchokes and water. Season the water lightly with salt and bring to a boil. Reduce the heat to low, cover the pot, and simmer until the sunchokes are just tender throughout when pierced with a knife, about 15 minutes. Drain the sunchokes, reserving the cooking liquid, and transfer to a blender. Puree the sunchokes, adding a splash of cooking water if needed to loosen it up. Season to taste with salt and keep warm.

——— FOR SERVING ———

2 tablespoons extra-virgin olive oil, plus more for drizzling	4 thyme sprigs
	1 cup Sunchoke Puree
Four 5-ounce salmon fillets with skin	Sweet-Sour Onions
Kosher salt and freshly ground black pepper	2 teaspoons thyme leaves
	2 teaspoons finely chopped chives

PREHEAT THE oven to 250°F. Brush the bottom of a baking dish with the olive oil. Season the salmon on both sides with salt and pepper. Arrange the salmon, skin side down, in the baking dish and slide a thyme sprig under each piece of fish. Cover the dish with foil and bake until the salmon is just opaque throughout, about 20 minutes.

SPOON A circle of sunchoke puree onto four serving plates (about ¼ cup per plate). Place the salmon, skin side down, on top (discard the thyme sprigs). Divide the onions over the fish, drizzle with olive oil, sprinkle with the thyme, and chives, and serve.

Index

Note: Page references in *italics* indicate photographs.

"I knew right away that Dan Kluger was a great chef when I saw him shopping at the Union Square Greenmarket three times a week. That is where we started a collaboration that lasted many years and many restaurant openings. Dan is a master of taking seasonal ingredients and allowing them to shine on the plate. His book *Chasing Flavor* is an approachable guide to creating balanced and bright dishes. The techniques he shares will guide you through home cooking and will get you close to feeling like you are dining in his restaurant."
—JEAN-GEORGES VONGERICHTEN, CHEF AND RESTAURATEUR

"Dan's cooking is beloved by so many because it is equal parts exotic and familiar. It takes a true expert to know (and to teach us move-by-move in this essential guide) that simple ingredients and simple techniques are the foundation of the perfect bite. Dan's genius is to use small but brave additions to make that bite sublime. Get ready for some delicious kitchen fun, led by the master of knowing just when a recipe needs a little something unexpected to be just what you wanted."
—DAPHNE OZ, NATURAL FOODS CHEF, *NEW YORK TIMES* BEST-SELLING AUTHOR, AND JUDGE ON FOX'S *MASTERCHEF JUNIOR*

"Chasing flavor is something that Dan Kluger has been doing for years, but luckily for us he's mastered how to catch it. This book is an instant cornerstone of my kitchen. Dan gives great lessons on building flavor through techniques like charring or balancing sweet, sour, salty, and spicy. *Chasing Flavor* helps us take everyday pantry items and unlock their flavor and texture, turning ingredients we see as ordinary into extraordinary dishes—in the simplest ways. Dan is one of the great chefs and people of our generation. If you love flavor, buy this book."
—SAM KASS, FORMER WHITE HOUSE CHEF AND SENIOR POLICY ADVISOR FOR NUTRITION

"Dan Kluger is a chef's chef—understated, focused, skilled in self-effacement, and immune to glitz, reserving his showmanship for the cooking line. Which is where you'll find him, night after night, creating dishes so delicious and remarkable I've spent many evenings staring at a plate of Dan's wondering, 'How did he do that?' *Chasing Flavor* is a manual on that; a treasure of accessible, technique-driven cooking, distilling for the home cook what makes a good dish great."
—DAN BARBER, CHEF AND OWNER OF BLUE HILL